Choose Happy

Find Contentment in Any Situation

Hope you enjoy the book
Sally Tippett Rains

by

Sally Tippett Rains

PHOTOS BY ALLEN AHNER

the PeppertreePress, LLC
Sarasota, Florida

This book produced for Rainbows for Kids

Information on Rainbows for Kids: RainbowsForKids.org
Rainbows for Kids is a 501 (c)(3) charity in the Greater St. Louis Area, which
works with families of children with cancer and other serious situations, serving
three pediatric hospitals: Cardinal Glennon, St. Louis Children's, and Mercy
Pediatrics. If you know of a family who could benefit by Rainbows for Kids or to
contact the author: Email RSVPRainbowsForKids@gmail.com

Thank you to NAILBA (National Association of Independent Life Brokerage
Agencies) Charitable Foundation who provided the grant to publish this book.
The mission of the NAILBA Charitable Foundation is to encourage volunteerism
among NAILBA members and provide grant funds to worthy charitable
organizations that serve to enhance the quality of life for those less fortunate,
with a special emphasis on children.

Additional copies of this book are available on
RainbowsForKids.org, STLSportsPage.com or Amazon.com.

ISBN: 978-1-61493-668-8
Library of Congress Number: 2019912912
Printed September 2019

Acknowledgments

Thank you to Julie Ann James of Peppertree Press and her associates, Teri Lynn Franco and Rebecca Barbier.

Much gratitude and love to Dreama Denver for doing the Foreword. Your words were so heartfelt and I know they will help someone.

Special thanks and love from the bottom of my heart to all who contributed to this book. I hope I did your story justice. I know it is more than a story, it is your life. Thank you for being willing to share your story in order to help others:

Ginger Alden, Paul Avery, Lexie and Clay Ashurst, Ron Barber, Teresa Barnes, Barbara Baxter, Heather Berry, Laura Compton Brandt, Angela Brunette, Jack Buechner, Amy Camie, Michele Carter, Suzanne Corbett, Dan and Elizabeth Crum, Cindy Czaicki, Trisha Davis, Dixie Dawson, Sandy Elfrink,

Rainey Fahey, Lisa Flittner, Karen Fox, Wendell Fry, Karen Garrett, Susan Genz, Sheryl Godsy, Karen Gore, Tessa Greenspan, Karolyn Grimes, Jake Gronsky, Lauren Haeger, Debbie Hammond, Ross Hammond, Denise Heidel, Patrisha Henson, Karen Hoffman,

Bob Ibach, Kelsey Ibach, Nicholas Inman, Darlene Kassen, Pat Knox, Karen Kroger, Lizzie Kurowski, Richard LaMotte, Charlyne "Chuck" Miller, Liz Oliver, Jan Orlando, Joanie Protzel, Maria Rodgers O'Rourke, Dr. Debra Peppers, Tyler Poslosky, Ryan Powell, Wendy Powell, Christopher Radko, Steve Savard, Jack Scaife,

Angela Scoggins, Dana Scott, Derik Scott, Kristie Breeding Scherrer, Dawn Roberson Shaver, Laura Sleade, Jill Sutherland, Barbara Tippett, Stephen Von Rump, Lesia Waggoner, Laurie Wasserburger, Patty Wilke, Kathy Witt, Samii Taylor Yakovetic,

Thank you to those whose stories were so personal they didn't want me to use their last names.

A world of thank yous to Allen Ahner. Your photos are so beautiful. I appreciate you for working with me on this book. I know the pictures bless the readers as much as the words. (AllenAhner.com)

Special thank you to Alan Protzel and N.A.I.L.B.A.

Much love and thanks to Karen Rains and Lori Rains, my two daughters-in-love; how lucky I am!

Infinite love to my "boys" who are the lights of my life: My husband Rob, and sons B.J. and Mike-- I tried as hard as I could to give you a happy life every day and you give it back to me every day; and my new sources of happiness Naismith and Nelson.

I hope these stories bless all who read them. All glory and credit goes to God.

What Others Are Saying About Choose Happy

"Sally is the authentic "real deal" in choosing happiness. She lives what she writes, and draws others who are either like her, or who want to be like her! This God-inspired book is a gift to be read, cherished and shared with others who need to "choose happy!"

— Dr. Debra Peppers,
Motivational Speaker, Radio/TV Talk Show Host,
National Teachers Hall of Fame

"Sally Rains has put a smile on my face through all the challenges and disappointments of raising a child with severe complications from his illness. In this book she is sharing her encouragement with others."

— Ronnie Herman,
Mom of Ethan, Leukemia survivor

"Sally Rains is always smiling and a joy to be around. Her book "Get Going Girl" was a good pick-me-up and helped me see things in a much simpler manner. Choose Happy *does the same thing."*

— Amy Gass Schult,
Mom to Luke, childhood cancer survivor

"Sally Rains is a God-send to many families and so will this book be."

— Jennifer Thorpe,
Mom of Ashley, childhood cancer survivor

Table of Contents

Introduction   1

Foreword   6

One: Forward: *Keep Moving Forward*   11

Two: Initiative   27

Three: Now is the Time   39

Four: Determination   53

Five: Community: *Accept the Help of Others*   75

Six: Optimism: *Don't Give Up on Yourself—or Others*   91

Seven: New Ideas: *A New Way of Looking at Things*   109

Eight: Tenacity: *Stay in the Game*   129

Nine: Energy: *Find Your Get-Up-and-Go*   141

Ten: Normal: *Achieving Normalcy When Nothing Is Normal*   155

Eleven: Trust Yourself—*And Others*   175

Twelve: Mindfulness: *Less Worries, More Gratitude*   193

Thirteen: Encourage Yourself—*Encourage Others*   199

Fourteen: Nutrition and Health: *Take Care of YOU*   211

Fifteen: Tranquility: *Learning to Relax and Be at Peace*   231

"If I can stop one heart from breaking,
I shall not live in vain;
If I can ease one life the aching,
Or cool one pain,
Or help one fainting robin
Into his nest again
I shall not live in vain."

-- Emily Dickinson

"A simple shift in our thoughts
can positively affect our whole day.
There is beauty to be found in the world,
just look around you,
and find the beauty in yours."
--Christopher Radko, Artist

Introduction

I wrote this book for one reason: to try and help someone out there get through a tough situation and to let you know that while there will be tough times for everybody, we have a choice as to how we live our life. We really can have happy times, no matter what we are going through—if we choose to.

Who am I to even write this book? I'm nobody, but I am in a family who has faced some unimaginable times and yet when I look back on the worst days, I know we had at least that many great days. As low as the lowest low was, we had the highest of highs and it was due largely to the family outlook that we were brought up on—always open to the possibility of happiness.

If any of my family's experiences or the people interviewed here can help someone, even one person, I will be happy.

Because I was a Tippett, I—along with the others—learned how to cope with and graciously accept all that has come our way, and I'm talking medical diagnoses, suicide, job loss, divorce, deaths, (and the list goes on). Every minute of your life is not going to be rosy—in fact, some of it will downright stink—but we have the power to choose how we will react to the situations with which we are faced.

When faced with a challenging situation, I choose **Happy.**

"One day you'll be 80 years old and many of your family and friends will be gone and you'll look out and say, 'Why am I here?' and then you'll hear a bird chirp or see a sunset and you'll know."
— *Jack Tippett*

That can apply to so many of our circumstances every day. I hope you hear the birds chirp tomorrow morning or notice the sunset tonight. There's a bird I hear in my backyard every day, whose chirp sounds like "pretty, pretty, pretty."

On my worst and most unattractive days, I hear that bird and pretend it's Pop saying, "Pretty, pretty, pretty!" I just looked up what bird says, "Pretty, pretty, pretty," and it's the Cardinal. Wow!

For all of you who are out there doing your best, I hope this book gives you strength and gumption. There is nothing wrong with turning to others for guidance and help. You have all the tools you need, but sometimes you spend so much time feeling responsible for others that you don't take the time to care for yourself—and realize how special you are.

Some of the strongest people I know are strong, because they have silently endured life's challenges. Maybe that's you. You are amazing. And at times, you are stronger than you ever thought you could be.

Keep striving for excellence, even if sometimes you don't know what the right thing to do is. Don't compromise your integrity— no matter what. Don't dwell on the negatives.

As my son Mike says, "Our minds are like a VCR—never replay the bad memories—only replay the good ones." Throw the negatives away.

One time I thought someone had treated my husband Rob badly. I was dwelling on it, but then I noticed he was on to the next thing. It was eating me up that a person could do that to such a nice person. When he realized I was obsessing about it, he said, "Don't think another thought about that. That guy is a speck. He's like a piece of lint and not worth our time to worry about," and he made a motion like he was flicking a piece of lint off his shoulder.

We shouldn't let others' bad actions toward us make us turn bitter—we should flick them off like a piece of lint and keep going, doing our best. Rob is a shining example of that. He's faced a lot of challenges, but just keeps doing the best he can with a positive attitude and is a great example for those who know him.

My sister, Barbara, is another good example. She's the type of person people love to be around. She just makes you happy because of her huge smile. Having Barb for a sister has really enhanced my life. As I like to say, "Things are always more fun with Barb." And she has raised some pretty awesome daughters, my nieces.

During the four-year period when her daughter—our six-year-old niece, Anne—had cancer, it was a very scary time for our family, but we stuck together and helped one another.

It was four years of everyone's life and what a shame if those four years were looked back on as a "dreadful time," because it was junior high and high school for some members. Anne's parents and the rest of the family kept going, and they gave Anne and her sisters and cousins the best life they could have during that time.

When faced with an uncertain situation, keep moving. Those five little cousins—with one sometimes in a wheelchair and tired from chemo—kept living their life. Each one of them had some notable successes during their high school or junior high years, despite what they were going through.

Our parents did so many things so that we could all continue having happy memories together, as the family went through that time, so it wouldn't be so awful. Throughout her treatments and the ups and downs of her disease, we had little parties and the grandparents always showed up at the kids' school or sports events. My dad even surprised my mom with a red convertible, because who doesn't love riding around in a red convertible! We all did.

That's living your life. We would say, it might not be the party we would have asked for, but as long as we are here, we might as well dance—and we might as well ask others to dance with us.

The year Annie passed away, we got a few female family members and friends and started the "Jingle Belles." What started as Barb's close family and friends wanting to help her get through the first year ended up being a huge blessing for all of us. Truth be told, we all thought we'd need help; so we did it for all of us. Each person took one month and each month someone planned a fun party or event. The reason it was called Jingle Belles was because Anne loved charm bracelets and loved to "jingle." After she passed away, Barb and I were at a craft sale and we tried on some charm bracelets. Barb looked at me and said, "We're just going to have to 'jingle' for the rest of our lives!"

In order to be a Jingle Belle, you had to wear a feather boa, lots of jewelry and/or a tiara—because Annie liked those things. We called our parties "meetings" and exchanged gifts each time. We laughed so hard and had so much fun that we kept Jingle Belles going for years. If you are going through a tough time (or even if you aren't), I encourage you to make more time for fun.

Several of our out-of-town friends started Jingle Belles chapters, so feel free to do it. It's fun. One of the things my sister and I do to "choose happy" is celebrate Christmas to the max. We are the first to put our decorations out and the last to pack them up, so you can imagine the happiness I got from meeting Christopher Radko, the artist who designed all those Christmas ornaments. He loves Christmas as much as we do, and when he told me, "A simple shift in our thoughts can positively affect our whole day" I knew I had to include that.

With all the negative that is going on in the world, I present this book as my contribution of positive-ness. People spend so much time being negative and criticizing. I remember once I was frustrated with someone and I complained about them in front of my son, B.J., who said, "Don't say that—he's our friend." I always remembered that, because at a young age he knew the importance of speaking up and sticking up for people. And it helped me remember to give people the benefit of the doubt and not be so critical.

This book was easy to write—God gave me all the ideas and put me right in front of all these great story contributors, so His name should probably be on the front cover. All the people who contributed—some famous, some not famous—were so brave to share their stories and each one of them continues to be a beacon of hope and light to others.

I dreamed of doing this and with the grant from NAILBA, it happened. I took no pay and wrote it in hopes that it would provide comfort, support, courage, hope and strength to anyone who reads it.

Everyone has their own way of getting through a tough time and for me, it is my Christian faith, but I don't mean to push any religion, lifestyle or idea, it is just my attempt to help someone get through a tough time, and to let you know you can be happy and have a positive outlook for your life no matter what you are going through. Maybe you will read something that will give you an idea; try it.

There is way more good out there and when we make up our mind to stop focusing on all that is going wrong, we start to see all that is going right.

I've found there are 15 keys that will help, and I've broken them down to correspond to the letters in the phrase Find Contentment

Sally's Fifteen Keys to a Happy Life

F orward - Keep moving forward

I nitiative - Take the initiative and start things

N ow is the time - Do it now, live in the now

D etermination - Stay determined to making it

C ommunity - Accept the help of others

O ptimism - Don't give up on yourself or others

N ew Ideas - Maybe it's the time to try new ideas

T enacity - Stay in the game, you can do it

E nergy - Do what you need to do to have energy

N ormalcy - Embrace your "new normal"

T rust - Trust yourself and others.

M indfulness - Less worry, more gratitude

E ncouragement - Encourage yourself and others.

N utrition and Health - Take care of yourself.

T ranquility - Learning to relax and be at peace.

There is light at the end of the tunnel—a light so bright it will amaze you. If you keep looking, you will find it. No matter what life hands you: Choose Happy. You can do it—you can live a life full of contentment in any situation. God bless all who read this.

— STR

"They who wait for the LORD shall renew their strength; they shall mount up with wings like eagles; they shall run and not be weary; they shall walk and not faint."

— Isaiah 40:31 ESV

Foreword

By Dreama Denver

There are times in life when you cross paths with someone who is "meant to be" in your orbit … for a reason, a season, or a lifetime. Often these connections are totally unexpected. You meet and you instantly like each other, you find commonality and you make a choice to stay in touch. That's how it happened with Sally Rains when both our books were honored with the Ella Dickey Literacy Award. As we got to know each other better, we realized, not only were we both authors, but we both ran nonprofit foundations that assisted people in challenging, life-altering situations. A friendship was born.

When she asked me to contribute to this book, I thought about my life challenges and where they had led me. I had no idea my thoughts were aligned with hers in a way that neither of us could have imagined: I was writing what she was thinking. Each of her chapters starts with a letter from: FIND CONTENTMENT. I had written my piece without knowing this and when I saw the titles of her chapters, I knew we were, not only part of the same book, but mentally on the same page.

You can read my original submission and judge for yourself.

"The only thing certain in life is change. Sometimes change is subtle, skimming the surface of your life in ways that cause the tiniest of ripples, barely noticeable to the naked eye. Other times change is a gentle wave that moves you forward, lifts you upward and caresses your life with a lover's gentle touch. But there are those times when change arrives at your doorstep with hurricane force, ripping away foundations, uprooting what has been planted and nourished, lovingly and tenderly throughout a lifetime."
— Gilligan's Dreams, by Dreama Denver

You've just finished reading the first paragraph of my book, *Gilligan's Dreams,* written about my life with my husband, Bob Denver. I'm guessing that most of you can remember changes in your life that fit each of these descriptions. Like you, I've had my fair share (sometimes it feels like more than my fair share) of hurricane force changes - the death of my brother at the young age of 31 and my sister-in-law, Kathy, whom I adored; my son's diagnosis of severe autism when he was a beautiful two year old toddler, and the death of my husband after almost thirty years of marriage.

In my young life, I was an actress, on the road, having the time of my life. After eight years of touring solo, I was asked to audition for a show starring Bob Denver of *"Gilligan's Island"* and *"The Many Loves of Dobie Gillis"* fame.

I auditioned and got the part of Bob's love interest and the rest was history. Our stage romance turned into the real thing and for the next seven years, we toured all over this country and Canada, living the dream together! Bob was the love of my life.

When our son, Colin, came along in 1984, he became the love of both our lives. His diagnosis of severe autism in 1986 turned our world upside down. Everything, and I mean EVERYTHING, about life as we knew it changed. In the blink of an eye, we went from playing pretend for a living to living the reality of our new normal.

In the years since my husband passed away, I've survived. I survived when I thought I couldn't. I survived when I honestly didn't want to. I survived in spite of myself and my heartbreak.

To those of you who are surviving, please, please give yourself the credit you deserve. You're still standing despite the odds and that takes enormous courage. The fact that you're a survivor also means you're capable of becoming a thriver. How? By digging deep inside yourself to find strength you never knew you had. By stepping outside your own pain and focusing on the needs of others, especially in the face of loss.

In my case, I founded West Virginia's Always Free Honor Flight, which honors our WWII, Korean and Vietnam veterans with trips to our nation's capital to visit the memorials built to honor their service. Honor Flight became a passion and helped me thrive.

But, trust me, the thriving part took time. It didn't happen overnight. I remember how some days I could barely place one foot in front of the other or string words together to form a sentence. When it seemed all I could do was to survive, how could I ever imagine thriving? That's a question that took me decades to answer.

I give myself credit for being a strong woman over the years. To family and friends who loved and supported me through everything, I give credit, which they absolutely deserve. In the case of my son, who needed full time care—care that Bob and I provided 24/7 for 21 years—I give the lion's share of the credit to my husband, who was steadfast and committed to both of us every step of the way.

I was blessed with so many selfless, loving people in my life. I was blessed with good health that allowed me to be physically capable. I was blessed with a tenacity that made me determined to navigate my way through the muck of life. And I was blessed by challenges that forced me to dig deep to find the strength to keep going.

Yes, you read that right. I was "blessed" by every challenge I faced. It was difficult to see the blessing when I was in the middle of the trial, and I didn't really understand that concept until five years ago.

I was out walking my dog, giving thanks, expressing gratitude as I do every day, for all the positive things in my life, when suddenly, out of nowhere, I fell to my knees. There, in the grass … on my knees, a torrent of tears came. I couldn't stop them. Please know, there was no forethought—it just happened. Every sad memory surfaced. A geyser of hurt poured out of me.

I cried for the pain and the sadness, the emptiness I had felt since losing my husband. I cried for the conversations I had never had and would never have with my nonverbal adult son. I cried for all the mommy experiences I had missed—the first day of school, graduation, proms, the girlfriend he would bring home that I wouldn't like and the one he would bring home that I would love. I wept for my son's marriage that would never happen and the grandchildren I would never have.

But the Tables Turned

Suddenly came more tears, but this time tears of gratitude, even joy, for my son EXACTLY the way he is because, honestly, he's the purest soul I've ever known and what I've learned by having him in my life is immeasurable—compassion, patience, joy for the tiniest accomplishment and most of all, how to love, with no expectations.

I cried tears for my husband, not because I lost him, but because I was beyond blessed to have spent over half my life with this decent, loving, honorable human being. And then, unexpectedly, tears of gratitude to God for His grace, which saw me through, and continues to see me through, the most difficult times in my life.

If I'm being totally honest, for most of my adult life, I hadn't given much thought to God's grace. I hadn't really given Him much credit at all. Like so many of us, I cried out to Him in desperation when things weren't going well and thanked Him a bit offhandedly when things were.

On my knees, in the grass, something inside me changed that day. I started looking back over my life and could clearly see His hand in every part of it—the people who came into my life for a reason or a season, the ones He sent to teach me valuable, sometimes painful lessons. Since my husband's death, the perfect people who had come into my life at the perfect time. There were endless examples. I began to see how every experience had shaped me.

I realized I wouldn't be the woman I am today had I not spent time in life's valleys. The valleys taught me so much more than the mountaintops.

A friend recently told me that was my lightning bolt moment and I was changed! I began Bible study and was flabbergasted by how little I knew.

Have you ever noticed that when we get what we think we want, it's never quite enough? The new outfit, the expensive shoes, the bigger house, the promotion, the new car … these things give us temporary satisfaction, but at some point, we always find ourselves wanting more, bigger, better.

We will never be satisfied fully in our earthly existence, because this earth is not our final destination. We're just passing through. We're homeless, all of us, and only our 'home' with Him will bring total contentment. Heaven and the New Earth will finally give us the elusive 'more' we seek, in our human existence.

Every trial I've been through, every challenge I've faced has led me to a greater understanding of God's original plan for us; being heaven bent, always looking up, knowing this earthly life is temporal is the greatest hope we have.

"For I know the plans I have for you," declares the LORD, "plans to prosper you and not to harm you, plans to give you hope and a future."
— Jeremiah 29:11 (NIV)

What a glorious future He has in store for those of us willing to accept His gracious gift of eternal life.
— Dreama Denver

You are doing a great job. Just keep moving forward. Whatever you are faced with, you can do it. Believe in yourself. You are amazing. You have a choice in how you will live your life. Choose Happy.   --STR

CHAPTER ONE

Forward, Keep Moving Forward

In a note I found on the day I finished writing this book, my father had taken a year from my mother's diary and summarized it to what he thought she would have wanted us to remember. Her memory was starting to fail at this time and he wanted us to have this. She kept diaries all her life, and while she wrote what happened, she never looked back with regret—she always kept moving forward.

I had already listed my "Fifteen Keys to a Happy Life" and coincidentally in the printout, she listed fifteen things she felt were important for a happy life, and many were basically the same thoughts as mine.

In the note, she said one of the keys to happiness is accomplishing what we can.

"Accomplish whatever we are capable of and whatever makes us feel fulfilled."

— *Margie Tippett*

When we are stuck in a rut, it's hard to accomplish anything, but if we keep moving forward and do what we can, we can have a happy life.

When I was a child, I was like many kids—I didn't like to read and my mom, who always had a book going, tried everything until she finally figured out a way to get me to read. She checked out a book at the library called, *Good Dog, Forward*—it was the turning point.

I was so interested in that book, Mom continued getting me books about young girls and women going through tough situations, but having the courage to endure. She once told me she got me every book about "blind girls and orphans" the library had, but it all started with *Good Dog, Forward.*

I couldn't find the book on the internet, but I remember it well—my first favorite book. It was about a girl who lost her sight and all she went through before eventually getting a guide dog. At first she was bitter and resistant to everything, but once she got her guide dog (support dog), it gave her confidence. Whenever she wanted to start walking, she would say "Good dog. Forward," and the dog knew to lead her. "Forward" meant they were going places.

Her support dog was taking her places and walking her home—just as we can offer support and take it from others.

"We are all just walking each other home."

— *Ram Dass, Author*

Wouldn't it be great if we had that sort of confidence when we were going through a situation? We could hold our heads up and say, "Forward!" and we would keep going without fear.

My love of reading about strong girls and women led me to as many Helen Keller biographies as we could find. After there were no more Helen Keller books, my mom introduced me to Amelia Earhart—who wasn't blind, but was a person who made up her mind to succeed. Both of these women displayed the mantra, "Forward!" throughout their inspirational lives.

Annie Sullivan, the woman who taught Helen Keller to communicate and brought her out of her proverbial darkness into the light, was as much of a hero to me as Helen was. She saw the potential in Helen and it was because of her belief in the young girl that Helen was able to do so much in her life. It was also because of her belief in herself that she succeeded.

Amelia Earhart had many doors closed on her, but she kept going forward.

"Never interrupt someone trying to do what you said couldn't be done."

— *Amelia Earhart*

No one was going to stop her and I'm sure many of you are like me—if someone tells me my idea won't work or I can't do something, I set out to prove them wrong. If you set your expectations low for me, I will exceed them every time, but if you say I can't do something, I'll say, "Watch me."

I had a college professor who told me I couldn't write and that I should change my major. Don't let anyone's words or opinion stop you from moving forward.

Once I found the joy of reading, I found out about others who, despite the situation given to them, found a way to move forward and find some joy in their lives.

As Anne Frank and her family were cooped up in an attic from 1942-1944 hiding from the Nazis during World War II, she kept notes in her diary and one cannot imagine a more dismal situation than her family faced—yet she found a way to live her life, such as it was, during that time. How was it that despite living every day with the fear of being found and killed, she was able to find some good in her life?

"I don't think of all the misery, but of the beauty that still remains."
— Anne Frank

It wasn't the life she would have wished for but she kept a positive attitude, and though she is gone, her words live on to educate and inspire generations. Anne Frank, along with Helen Keller and Amelia Earhart all refused to quit; they kept moving forward—and we can, too.

It's happening every day. People are choosing hope over despair. They are choosing power over being a victim; strength over weakness; and happiness and contentment over pity. Life is so much better when you choose happy over sad—and you have the power inside you to choose.

ARE YOU HEARING VOICES?

If you ever feel that little voice inside you telling you to do something, if it's good, you should do it. You never know how much the smallest thing can mean to someone, and that's what happened with the gift of a book.

About three months after I lost my father, I entered a period of time that was not optimistic. The day he passed away was the day before the big eclipse in August of 2017.

We had some family members staying with us and I had planned a big eclipse-themed party for them. Unfortunately, I had to tell them my dad had just passed away. One of them asked, "Are we still having the party?" Well, I had all the food bought and people had traveled to get there, so I said, "Sure."

I put on a dinner party that night and had family over the next day to view the eclipse, so there was no time for me to break down and cry. It wasn't like I put it in a box to get through those two days—I put it in a box, set it on a shelf and forgot to take it out. Soon it was Christmas and I tried extra hard that year, buying everyone in the family matching holiday pajamas. I wanted everyone to have a fun Christmas and then a Happy New Year.

But one day in January, a big sadness came over me and I could barely function. This was not like me at all. I didn't feel like I had anyone to talk to about this, because I didn't want to upset them—I felt I was the one who should be helping everyone else. I'm sure many of you feel that way sometimes.

For several days in a row I felt depressed and began to think, "No one cares about me."

Has that ever happened to you, where you feel bad and then you start placing blame on others for not caring about you? However, in reality, of course they do care about you—lots of people do. I was not asking for help or telling anyone how I felt, so how could they have known to reach out and help me?

Then one day, my son Mike's girlfriend, Lori (who was to become his wife), gave me a book called *Love Does: Discover a Secretly Incredible Life in an Ordinary World* by Bob Goff.

Lori said the book made her think of me, and this really touched my heart. I started to read the book—and by the first few pages of the first chapter I was in tears—tears of happiness.

The box had come down from the shelf and was opened! All those emotions came through with this book full of experiences from Bob Goff's life. Just reading the book gave me great enthusiasm for things I could do. Maybe if Lori never gave me that book, I would never have written this one.

I'm not sure if it was completely the book that helped me. I think it was the fact that Lori made the effort to give me the book. The book provided just the encouragement I needed at just the right time.

She had no way of knowing that I really needed some encouragement at that time. When others saw me, I was always the happy, friendly hostess. But when everyone left, I felt I had no purpose.

I had loved being a mother to my sons, but now they were grown and it seemed like they didn't need or want my help. I had been a caregiver to my parents, but once they were gone, it was like I was experiencing the empty nest feeling all over again. It seemed everyone had their life going on, and I was just watching. I will bet you have felt like that a time or two in your life—maybe even now.

"Living a life fully engaged and full of whimsy and the kind of things that love does is something most people plan to do, but along the way they just kind of forget."

— Bob Goff

Wow, that really hit me and a huge burden was lifted. In my own little doldrums I had forgotten to be my old self—my fun-loving whimsical self. Even if you are going through something like a sick family member, a health crisis for yourself, a big time of decision-making, a loss of job, a stressful time at work, death of a loved one, you can live through it and you can do it with contentment, and maybe even a little whimsy.

I like Kevin Costner's quote, "You have to decide if you will wilt like a daisy or are you going to live the life you've been granted?" Don't wilt when you can be happy.

There is great power in being content, because when we are restless—always looking for something else—it steals our joy. How can you have a good day, if you are constantly mulling over all that is going wrong with your life? Being content doesn't mean you are ecstatic—all excited about life every minute. We all have down moments and we have to be able to respect our feelings (or someone else who is going through something and seemingly having a bad day), but then get back up.

If you find yourself in a deep valley, don't expect too much out of yourself right now. If you do, you will begin to feel bad about yourself, because at this time you are not at your strongest. Stop beating yourself up—this is not the end of your story. You'll be back—and you will be stronger than you ever thought you could be.

How Can I Calm Myself Down?

Right now, just take a breath and be open to a new feeling. Visualize yourself being content.

Here is a little exercise you can do right this minute to calm down. Calming ourselves down puts us on the road to *Happy.*

Picture yourself in a wonderful place. Water can sometimes help: the beach with the peaceful tide, a lake surrounded by mountains, a stream or brook.

As you visualize your happy place, take deep breaths. Breathe in, breathe out. Breathe in and hold it a few seconds, breathe out. Do it again. Now, make your face into a smile. Hold that smile, keep smiling, showing your teeth and tricking your brain into thinking you are happy.

Smiling Improves Your Health

Even if you don't feel like smiling, do it. A fake smile will do the same as a real one with lifting your mood, lowering your stress and even boosting your immune system. As an article on NBC.com says, " … smiling can trick your brain into happiness."

"What's crazy is that just the physical act of smiling can make a difference in building your immunity," Los Angeles-based Dr. Murray Grossan told the website, "When you smile, the brain sees the muscle [activity] and assumes that humor is happening."

A great day is when we can contribute to it, as much as we get back. Sometimes our smile is our contribution to make the world more happy— or even the world of just one person.

When we are fighting battles every day it can get tiring, but when we make an effort to wake up with a smile on our face, the world smiles back at us.

Being content gives you peace in your heart. When we have peace in our heart, others see it and it can in turn help to strengthen them.

"Having an attitude of peace and calm is priceless. It's an attitude that says, 'I'm trusting God,' and it speaks powerfully to people."
— Joyce Meyer

The "I'm trusting God" attitude will get you a lot further than the desperately hoping, "Oh please God, help me!" or the ever-popular, "It's no use," or "I'm having a bad day." If we ask Him for help in our distress, then we should trust that He will be there with us—that trust is what gives us the power to go forward.

Keep Going No Matter What Happens

Tessa Greenspan, who once took a business from a million dollars in debt to $10 million dollars in sales is the most positive person that most people will ever meet. She is known for being positive and says she has 35,000 positive sayings stored in her phone.

She travels the world, has impeccable taste in clothing, and always has a smile on her face and a hand to reach out to someone. However, those who know her would be surprised to know how she came into the world: a product of her mother's rape at age 14.

It was the 1940s in a small farming community in Arkansas and after the harvest, the farmers in the surrounding towns would get together for a big celebration. Her mother, Susie, was 14 and she met a boy who she thought was cute and they took a walk, but the boy overpowered her and took her into the woods and brutally raped her.

She had no idea what to do; she was devastated and felt ashamed with no one to talk to about it. Finally, when she was six months pregnant, her stepmother noticed what was happening and asked her about it.

She was encouraged to have an abortion, but she wouldn't do it. Tessa was born in Arkansas, in a shack with no running water, a dirt floor and an outhouse. Susie's parents found a man for her to marry two weeks before Tessa was born, and she had another daughter by this man two years later.

"Most children of rape are resented, but for some reason my mother loved me unconditionally," Tessa said.

But the story doesn't end there. Six years later, when Tessa's mother Susie was 20, she was in a horrible car accident.

"She was crushed in that accident and spent 13 months in the hospital," said Tessa. "The gangrene settled in and the doctor came in. Before he could say anything, she said, 'Go ahead and do what you need to do, I've got two kids I have to get back to.' "

The doctor amputated her left leg.

"There she was, two kids, one leg and no money," said Tessa.

"But she had initiative.

"While on crutches, she found a program and was able to go to secretarial school. At the time, we lived in the projects in East St. Louis. When put into a situation, you can either overcome or succumb. You have a choice. My mother chose to overcome. I choose to overcome."

Susie took the bus while on crutches for more than a year to go to school. Tessa says she got her positivity from her mother.

"It's all about your determination," she said. "It's about the choices you make when you have decisions to consider."

And the little girl watching her mother get an education stuck with her, too.

"I work on myself every day," she said. "When I wake up, I read, I meditate. I've been a lifelong reader and searcher."

Why is it that some people are able to endure so much in life and others seem to be crushed by it? Many feel having a foundation to hold on to is a big factor.

"I think it is a God thing," said Tessa. "My mother sang gospel songs to me all the time. I always convey my positivity to others. Every day I post something positive on Facebook."

While she is constantly learning and traveling and doing, she does not watch television.

"In fact, I have a plant sitting in front of my television set," she said. "I am very protective about what I put in my mind. I am only going to put positivity into my mind."

How was Tessa's mother able to give her such a positive life with such an unspeakable beginning? She worked at it. She never stopped moving ahead, first with the decision to keep her baby, then with going to school, and then raising her two children despite having a leg amputated.

What if Tessa's mother had given up? What if she had gotten an abortion or taken her own life before anyone found out about the pregnancy? The world would not have Tessa.

"We all have opportunities every day to make choices that would make a difference in our lives," she said. "I choose to live a life of significance and leave a legacy of positivity."

Tessa had a sister who was raised in the same house—with the same mother—and Tessa went one way and her sister took an unfortunate "poor me" attitude turn in the road. She ended up on drugs and had an early death due an overdose.

"I tried every way I could to help her," said Tessa. "I gave her money, I was there for her. She died of an overdose of methadone. I paid for her funeral."

She wanted to tell her story in hopes it would help someone.

"You can be a victim or a victor," said Tessa. "You have a choice." (Contact Tessa Greenspan: Tessa@TessaGreenspan.com)

SOMETIMES YOU ARE A LEADER, SOMETIMES YOU ARE LED

Tessa is seen by her peer as a leader, largely because she is always moving forward. Forward thinking is a good quality in a leader. Recently, a friend told me she had read the latest book on "leadership" and it got me thinking what really is leadership and how can we be leaders?

"Leadership is the ability to adapt the setting so everyone feels empowered to contribute creatively to solving the problems."
— *Steven M. Smith*

Often we see leadership as one person who is all important leading the flock. Is the leader the most important person in that setting? No, because if there were no "flock," then who would the leader be leading? The most important part of being a good leader—whether it is the leader of your family, your business, or your community—is to see the flock as being as important as you are.

My husband, Rob, is a sportswriter and when he writes an article or does a speaking engagement or a "Facebook Live," he always considers the audience. In that moment, he is the "leader," as people are looking to him for information about the sports teams he covers, but he always remembers that if there were no readers or listeners, then he would not have a job. Many of those readers or listeners may be leaders in their church or community—where Rob is a member of the flock. We must always realize we are no better than anyone, and no one is better than we are—we can all fit in, if we respect others.

Feeling good about ourselves or having the ability to help others feel good or respected helps us move forward. When we stay grounded and are respectful to others, doors open.

Another example of leadership can be found in the sales profession. If you have a product to sell, don't talk down to your potential customers. It would not motivate me to buy something from someone who says, "If you say you can't buy it due to time or money, you are just wrong." Wouldn't it be better to say, "I understand your concerns, but maybe I could help figure out how to get it—if you want it." Good leaders realize they are not better than others, because it takes everyone for us to be successful.

In our families, if we are to be good leaders—good parents or siblings—we will get a more effective outcome if we live the examples we ask for in others and if we are constantly trying to move forward in improving ourselves. As a child, I have a better chance of not using profanity, if I don't hear my parents using it. There's a better chance I will make my bed every day, if my parents emphasize it and if they lead by the example of making their bed.

One of the most famous early self-improvement-type leadership books was *The 7 Habits of Highly Effective People* by Stephen Covey. On his list of habits, I like number seven the best: "Sharpen the Saw."

We buy a bright and shiny new saw that makes cutting wood so easy. It makes us want to be more productive, because we are moving along, but if we do nothing to that saw, years go by and the productivity goes down. Same with us. There are so many ways we can improve ourselves if we choose—stay physically fit, do things that help us emotionally and socially, as well as feed our mental and spiritual sides.

SHE MAKES MORE SALES BECAUSE SHE MAKES MORE FRIENDS

Susan Genz sells Mary Kay products and has a successful business going. In this type of business, it helps her to have customers come on as distributors under her. However, many who go into the multi-level business fizzle out, because their heart is in the wrong place. Their goal is to get more people to sell their product so they will make more money, but if your goal is to truly serve the individual, you will have more success.

"No one is under me—everyone is on the big team," said Suzie.

She looks at each person she deals with as a person not a possible client and her genuine-ness comes out. Instead of, "You should buy this to cover up those wrinkles," she is all about, "You are so beautiful," which then endears people to her. They love being around her and want her to come back, so they buy her products.

She ends up making more sales, plus she makes friends and has a happier life.

We look in the mirror and see our flaws—we don't need others telling us about them, just to get a sale.

A real leader doesn't try to tear others down—they constantly seek ways of including others and making them feel important. This is true in the most expensive mahogany boardroom at the top of an office building—and it's true in the family room of your house.

> *"There are only two ways to influence human behavior: you can manipulate it or you can inspire it."*
> — *Simon Sinek, author*
> *Start with Why: How Great Leaders Inspire Everyone to Take Action*

If you want people to respect you and want to be around you, you've got to employ the type of leadership that involves working with others. You must realize you aren't perfect and there are always ways you can be improving yourself.

> *"Leadership is about making others better as a result of your presence and making sure that impact lasts in your absence."*
>
> — *Sheryl Sandberg*

People who are able to live a happy life—at least most of the time—are those who choose to. Often their choice is through leadership, even though they may not even realize they are being a leader. No matter what your situation, you have the strength to endure it and lead yourself and others though it.

The person who receives bad news in the form of a diagnosis of illness in a friend or family member, yet keeps moving forward by fighting alongside their friend, is a leader. So often there are those who just "can't take it" and disappear. If you choose to join in someone's fight, you are a leader.

On that day you have a big job interview and you are alone in your bedroom getting ready, you can be a leader to yourself. Don't let your head get filled with fear, "What if I mess up the interview?" "What if I'm not qualified?" Instead, psyche yourself into, "I know I can do this." "The person interviewing me is no better than I am—he/she had to go on a job interview once upon a time or they would not be there."

> *"You gain strength, courage and confidence by every experience in which you really stop to look fear in the face. You are able to say to yourself, 'I have lived through this horror. I can take the next thing that comes along.' You must do the thing you think you cannot do."*
>
> — *Eleanor Roosevelt*

Our challenges, roadblocks and detours in life don't have to define us or keep us from moving forward. Just because someone around us chooses to be negative and see things from a "helpless" perspective, we don't have to.

Make up your mind that you are going to thrive. You are going to move forward in life and have a positive impact on others. By doing this, you will have a positive impact on yourself. You are going to be great.

"Tough times never last, but tough people do."

— Robert Schuller

Think of the most awful thing you have lived through. You made it through that, so you must be a pretty strong person. Look down at your feet. They are right where they are supposed to be. Whatever you are doing, if you are doing your best, you are doing a great job.

WE CAN ALL BE LEADERS IN THE CLUTCH—LIKE IT OR NOT

Lauren Haeger of Peoria, Arizona, was a two-time National Champion softball pitcher for the University of Florida. Seeing her out there in the national spotlight, she looked so powerful leading her team to victory, but in reality it came with a role she did not ask for.

She was put in a position of leadership—whether she wanted it or not—but a conversation with her coach changed her life as far as her attitude on being a leader goes.

"I was in a meeting with the coach," she said. "We got into a passionate conversation and I said I thought it was unfair that everyone else can have a bad day and they can have it show, but I can't. I felt frustrated and said, 'Why can't I just have a bad day? Why can't I just have a bad day and go to practice and have it be over?' "

That is a feeling we all get in every aspects of life. Why can't I just fall apart? Why do I always have to be the strong one? Because we are called to lead by our actions and we have the strength to do that. A leader knows how to handle that which is thrust upon them and as a young college student, Lauren learned some valuable life lessons.

Her coach understood what she was saying, but he abruptly interrupted her.

He said, "Because if you have a bad day, then everybody has a bad day. The entire energy changes. When you are happy and having a good time, everyone else is happy and having a good time—haven't you noticed?"

She told her coach "I don't want to do that (be a leader), I just want to do my job and do my best and win softball games."

She said that being a leader was not in her plan—playing softball was. But as it turned out her great skill in playing softball and her passion for the game led her to have leadership qualities she didn't even realize she had.

Coach was right—when she was happy, others were.

Happiness feeds off of happiness. Good attitude feeds off of good attitude. When someone is giving off good positive vibes, it is easy to buy into it and feel positive. The same thing can happen in reverse—a downer can bring others down with them in no time.

Lauren and her Florida Gators teammates won the NCAA Championship for the second year in a row in 2015. Lauren became known for her famous "Haeger Bombs"—the home runs that came just at the right time.

She was clearly the leader of the team, whether she chose that role or not. Lauren thought about what her coach told her and realized that when she really wanted to win, she would develop a "let's go!" attitude with her teammates and they felt that enthusiasm and fed off of it.

Lauren didn't even realize she had taken on a leadership role merely by having a positive attitude. We all do this every day. When we go through an illness, lose a job and face financial woes, experience a death, we will either crumble or rise up. We will either assume a positive attitude to help the others get through the situation or we won't.

She had played on teams internationally and had the winning spirit, but up until then, she had never thought of herself as a "leader."

"I just thought I was doing 'me.' The coach helped me see it more clearly and I learned, and I matured. I learned that when I was not in the best mood to just let it go. I realized the mood of the practice was a lot on how I was acting."

We all go through similar struggles in different settings. If you are sitting in a hospital waiting room, you have suddenly been thrust into a situation. Your "coach" is saying, "It's time to be a leader."

Lauren, who played professionally after graduating, says she always gravitated towards leaders, but didn't realize she could end up being seen as one to others.

"One of the secrets to wild success is honing your leadership vision and communicating it to others."

— Tony Robbins

Sometimes we are put in the role of leadership for something we did not want to do. Those around us see us moving forward. They see us picking up the ball and saying, "Let's go!"

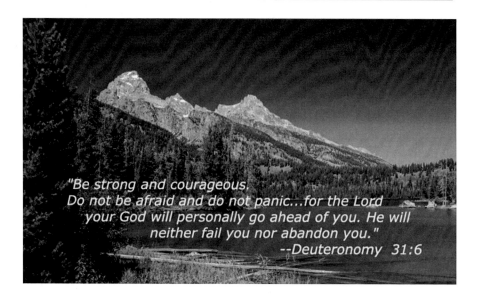

"Be strong and courageous.
Do not be afraid and do not panic...for the Lord
your God will personally go ahead of you. He will
neither fail you nor abandon you."
--Deuteronomy 31:6

THE CLUTCH GENE

"It's like the clutch gene," said my son, Mike Rains. "Some people just have the ability to come through in big moments. For whatever reason, they seem to have success when they are needed most."

Once again, it's a sports analogy that can apply to our everyday life in our quest to keep moving forward.

"Matt Holliday (the baseball player) has the clutch gene," Mike said. "Whenever the team was in a crucial situation, he was the man you would want up at the plate."

We all have the ability to come through in the clutch. We do it every day.

It is something some people are born with, but can we all try to find our own clutch gene. It allows a person to stay relaxed. When things are chaotic, there are some people who are able to stay grounded or force themselves to remain calm. They don't let the situation overwhelm them. If they are born with anything, it is the ability to make the right choice.

When others see they are able to stay calm in a stressful situation, it enables them to try to emulate that, to realize they can do it, too. They don't have to panic and be overwhelmed with the situation.

Be a clutch hitter, a leader. Be the person who helps everyone else operate as a team, because you have the guts to step up.

You might not think you have the guts to do it, but you can do anything—even if you are afraid.

"Whenever I feel afraid, I hold my head erect, and whistle a happy tune—and no one will suspect I'm afraid. Make believe you're brave. And the trick will take you far. You may be as brave as you make believe you are."

— *Rodgers and Hammerstein, The King and I*

When I was a kid, I was afraid of the dark. If it was dark by the time I left my friend's house to walk home, I would sing that song and it helped me not to be scared. Sounds silly, but I still sing it sometimes when I need it.

Even the people we think are the strongest can get scared. You might be that person to someone else. To others you are perceived as strong, powerful, successful, but you could be facing a situation filled with uncertainty, and you feel unsure or afraid.

Make believe you're brave—and the trick may take you far. You might even fool yourself. Look towards the light and keep moving forward. Sometimes it may seem difficult, but take the initiative.

They asked the wise old man, "What is your secret for a happy and productive life?" "Why don't they ask something more meaningful," he grumbled softly to himself, "Such as, 'How do you keep from falling?' The answer to both is just the same: You find something substantial and worthwhile to hold on to; and HOLD ON!"

— Jack Tippett

"I want it said of me by those who knew me best, that I always plucked a thistle and planted a flower where I thought a flower would grow."

--Abraham Lincoln

Chapter Two

Initiative

Taking initiative is what leaders—and happy people—do. It's the power to act or take charge before others do. It is the power to take control of a situation—or your life—before it gets control of you. Even in your weakest moment, you can be powerful—you have it in your heart, so don't give up—stay strong.

We have so much more power down deep inside of us than we realize.

No matter what you are going through, it is possible to have a wonderful life—at least some of the time. No one knows this better than my friend, Karolyn Grimes.

Karolyn Grimes has been in at least sixteen movies, including *The Bishop's Wife,* with Cary Grant, Loretta Young, and David Niven where she played Debbie; and Hans Christian Andersen with Danny Kaye, where she played the Little Match Girl. She also worked with John Wayne, Bing Crosby, Fred MacMurray, and Betty Grable.

But the movie she is most known and loved for is *It's a Wonderful Life,* where she played Zuzu, alongside James Stewart and Donna Reed. Karolyn had one of the most memorable lines from the movie: "Daddy, teacher says every time a bell rings, an angel gets his wings."

Despite the upbeat title, *It's a Wonderful Life* was at times sad, but the reason everyone loves it so much is that the theme touches us all. The basic premise is a man who is so down on his luck and feels the weight of the world on his shoulders to the point where he feels his family would be better off "without him," so he sets out to throw himself over a bridge.

He is rescued by Clarence the angel who shows us throughout the rest of the movie how our lives touch so many others, even though we don't realize it.

"Strange, isn't it? Each man's life touches so many other lives. When he isn't around, he leaves an awful hole, doesn't he?"
— Clarence Odbody

IT'S A WONDERFUL LIFE

Karolyn looked so adorable in the movies, but no one knew that behind the scenes, her mother had developed Early Onset Alzheimer's disease and her carefree child acting time came to an abrupt end with her mother's death and the subsequent death of her father in a car accident, not long after.

From her Hollywood life, she was sent by the court, as a teenager, to live in Osceola, Missouri, with relatives who turned out to be less than desirable as substitute parents. Even in those younger days, she knew she had to pull herself up. Karolyn told me, "We all have choices."

"I learned that at a very young age," said Karolyn. "I have followed the rule that life is what we make it. We, as individuals, have the power to make it dark or light; sad or happy."

With the help of teachers and people from that small town—and her own inner strength, she received an education at Central Missouri State in Warrensburg, was married, and had children—but more loss was to come.

"I lost my parents when I was 15 and then I lost two husbands," she said. "I have dealt with death, but for me the worst part was losing my son to suicide at age 18."

A month after his 18th birthday, her son John was gone and she was inconsolable for a time, rarely going out of her house. There is common thought among survivors of suicide (the families)—they wonder, "Was there anything I could have done?" In most cases, there was nothing. It was going to happen and survivors are left to live their lives as best they can.

"When my son died, I felt like a part of me died with him," she said. "A wise old priest encouraged me to turn away from my grief and pain. He suggested I volunteer, which at first I found very hard to do, but I made the effort and soon I realized how good it felt to give of myself to help others."

She started at the school her son had attended, then she did volunteer work at retirement homes and hospitals.

"Helping others makes you feel good about yourself and brings about healing," she said. "And sometimes it is a wonderful life!"

As difficult as it may seem, the best thing to do is take the initiative and keep moving, right foot, left foot, right foot, left foot. Volunteering and helping others seems to be a universal theme of happy people.

Karolyn now travels to speaking engagements about *It's a Wonderful Life*, sharing the message of the film and her message of faith, God and community (zuzu.net). She has lent her name to a home for homeless teens and participated in its opening.

In 2016, Karolyn told Country Living Magazine, that although she enjoys speaking about *It's A Wonderful Life*, her life has never been "wonderful."

"Maybe when I was a child, but not after age 15," she said.

No one's life is perfect.

"There are always ups and downs throughout life. It is how you choose to deal with each crisis that matters," she said. "I always try to look for something positive in a bad situation. It is always there and I focus on that. No one has a completely wonderful life.

"It's how you deal with the situations that you encounter that make the difference. Look for the positives. They will be there."

In *It's a Wonderful Life* when George Bailey is at the end of his rope, and about to jump off a bridge, he prays: "Dear Father in heaven, I'm not a praying man, but if you're up there and you can hear me, show me the way … show me the way."

How many "angels" save others from the same fate every day? Kevin Hines and Ken Baldwin are two men who jumped off the Golden Gate

"A Society grows great when old men plant trees whose shade they will never sit in."
--Greek Proverb

Bridge—and survived. Since it opened in the 1930s, more than 2,000 have jumped off and only 2 percent have survived.

They were interviewed on ABC 7 in San Francisco. They both said that the second they let go they wished they had not done it. Both suffered from bipolar and both felt they were in a black hole before the episode. They felt their life could not be fixed and that they were a burden to everyone and people would be better without them, but after this episode in their life, they learned a lesson: people would not be better off without them.

As he fell, one of them said he saw his present life in front of him and saw how sad his family would be. Due to his bipolar, he felt he heard voices telling him to do it—if only he had recognized that it was the wrong thing to do.

Both said the minute they left the bridge, they had an instant regret. Once you do it, you can't undo it—but God gave them that one more chance and it was enough. Times get tough and though they had depression, they knew they had to stand up to any urge in the future, because their despair and feeling no one cared about them simply wasn't true.

Their outlooks got better. They have both gone on to live happy lives—one finding a wife and one was able to walk his daughter down the aisle at her wedding. Their lives are not perfect, but they realize how precious life is.

"I just want to live happily ever after, every once in a while."
— *Jimmy Buffett*

If you're feeling bad, don't give up on yourself. Whatever you are going through—there is always a way out. If you are so scared you don't know what to do, try to calm yourself.

The song, *Be Not Afraid*, by John Michael Talbot can be very comforting.

If you feel like your life is spinning out of control, tell someone—get help. There is a lot of happiness waiting for you just around the corner from this depression.

There is never "no way out." There is always a way—you just have to find it. Keep trying. Don't give up.

WHAT ARE YOU LOOKING FOR IN LIFE?

When we are young and the whole world is in front of us, we might have big dreams and goals. We feel as though we can do anything. We are brave and take the initiative to try new things.

"The biggest adventure you can have is to live the life of your dreams."
— *Oprah Winfrey*

It is exciting to be pursuing a dream, but the reality is sometimes we land in a deep valley—a place we couldn't have imagined and plans just go by the wayside.

Dreams are great, but don't let the whole "motivational" world make you feel bad if you don't have a "dream" right at this moment. You might just be struggling to make it through the day. Maybe you are tired, and it's OK to rest when you are tired.

Is it OK to just try to be content where we are right now instead of making all that effort and initiative to pursue some big dream? Yes, it is. Sometimes we need to rest to get our strength back to get the initiative to do great things.

Your time will come for that. Maybe now is the time to just try to find contentment in what is right in front of you. You will gather yourself and get strong and soon you'll be taking the initiative to get on with life, and when you do, you'll have trouble staying still. Everything happens in the time it is supposed to.

One definition of contentment is "a state of happiness and satisfaction." You don't always have to be achieving or excelling—sometimes it's just enough to reach a state where you are moving through life in contentment. You will get strong enough to go achieve great things again, but maybe now you just need to try to heal yourself, and you can do it.

One night I woke up in the middle of the night. I laid there worried about our kids, worried about our finances, worried about our parents—you name it, I was worrying about it.

I looked over at my husband, who was sleeping soundly. He doesn't take his worries to bed with him. Before falling asleep, he reads a chapter or two from a book and it calms his mind down and he falls right to sleep.

Not me—I lay there stewing in my juices, thinking about all that happened that day and that leads to worrying about things I don't need to be worrying about—that I can't control. Finally I started keeping an inspirational book (like this one), the Bible, and a flashlight next to my bed so when I can't sleep, I can read and hopefully become peaceful and fall asleep.

The problem with not getting a sound sleep is you have no energy the next day. Take the initiative to calm yourself down. Calm down? That's easier said than done.

TEN (OR MORE) WAYS TO CALM YOURSELF DOWN

1. Walk away from the situation that has you upset
2. Concentrate on taking deep breaths and watching your chest rise up and down when you do
3. Count to ten forwards and then backwards
4. Take a walk
5. Take a bath
6. Distract yourself by watching a funny movie or calling a funny friend
7. Make yourself a cup of hot tea or hot chocolate
8. Find a quiet place and try to think of something else or meditate
9. Take a nap, listen to music, or look at peaceful pictures
10. Give yourself a hug

That last one, giving yourself a hug, is an important one. If no one is around to hug you, giving yourself a hug is the next best thing.

Did you know that the human touch is valuable in calming yourself or others down? When we are physically touched in a kind way, our bodies release a powerful mood elevator called oxytocin.

A hug can be a great thing. This is why I gave my mother a long hug every time I went to visit her in the memory care ward. She may not have known who I was, but I didn't want her to be afraid. I wanted her to feel the human touch of someone who loved her, whether she knew it or not. When I touched her, I sensed she felt at ease with a familiar person.

When my sons were little—and even still today—I told them if they ever needed me and I wasn't there, to cross their arms across their chest and grasp their shoulder blades and that was me giving them a hug. Little did they know I was getting hugs from them when I needed it by doing the same to myself.

Years later, I found out I wasn't the only one doing that. EverydayHealth.com suggests giving yourself a hug.

"Did you know that a 10-second hug a day can change biochemical and physiological forces in your body that can lower the risk of heart disease, combat stress, fight fatigue, boost your immune system, and ease depression? You can begin by giving yourself a hug."

After you've crossed your arms over your chest and reached your hands to the opposite shoulder blade, come back to your upper arms and grasp your upper arms. You will notice the warmth and comfort you have by giving yourself a hug.

You probably already do something similar when you cross your arms. When we are cold we often cross our arms. It's the same type of comforting gesture. Give yourself a hug!

In this busy world, you sometimes need to take the initiative—to make your life more peaceful. It isn't just going to happen. Do what you need to do to save yourself: spend time with happy people. Decorate a room that you like with new, happy pictures or colors, try one of the ideas listed earlier. Happy people don't get there by accident. They make things happen.

One way to take the initiative of trying to be happy is not to lump all your bad happenings in one basket. We've all heard people say, "This has been such a bad year, I can't wait until it's over!" Why would you want something to be over? How do you know the next year will get better? If you are looking for something else bad to happen, you can usually find it, but if you are looking for something good to happen, you'll find that, too. What you are looking for is your choice.

Some people become strong and content in their life and others just can't seem to make it—they seem to lack the initiative to pull themselves up by the bootstraps. They blame their circumstances. They blame other people. It's never their fault—they are always the victim. But that's not you. You are not going to fall apart, you are teaching yourself to be stable in any situation.

IT HASN'T BEEN A BAD YEAR

You should never remember time by years—
As a "great" year in smiles or a "bad" year in tears.
For each new day is a blessing you make
For the way that you live and the chances you take.

Each day is a chance to make a new start
But you've got to reach way down into your heart
And find that enthusiasm that life can give
Then you'll live the life you were meant to live.

Don't ever look back and wish you'd done "this"
Or wish you'd done "that." What fun you will miss.
Be here in your life, and live each day as new
This is my special wish for you.

— STR

YOU HAVE CHOICES.

Margie and Jack Tippett were great examples of contentment and positivity to all who knew them. They had the initiative to achieve great things with their life—and they did. Their version of "great things" may be different than some people's. Their name is not on a building, they didn't win a lot of awards and were not famous—however there is a YMCA building that is there in great part due to Margie's hard work behind the scenes, and there are a few medical advances that help orthopedic surgeons every day due to Jack's efforts.

But the greatest of all the great things they did was to make everyone who came in contact with them a better person. When we see positive, productive people, it makes us want to do more and be better—especially when they encourage us. Where we see kindness we want to be kind. Where there is light we want to contribute to it.

They faced problems just like everyone does in life, and there was a time when it seemed like tragedies began to pile up on them, but they did the best they could.

Through the most tumultuous times that life threw at them, they never fought with each other or others. They took the initiative to lead by example.

There was never a day that went by that one of them didn't remark on if the dogwood was in bloom, did you hear the bird singing this morning, how beautiful the sunset was, how many stars were out that night.

They saw beauty in every day (and night) and they smiled when they saw it, and often Jack used his favorite word, "Wow!"—although the biggest wow was saved for when they were getting ready to go out and Margie came walking down the hall. He would look up at her beauty and say, "Wow!"

HOW DID THEY STAY SO POSITIVE?

One way was not to dwell on the negative. They had a choice when something bad happened, they could go down the path of despair or they could just keep going and doing the best they could to try to live a positive life. They did all they could to help others. They devoted their time and attention to people when they needed help. They volunteered. They went to church.

While they spent much time helping people or attending to those who needed them, they also had the wisdom to do completely unrelated things so they could have some happiness every day. They never let the worries of the world rob them of their joy.

At the end of the day, after the kids went to bed, they would sit by the fireplace and listen to music every night of their life and just talk to each

"We only have a certain amount of time together, so we should make up our minds to be happy."
--Margie and Jack Tippett

other, or sometimes they would dance.

They put their worries in a box. They may have been worried about a family member or a friend who was sick, and while they helped them out, they did not dwell on that negative, they did not let it affect all areas of their life.

You see the opposite of this all the time. People get so stressed out, because they are taking on the problems of others. You might even do it. A friend or even just a person you know starts dumping their situation on you and soon you are all riled up about it.

When we allow the problems of others to infiltrate our lives to the point that it changes our outlook, it is time to step back. It's good to help others, but we should not let their problems consume us.

Think about Queen Elizabeth and her hats. She wears a different hat to every event she attends. If she had all the hats sitting out on her dresser, it could become very stressful with hats everywhere and not knowing what one to wear.

So after she gets home, she takes off her hat and puts it in a box and sets it on her shelf. Or probably her butler or footman or whoever does it for her, but it's a good guess that there aren't a lot of hats strewn all over her dresser.

Putting them in their appropriate box allows her to go on with what she has for the rest of the day without the worry that one of her corgis is going to chew at one of the hats. And then when she needs another hat, she opens the box for that specific hat.

Isn't it fun that Queen Elizabeth's hats can be an analogy applied to us? Just picturing all those colorful hats makes me happy.

We have so many things going on in a day—we are wearing so many hats—that sometimes it can become overwhelming. We need to learn to put things in an imaginary box, setting it on our imaginary shelf, and go experience all the good there is in life every day.

An example of this would be you have a loved one in a medical facility who you visit every day. You have two choices—you can see your life as one big negative, because you "have to" go visit your loved one complaining, "My life is so awful, I have to visit so-and-so every day … " or "another bad day at the hospital."

The second choice is to feel like "I GET to" visit that person. Go visit and give them the best that you have of your love and your time—and when you walk out the door, put that visit in the box and set it on a proverbial shelf.

If this is something you endure every day, then don't spend time crying or being sad about your visit, because your life will become all about that. When the visit is over, it's over. Once you leave it behind you, then you are fresh to do other things. You can be a parent to your children or a spouse to your husband or wife.

The same could be said of a parent with a sick child. Maybe they have to go to the hospital for treatment every day, but then when they get home, hopefully the medical appointment goes in a box, and some fun time begins.

You will open that box up later. You can get through a tough time, if you take the initiative to make good choices—now is the time to begin.

"Change happens when the pain of staying the same is greater than the pain of change."

--Tony Robbins

Chapter Three

Now is the Time

Is there something eating at you? Do you have a big decision to make or maybe you don't like the situation you are in, but can't seem to make your move. It could be a small change you have been wanting to make or it could end up being a life-changing event.

When we have a decision to make, yet we don't do anything, the stress of that decision just sitting there can cause us a lot of problems. If you really can't decide, now is the time to resolve you are not going to make the decision. Get it out of your mind for a while.

We aren't here to tell you to make a big change, but if you have been wanting to do something and you know in your heart it is the right thing to do, you might want to give it more thought.

Write down on a piece of paper the pros and cons. Why do you want to make the change and what would it accomplish? What would be the consequences if you don't make the change? Sometimes we get so restless, we decide to make big changes and in the end, it was a poor choice. If that's your situation, try to learn to bloom where you are planted and go for an attitude change.

There is also a time when we have put great thought into something and we know we are not living the life we could, but we are stuck for whatever reason. Now is the time to take control of what you can control in your life—choose happy.

She Knew in Her Heart It Felt Wrong

Brenda is a beautiful and smiling receptionist. She is the first person people see when they enter her place of business—a positive asset to her company. But who could know that behind her smile, she was hiding pain and only recently has she been able to feel joy.

Her life growing up was basically filled with love, but that changed one day shortly after the death of her grandma.

"We all loved my grandma so much that when she died, we were all kind of lost," Brenda said. "I was so sad. Around this time, I met a guy and his great personality helped get me out of the doldrums."

Initially they hit it off and it seemed like he could not do enough for her—until he did too much. What looked like devotion and loving attachment was eventually turning into smothering.

"There were a few red flags, but I ignored them," she said. "He came at a time I needed him and really picked my spirits up. In the beginning, it was all good, but I was not used to being attached to people the way he was to me."

He began isolating her from her friends and family, but it was disguised by all he was seemingly doing to make her happy. Sometimes she even felt confused about it.

Once when her cousin asked her to go out and celebrate her birthday, Brenda's boyfriend convinced her to stay home. Her cousin ended up being very hurt by the situation, yet still Brenda did what he asked of her.

It was a double-edged sword, as he was working and providing for her, yet she felt she was slowly slipping away from being her own person, to the point where she needed him—if nothing else, to pay the rent and for the finances—which he controlled. Slowly she went from having good credit to having bad credit due to the decisions he was making.

"It all built up, until one day he hit me," she said. "And he did it while we were in bed, while I was sleeping."

He was living in her house and would not leave, and he always made up with her—but he did it again. Each time he persuaded her it was her fault and he continued to make her feel smaller and smaller. He stole things from her, but most of all he stole her life and her self-esteem.

"I was feeling so low about myself and later I found out I was the victim of narcissistic abuse," she said.

Hearing the term "narcissistic abuse" makes you think the person is in love with themselves and that they think they are better than everyone, and from the way he treated her, it would seem so.

> *"Narcissists don't really love themselves.*
> *Actually, they're driven by shame."*
> —*Psychology Today*

Whatever their reason, they come in many forms. In Brenda's case, he would apologize and even cry after he hit her, making her believe it was her fault that their life was like it was.

Why did she allow someone to control her like that? Why do narcissists act the way they do?

Psychology Today says, "Deep down, narcissists feel the gap between the façade they show the world and their shame-based self. They work hard to avoid feeling that shame. To fill this gap, narcissists use destructive defense mechanisms that destroy relationships and cause pain and damage to their loved ones."

If you are involved in a destructive relationship, whether it is domestic or even at work or with a so-called friend, now is the time to figure out what you are going to do.

Whether abuse is physical or mental, it is still abuse and no one deserves it.

"He was forcing me to do a lot of things I knew in my heart were wrong," said Brenda, "but I pretended he was a different person—a better person. I kept hoping he would change and we could go back to our happy life."

If you find yourself in a controlling situation, the time to get out is now. You deserve no blame, no judgment. What you do deserve is a "real" happy life—not someone's controlling version. If you are in a controlling situation, tell someone so they can help you. It will do no good to keep this all to yourself because you feel like a failure for landing in this situation.

"It was embarrassing that something like this could happen to me," she said, "that a person could take everything from me. For much of the time, I didn't tell anyone, because I was in protection mode. I just went through the motions of life with no enthusiasm and finally no emotions at all."

She finally decided enough was enough and now was the time. She made herself grow stronger and left.

"He stayed the same, but I changed," she said. "Somehow reality hit. I got smarter."

Maybe there is one person reading this who needed to hear it. Maybe Brenda's experience was not in vain.

Sometimes just deciding to make our move—and doing it now—can make all the difference in the world to us.

MONEY AND POWER DON'T ALWAYS BRING HAPPINESS

The Tony Robbins quote, "Change happens when the pain of staying the same is greater than the pain of change," really touched the heart of Stephen

Von Rump, a long-time executive who has recently made a life change.

Stephen has been a successful CEO of several international companies, dressing the part, looking the part, and giving off the air that he is a happy, successful person.

Underneath that layer was a man wishing to simplify his life and get back to his family and a less hectic, more meaningful life. But how could he walk away from a six-figure salary with his head held up high, when he knew people would think he was crazy?

He spent many sleepless nights and there were endless ways the stress affected his health and family life. Was he going to stay in the situation and be miserable or make a change? He pondered the situation and fretted about it.

"You're the CEO of a company and you're taught that based on your career path, that is what you aspire to," said Stephen. "That's what you're destined to be, a leader, a CEO of a company—it's something many people aspire to, and there I was."

But he wasn't happy. He found he was spending more and more time away from home all in the name of making money and keeping that prestige.

"In the type of work I did, I tended to check out of life—especially the community of my family and friends," he said. "I used the excuse that the pressures I faced were greater than everyone else's, and in doing so I missed the cues of people that needed my help and support, and I robbed myself of that same privilege."

Whenever he would entertain the possibility of downsizing in his career, he would be met with negatives from those in the business world.

"I'm a CEO—why would I want to walk away from that?" he said. "Because I'm miserable. I realized I'm trying to meet someone else's expectations for my life. I wanted to be there for those I love and I wanted to live the life I desired—not the one others think I should."

Finally, he did it—he quit his job as a CEO and made a choice to start doing things he wanted to do.

"Making the change was a leap of faith," said Stephen. "But I'm so glad I did it. I'm not completely sure where I'm headed, but I know the timing was right. I felt I had to make that decision now or my soul would die. I am so excited about what tomorrow will bring."

Stephen's Reasons Why People Don't Leave a Job They Are Unhappy With

1. Money
2. Prestige
3. Living the expectations the world has created for you
4. Fear of the unknown (such as, what happens if you leave)

Once Stephen rebelled against the world's expectations, he felt a great relief roll off his shoulders.

"I love music and I have been writing songs and recording," he said. "I even built myself a sound studio. And I'm also working with local entrepreneurs to help them plan and build their companies, something I have always been passionate about."

Stephen's story of being in a dilemma can apply to many of us. Are you stuck in a situation you don't want to be in? We all have the power to change our circumstances, whether we leave them or change our attitude towards them.

Sometimes we need to make a change in our life and we need to make it now. Change can be any small thing—like changing the side you part your hair on, to a big thing like moving to a different state to be near a loved one. Sometimes making a change or a decision to do something "now" can be a life changer, and sometime it can just be fun.

My sister, Barb, reminded me of a time when she was younger and her friends were contemplating a last-minute road trip to Kansas City—a town about four hours from our home. They were in our living room talking about it. She says, I walked through and heard them talking and said, "If you don't go now, you never will." They decided to go.

Every day we are presented with opportunities, and we are also given just as many excuses why we "can't" or "won't" take advantage. If you are waiting for the perfect time to take action, it will probably never come.

Have you ever turned something down, because the "timing was wrong" or not done something for the same reason? The right time may never come and you will have missed a great opportunity. Make that decision, and then rest and watch it happen.

"Don't wait until everything is just right. It will never be perfect. There will always be challenges, obstacles, and less than perfect conditions. So what? Get started now. With each step you take, you will grow stronger and stronger, more and more skilled, more and more self-confident and more and more successful."

— *Mark Victor Hansen*
Creator of Chicken Soup for the Soul

Cardinals Hall of Fame broadcaster, Jack Buck, was one of the most beloved citizens of St. Louis and was known for the kindnesses he showed, the charity he did—along with his great broadcasting.

He was powerful in that he had great self- confidence, which commanded respect, yet he was content with what he had and did not continually look for more. He took great joy in helping others.

The night before he was admitted to the hospital for the last time, he was the keynote speaker for a big dinner. My husband, Rob, was in charge of the dinner and as they sat in an office before Jack was to go on stage he told Rob, "I am going to check into the hospital after the dinner—I have lung cancer."

Here was this man, the emcee of the dinner, who had every excuse in the world to cancel out. How easy it would have been for Jack to have told Rob, "I can't make it." But he knew the "now" might be his last and he wanted to take advantage of it—and to our knowledge, it was his last public appearance—one full of his typical jokes and conversations with every fan who came up to him. He went out swinging.

"Things work out the best for those who make the best of the way things work out."

— *Jack Buck*

In Jack's autobiography, which Rob co-wrote, he said that he had one question he looked forward to asking God when he saw Him: "Why have you been so good to me?" Maybe because you were too good to others, Jack.

We don't have to be as famous as Jack Buck to be an example to others—we just have to keep trying as we go through life. There are those who seem to fall apart with a sinus infection, and those who make the effort to show up at an event with Stage Four cancer and keep on smiling through what seems to be the biggest challenges.

"Go for it now. The future is promised to no one."

— Wayne Dyer

Sometimes your "go for it now" can be as simple as starting to live in the "now." Do something that makes you happy right now.

I remember when the doctors found my little niece had a brain tumor and it felt like our life was crashing down around us. Nothing was the same and life felt so strange.

Shortly after she was diagnosed, I went to a woman's "networking" seminar I had previously signed up for, and they asked us to write down our greatest dream. It was a great idea for those trying to get inspired to start a business or do something they want to do, but it hit me very hard: I didn't have a dream. On that day, I only wanted my niece to get well and my family to be happy. I was not thinking past the little cocoon I had built around my family—I did not have a dream that day.

You don't have to have to be pursuing something amazing at all times in your life. Don't let anyone make you feel not as important because you aren't doing something "they" think is "important."

Often when a child gets sick, the mother has to quit her job to take the child to treatments. It should be a time to surround oneself with family and peace—not a time to feel bad, because you don't have a job, or you have gained weight due to your worries, or you think you are unable to be the perfect mom or dad. You are enough. You are perfect. There will be plenty of time to address those thoughts later, but you need your strength to do what you need to do now.

You will get through this and you will be even more amazing than you were before. Our obstacles tend to make us fight harder and in the process, we become stronger and more empathetic to others.

"What Doesn't Kill You Makes You Stronger."

— sung by Kelly Clarkson

Our life takes us through a lot of twists and turns—times I like to call "adventures." If you go on an adventure you don't know exactly how it is going to go—but go with an open mind and who knows the marvels you will see along the way.

"Life is a daring adventure or it is nothing at all."

— Helen Keller

In The Wizard of Oz, Dorothy and her three friends have every chance to give up and turn around. There were all sorts of obstacles along the way, but they wanted to get to Oz and they wanted to do it now, so they each dug down into their hearts and found what they needed to succeed. The Scarecrow used his brain, the Tin Man used his heart, and the Lion his courage. What did Dorothy have? She had an optimistic outlook and the will to make her move. Once she got home, she realized it was a pretty good place to be.

"If I ever go looking for my heart's desire again, I won't look any further than my own backyard. Because if it isn't there, I never really lost it to begin with."

— Dorothy, The Wizard of Oz

We are often looking for something that is out there—happiness, financial security, a bigger house, a new job. During our trials, it is good if we just find the happiness and contentment that is right in front of us—right now. We get so busy, we don't look around to see what is right in front of us.

Maybe now is the time you bloom where you are planted.

"Therefore we do not lose heart. Though outwardly we are wasting away, yet inwardly we are being renewed day by day. For our light and momentary troubles are achieving for us an eternal glory that far outweighs them all. So we fix our eyes not on what is seen, but on what is unseen, since what is seen is temporary, but what is unseen is eternal."

— 2 Corinthians 4:16-18 NIV)

Are you all cocooned up with your family because of a situation? Job loss, someone is sick, it's a blizzard outside; these are all times like that. Try to just do things to help you get through; live in the now. Play games, watch funny shows, read magazines.

"Life may not be the party we hoped for... but while we're here we may as well dance."

— Jeanne C. Stein author

We all missed the day we got to sign up for the life we wanted; but we have been given the life we have for a reason and we should make the best of it.

CONSIDER THE SUNFLOWER

One sunflower is pretty, but a whole field of sunflowers is amazing. It is a heliotrope, which means it follows the path of the sun each day. Our lives would be so much better, if each day we followed the sun, meaning we turned towards the light, and kept our heads up.

One single sunflower can have up to 2,000 seeds. They provide food products, and some of their seeds provide healthy oil, while other seeds wind up on the floor after being chewed and spit out by baseball players. One sunflower can do so many good things.

How about that? Each one of us has the potential to have a positive effect on so many in our lives—these are the seeds we produce—and we have the ability to provide nourishment to others.

And what about the strength of a sunflower? The stalk is thick enough to withstand bad weather. We may not realize it, but we are built to make it through the storms of our lives, too.

The 2,000 seeds of a sunflower can symbolize the many facets of our life. Some days we feel strong, some days not so much, some days we are creative or crabby or excited. Good or bad, it is all a part of us and God loves us the way we are. Let the sunflower give you strength. Whenever you see one, let it be a reminder to keep looking towards the sun.

Good or bad, it is all a part of us and God sees and loves us as the whole, not the tiny 2,000 parts of us. He sees the good in us and wants us to see the good in others and in any situation we are faced with. Let the sunflower give you strength. Whenever you see one, let it be a reminder to keep looking towards the sun.

> *" ... Let your light shine before others, that they may see your good deeds and glorify your Father in Heaven."*
>
> — *Matthew 5:16 (NIV)*

I have a sign on a wall in my home that says, "You were given this life, because you are strong enough to live it."

If you are going through a tough time, you might be fed up with people saying, "God doesn't give us anything we can't handle." You might be saying, "Hey, God, I can't handle anything else." It's about this time that the negative thoughts start to creep in and you think, "Why are these things happening to me?" "What else can happen?"

The best thing to do in these situations is not to think those thoughts. What else can happen? A lot, so don't start dwelling on it. Why is this happening to you right now? Because it's happening, that's why.

You might not even be going through a "tough time." Maybe you are just wishing your life was in a different place than it is right now. Maybe you wish you had the nerve to get a different job, but you are afraid. Are you in some sort of situation that you wish you could get out of, but you are afraid or feeling like you can't do it?

It happens to everybody. Being negative and feeling sorry for yourself doesn't help. Being scared and nervous doesn't help. The only thing that will help is trying to find contentment during this time, or if you really don't like your life, now is the time to make a change.

You may be thinking, how do I find contentment when I hate my kitchen cabinets or my house is too small or I wish I went to college, so I could get a different job? If you can find a way to accept your situation with grace, yet also work to improve it, you will live a happier life.

There is always a way to fix our situation. Paint those cabinets, re-arrange your rooms, and throw things away in that small house to make it seem larger, take some online courses. When we do these things with a positive attitude, it goes from "I hate my cabinets" to "Wow—look what a can of paint did for both my cabinets and my frame of mind!" We can go from, "I hate my job" to, "Things are starting to get better."

You can go from hating your situation to figuring out how you can accept it and in the end, you will become proud of yourself for what you achieved in the process.

If you don't like your job or someone at your job is making it unbearable for you, now is the time to do something. Don't become a negative force— either quit or adjust the way you look at the situation.

Don't Lose Your Integrity

If others at work have a bad attitude, don't join in their negative actions. One of the best pieces of advice I got in my young work-life was "Don't bad-mouth your coworkers." If others are complaining in the lunchroom, don't join in their negative actions.

"Sometimes the pressure to succeed can make the most principled person chuck their integrity to the wind," said Pastor Matt Herndon of Rooftop Church in Affton, Missouri.

He says integrity is important to have every day and despite a troubling period at work, we should adjust our attitude. Sometimes we feel disrespected by our boss or a coworker. What if you don't like your boss?

"Pretend you are working for God, because you kind of are," said Matt. "If everyone else at your work has a bad attitude that doesn't mean you should."

Matt's Four Ways to Keep Your Integrity at Work in Tough Times

1. Live by God's standards—not your own.
2. Find some workplace support and accountability.
   Sometimes it is worthwhile to find others who feel like you do, but are sincere in improving the situation and meet with them, but be careful that it doesn't turn into a slam session against your employer.
3. Take a stand for righteousness.
   Do you see someone at work doing something wrong? You don't have to report them, but you could gently tell them what they are doing is wrong.
4. Repent and be forgiven.

Maybe you are the one who has done something wrong—have you been bad-mouthing an employee or co-worker? Did you take some office supplies for your personal use? Do you take extra time on your breaks when the boss is gone? Integrity is doing the right thing even when no one is looking.

"In the Bible a person with integrity is referred to as a righteous person," said Matt. "If we live a righteous life on earth, we will be rewarded in Heaven."

I've always taught my boys to strive for Excellence. That does not mean perfection, it means you are proud of where you are and you are always looking to get better. Since life is a process, there is always a way we can be better.

If we strive for perfection, we will just disappoint ourselves, because we will never reach that goal. If we try to be excellent, we can be excellent right now. If every day we are doing our best in whatever it is (work, raising our children, living our life) and doing it in a respectable way, then we are Excellent.

> *"Excellence with integrity is more than doing a good job ... more than performing the bare minimum ... a person with a spirit of excellence, who walks in integrity, can be trusted to do quality work every time without question, no matter the task. Excellence goes hand in hand with integrity. The character of an individual can be judged by what they do when no one is watching."*
> — *Alan Bullock, Daystar.com*

Be your best, even when no one is looking.

DON'T STOP WHEN YOU'RE TIRED, STOP WHEN YOU'RE DONE

It's all about choices we make and there's no better example than Brian Garner. He never puts things off. He is always doing things "now."

"I had leg and hip reconstruction at age one, then my right leg amputated at age four—then more surgery when I was 12," said Brian, husband and father of two who takes frequent road trips either by himself or with his family to see his favorite sports teams play. "I've had to learn to walk three different times in my life. From the beginning, I CHOSE not to be different from others. I played ball with all the other kids in school and chose to participate in sports in high school. I chose not to be different, no matter the outcome."

If he fell, he just picked himself up—and the prosthetic leg too—and continued. As an adult he joined sports teams including hockey and softball, and he coached baseball for 27 years. He volunteered to work with children with cancer and on his first day—when he knew none of the kids—he sat waiting on the bench and as he looked over to his left, he saw a prosthetic leg! It was a miniature of his own and belonged to a young girl who had the same attitude as he. She had signed up to be on a softball team.

"I chose to never stop when I was tired—but to only stop when I was done," he said.

What a great mantra for all of us—Don't stop when you are tired; stop when you are done.

"My prosthetic leg allowed me to be as great as I wanted to be," he said. "If you truly believe in yourself and have the courage, it can be done. Some may consider my prosthetic leg a handicap or disability; but not me!"

Garner actually uses his leg to meet people. Rather than let it be a crutch in his life, he gets sports autographs on it.

"My leg has brought me friendships with athletes, their families, and coaches from the Oregon State baseball team to Mizzou football to the SEC to a Cardinals writer who I've admired since the 80s," he said.

He will stand in line at Spring Training in Jupiter, Florida, and when he sees a player whose autograph he wants, he plops his wooden leg up on the ledge and who can resist him.

"Impossible is just an opinion," he said. "I choose to forget all the reasons why I can't and believe in all the reasons why I can."

Life is a series of choices; it's a series of decisions, and you have to make them now. Now is the time.

"I may not always make the right decisions, but I make the correct choices for me at the time," he said. "I make it a choice to rule my mind, so it doesn't rule me. Of course this path is difficult. If it were easy, everyone would do it. Hard is what makes it great.

"Your dreams don't have an expiration date. Take a deep breath and try again. I'm living proof."

"For after all, the best thing one can do when it is raining, is let it rain."

— Henry Wadsworth Longfellow

You are stronger than you think you are. Be determined to be happier than you think you should be—now.

"A dream doesn't become a reality through magic; it takes sweat, determination, and hard work."   --Colin Powell

CHAPTER FOUR

Determination

Have you ever decided to do something you really intended to do it, but somehow it just fizzled out? At the beginning you were gung-ho, but as time went by, you let the idea go by the wayside.

It happens to all of us. We have the best of intentions, and when we get started, we are super-motivated, but then something causes us to go off track. If there is something you really want to do, it is good to realize that motivation and determination are two different things, but both are needed to accomplish a goal.

Motivation is that exciting feeling that propels us to do something. An online dictionary definition of motivation is: the general desire or willingness of someone to do something. In contrast, determination is defined as: firmness of purpose; resoluteness. You could say motivation is what causes us to try to make a change and determination is what actually carries us through to actually do what we intend to do.

An example would be the motivation of looking good for a special occasion to cause a person to go on a crash diet. The person is strong when they start, but can't stand the hunger pains and the way they feel so they quit, as opposed to a person who is determined. "I am determined I am not going to continue going on diets all my life, so I am going to start living a healthy life, rather than go on a crash diet. If I want to lose weight, I'll do it slowly, so it will stay off"—and then they do.

If a person is truly determined, he or she will see it to the end, unless there are unforeseen circumstances which prohibit it from happening.

You can do anything if you are determined and no one can stop you. Make up your mind to be the person you want to be. Strive for excellence every day of your life and be determined to succeed.

WE CAN ALL BE TITANS

Derik Scott was a finalist on the nationally televised "The Titan Games" with Dwayne "The Rock" Johnson in 2019. It was a show full of so-called "everyday people" competing in near impossible-looking physical challenges—all in hopes of winning the coveted title of "Titan." In Greek mythology, the Titans were above all, they were a race of gods and to be called a titan today is someone who is powerful or influential in their field.

Derik has always been determined to succeed when he was competing in sports, but during his senior year, his mother noticed he never said anything about what he planned to do after graduation. He had always excelled at gymnastics and every sport he participated in, but due to extenuating circumstances, his grades were not where they normally would have been, and he was uncertain about his future.

Perhaps his uncertainty had to do with the fact that he lost his older brother six months after the brother graduated.

He decided to take some time off and went to stay with a relative in South Beach, Florida. For a time he was living the good life—and he liked it. After that trip, Derik was determined to live the life he wanted, so he got busy.

First, he worked for and achieved his master's degree, then went to law school and got his law degree, opened up a training center with his brothers, and eventually moved to Los Angeles where he landed a spot on the highly publicized athletic challenge show. He ended up coming in second on the show and right after that he was booked on an MMA Fight. He was living the life he dreamed, because of his hard work and determination.

We can all do that on a smaller scale—or even a larger scale. The point is, you get to decide what you want to do with your life. If you are in a situation where you feel trapped by your circumstances, don't ever give up on yourself. Maybe this isn't the exact time to make a change, but you can be preparing for your future whatever you are doing.

Don't just be motivated in your life, be determined and see it through.

During the taping of the show, Derik decided to dedicate his performance to his brother, Ian, the one who had passed away. As his family watched the show, they were all so proud, but it was an emotional time and their thoughts could not help but go back in time.

When his parents met years ago, they were gymnastics coaches at competing gyms in St. Louis.

"I had previously worked with gymnasts in New Jersey and Pennsylvania, and he in his home-state of Minnesota," said Scott's mother, Dana Scott. "Kevin had recently moved here."

They fell in love and when she found out he had been married before and had a four-year-old son, she practically jumped for joy.

"I wanted children and I was very happy with this news," she said. "It was love at first sight with Ian, I just fell in love with him."

As with many divorced families they faced the situation of where the child would live; as the mother lived in Minnesota. When he was in first grade he attended a year of school in St. Louis, then spent second grade with his mother in Minnesota.

"He spent third, fourth, fifth, and sixth grade with us in St. Louis," said Dana. "Our three other boys were born during this time and the brothers loved each other."

They missed their brother and the parents missed their son (and vice-versa) when he was in Minnesota and that was where Ian finished high school.

"It was heartbreaking to not be with him," said Dana.

Six months after Ian's graduation, they received the devastating news that he was involved in a single car accident.

Dana remembered that just a year earlier, her son Shaun's third grade teacher had passed away and she and her husband had gathered the three boys on their living room couch to break the news to them and here they were doing the same thing, telling them about their brother.

"The last time we were all together was at a gymnastics event in Minnesota earlier in the year and we made plans for him to come to St. Louis for Christmas."

She didn't know how she would make it through the funeral and aftermath, and worried about how Kevin and the boys would do.

"Then the most amazing thing happened," she said, "We were staying in Kevin's dad's basement and I looked on the wall and there was a rainbow. There was no light at that end of the basement and there should not have been a rainbow on that wall—there was no explanation for it."

Then they got into the car to head for the funeral and she lifted the cover of the mirror above her side in the front seat. For the first time in six months, the light went on!

"It was that day that I realized Ian is always with us—the rainbow and the light was my sign," she said. "All that time I felt I could not be with him when he was in Minnesota, but suddenly I felt him with me."

After that she felt she was not saying goodbye, because she could feel he was still with her in her life.

"It's like electricity," she said. "You can't see it, you can't feel it, but you know it's there. I'll be driving down the highway and a light will go on and I know he's there. So now I feel like he's our guardian angel."

Dana was determined her sons would live a happy life despite losing their brother and they have become champions in many different ways, excelling and always moving forward.

Ian will always be in their hearts, but they have chosen to continue to live their lives.

Living a happy life and staying active is not an insult to a person who has passed away. It is actually a compliment. If you take their good points and live the life they would like to see you live, it is a tribute to them. The more of them that you pour into the world, then they can never really leave.

Often, after we lose someone, it is hard for us to move forward, because we feel guilty having fun when they are not there—or worse yet, maybe if we live our lives, others will think we don't care or miss that person.

Despite what happened to the Scott family in the past, they have so much joy and excitement in their lives while also honoring Ian. A death in the family can cause several different reactions. Sometimes it can tear a family apart. They chose to stick together and were determined to live their lives to the fullest

"My sons have sort of banded together," she said. "It's like 'all for one and one for all.' They know how hard it can be."

In an interview before the Titan Games was about to air, Derik Scott said, "I feel like every day of my life is about how I can improve my life and the lives of those around me. I lost a brother who didn't get to fulfill his potential as a person, so I feel obligated to fulfill mine as a tribute to him."

One of the tasks Derik was faced with on the show could be a good example for all of us. He and his opponent stood on a bar 30 feet above the ground and they were to push a very heavy object in hopes of pushing it so far it would cause the other person to fall off.

This task proved to be grueling even to those who watched. Back and forth they pushed—his opponent was so strong and at one point, it seemed Scott could not take it anymore and would give in. One mistake and he would fall 30 feet. He was within inches of going and it really looked like there was no way out. Suddenly he found the strength and with one big push, he started reversing the situation. Slowly and with every ounce of strength he could muster, he started going towards his goal—and he ended up winning that task.

Think about your own life in this instant. One could say our lives are on a smaller scale than a television show with millions of people watching—but really it isn't. Your situation is every bit as important as theirs was.

You can be a Titan, even if it is just being determined to handle your situation in a positive way. Hang on—no matter how impossible your situation seems, it will change. To you, your challenge may seem as impossible as Derik Scott's challenge was, but remember when it looked like he was done—he wasn't. Don't let anything get the best of you.

"We are not given a good life or a bad life," said Derik. "We are given a life. It's up to us to determine whether it's good or bad."

Every day we get the opportunity to fulfill our own potential as a person. Each new day that we wake up in the morning provides us with a new chance. We are never going to live a happy life, if we sit around feeling sorry for ourselves and the situations we are in. You've got to get up and press forward.

SHE'S COMMITTED TO "WEALTH"

Liz Oliver is the general manager of a hotel in Florida and is raising her daughter as a single mother. She was determined and her determination has landed her a successful and happy life—although, as with all of us, it is a process we go through every day. Liz has not rested on her success; she is constantly trying to improve herself, learn new things, and strengthen the already strong bond with her daughter.

She is dedicated to being good at her job, all the while determined to put her family life first. What is her advice?

"First of all, you should set goals on what you want to achieve," she said. "Focus on those goals."

While it's important to focus on work and family, Liz feels it's also vital to focus on improving yourself and says that begins with a commitment to yourself.

"Commitment is that thing you do when you come to the realization that this is about self," she said. "Whether you commit to a person, a task, school, a business fitness path or self-growth, commitment is that thing you do when you inflict self-love."

Commitment is what can get us from motivation to determination. If you are committed to your goal, you become determined, and will not waiver—you will see it through. Liz thought about what her goal in life was, and for many, it is wealth. As she thought of what was really important in her life, she said it all boils down to W.E.A.L.T.H.—but her wealth is very different from many others.

LIZ'S DEFINITION OF WEALTH

W hen
E verything
A round
L eads
T o
H appiness

"Wealth as I know it is when everything in life leads to happiness," said Liz Oliver, who writes a blog about it (yourwealthyself.blogspot.com). "It's that simple. When your career, love, finances, friendships, health, and family lead to your happiness and the happiness of your family, that is true wealth."

"Connecting is a key to surviving and being happy," said Liz. "Connect your head to your heart, your heart to your soul, and your soul to the Almighty. The key word here is connecting."

When she says "connect your heart to your soul" that is where your passion for life comes in. What is it that you really want out of your life? Do you just want to exist and go through life doing what you are supposed to do?

HOW TO PUT PIZAZZ BACK INTO YOUR LIFE

One of the things Liz does at her hotel is hold periodic karaoke nights. She has a great voice and so much enthusiasm when she gets up there in front of the hotel guests at these special parties. You can tell music is a passion to her and she lights up when she sings.

One night I was in the audience and she stuck the microphone in front of me. I had never done anything like that and I really don't have a very good singing voice.

As she approached me, I could see what was happening. She was headed right towards me and handed me the microphone. I had never done karaoke before and I was nervous, but I started singing.

Then she motioned for me to get up, which was way out of my comfort zone, but pretty soon I started enjoying it. I learned something from that experience—you don't have to be good at something to have fun doing it. And likewise, you can provide fun for others, if you just have fun doing it and have confidence (or at least pretend to have it).

MUSIC CALMS US DOWN

"My mom always responded to Frank Sinatra music," Maria said. "I played some of his songs for her the day before she died. I put my phone on the bed next to her and I could see it brought her such comfort. Her breathing was so calm and she wasn't agitated as the music played."

Now that's tranquility. That's peacefulness, and if music can help a person at such a stressful time, then think what it can do to bring us tranquility in the middle of a busy day.

The singer, Sandi Patty, has a song called *Peace, I'll Give You Peace.* It's a very calming song, and often when the day gets too hectic, I will just go to YouTube and turn on that song.

> *"Peace, I'll give you peace, When the wind blows on. Peace, whenever you call Me, I'll give you peace, When the wind blows on."*
> — *Sandi Patty*

If we are determined to be happy, we must learn to be peaceful, but it goes the other way, too. Our life will be so much more peaceful, if we are around those who make us happy.

MUSIC IS THE UNIVERSAL LANGUAGE

One day I took a karaoke machine over to the memory care facility where my mother was and I took my chances. As I said, I'm not the best singer and I wasn't sure what my audience would do. The people loved it! We sang old songs they knew and then some of the residents asked if they could sing.

I've come to learn that music is a universal language and even when my mother's mind was behind the trapped door of Alzheimer's disease, her face would light up in a smile when I sang to her—and sometimes she joined in. My sister, Barb, would sing to her too and get the same happy response.

Isn't that amazing? A person unable to put together a complete sentence can sing a song. I would start singing White Coral Bells, an old song she had sung with her mom as a child and then sang with my sisters and me. She remembered every word and sang it with me. Think of the fun I would have missed by not making this connection of communicating with her in this very special manner.

The workers at the Memory Care center would look up with surprise as my sister and I started singing to our mother. And you know what? It made them happy, too.

Because I saw how happy the music made everyone, I now have the nerve, the gumption, and a karaoke machine to provide happiness to others—and I never would have thought I had it in me, if Liz had not stuck that microphone in my face.

What happened to your passion? What happened to your joy and your excitement? Do you ever do anything crazy anymore? Where's that pizazz your life used to have?

What do you say, if someone asks you, "What do you like to do?" or "Do you have any hobbies?"

Sometimes in our efforts to escape our own everyday world, we spend too much time watching mindless television, or scrolling on our devices. Why do you think there are so many reality TV shows?

And by the way, sports is a "reality" show, too. If you are on the couch watching show after show (or game after game), maybe it's time you get a hobby. You have a passion in your heart, something that makes you excited. It's time to find it or recapture it.

"Everyone has passion," said Liz Oliver. "Sometimes your passion lays dormant and what you need to cause a resurgence is a muse."

What is a muse you ask? Google it and you get, "a person or personified force who is the source of inspiration for a creative artist." Liz's daughter is her muse.

"You won't know beforehand, but when your soul finds that muse and if your heart is open and receptive, watch out for the explosion."

She Decided to Live a Life of Passion

Sheryl Godsy has had that explosion. She is a person who is excited for life every day, because she does things that make her happy.

"We all have dark times in our lives where the stress gets heavy and major life things just bog us down," said Sheryl Godsy a retired teaching professional in Liberty, Missouri. "When we're so busy with work and kids, we sometimes forget to make room in our life for the passions that we have—you know—those things that light up your soul.

"I have always loved and found solace with music—learned to play guitar as a teen, used to sing to my babies, and found joy singing and playing music with others ... but now the guitar gathered dust in a corner of a room."

Sheryl said life happened and music slowly slipped out of her life, but then a turning point came. Her parents, Loretta and Fred, had always had a fun-loving attitude, always providing new adventures in her life, but when her dad got sick and then passed away, the wind was taken out of her sails.

As many of us do we do when we hit a certain age, we have double the concerns—how would Loretta go on without Fred and how what would this mean to the grandchildren that Fred had doted on? Life became so serious. It seemed at times there were more worries and fewer adventures, until one day it hit Sheryl.

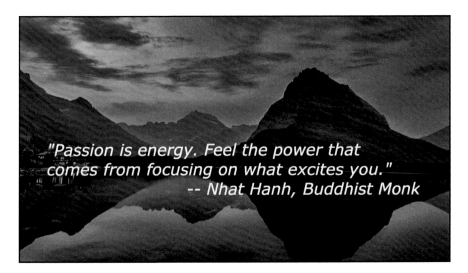

"Passion is energy. Feel the power that comes from focusing on what excites you."
-- Nhat Hanh, Buddhist Monk

"After I lost my father, it was a turning point in my life," she said. "That time in my life made me realize that life is short and rather than just dream of the things you want to do—it's time to start doing them."

She thought about the things that make her happy—that "light up her soul" and it came down to having adventures and getting more music back into her life.

"So I bought a gypsy wagon camper," Sheryl said. "The intent of this 'gypsy vardo' was something fun for me 'glamp' up and to take it to music festivals and spend time in the summer camping and singing around a campfire."

Glamping is "glamorous camping,"—also called luxury camping—it's a fun way to leave your cares behind and it provides that escape you've been meaning to take.

A vardo is from the old traditional gypsy wagon, but it is a small trailer that can fit a double bed and a few other things can be towed easily to campgrounds. Sheryl likes the idea of the vardo, because she can manage it by herself.

"Around the time I bought the vardo, I somehow had an additional $700," she said. "Then I was torn between buying a new leather couch or a hammered dulcimer—an instrument I had always wanted and dreamed of. Well, I bought the dulcimer and have never regretted it."

Then she found other like-minded people and joined groups, which do several things—they helped her make new friends, but groups also keep her accountable that she will actually practice. She joined the Prairie Dulcimer Club, Midwest Glampers, community choir, Harmony singing class, and KC Women's Music Network.

"I believe that making those leaps of action on passion has brought me to a most wonderful time of my life," said Sheryl. "These groups have brought me new friendships and experiences with people who have the same interest. I have had amazing travel and events to attend. I've acquired multiple instruments and have even bought my family members instruments, so we can have fun playing together. Being excited gives you energy. I'm always excited to see what is next in life."

Sheryl has new adventures every day because she made the choice to include hobbies and other interests in her life. She was determined to really think about her passions—what makes her soul light up.

"My advice to others is to try and find a way to do the things that you are passionate about," she says. "Even taking a little step in that direction, such as buying an instrument or finding a group with similar passions, can help lift your spirits."

SHE LIKES HORSING AROUND

Another person whose life has been enhanced by having an outside interest is Dawn Shaver of Millstadt, Illinois. Dawn loves horses and when she first bought a horse, she got more than she bargained for—along with the horse, she learned some life lessons and got a longtime friendship with the stable owner.

"Charlotte Traiteur was the strongest woman I ever met," said Dawn. "She didn't have a high school education, but when it came to life, she was hands down the savviest person I have ever met. She knew a lot about horses, but she also knew a lot about life, and I learned from her."

Dawn started out getting involved with horses to help her family have more together time outdoors and teach them some life lessons—but she ended up learning way more herself.

"I did it so that my family could get away from the city and get some fresh air, and it wasn't too far from home," she said. "I've had an interest in horses dating back to sixth grade when my friend, Sharon, had one. So I got the horse and brought my family out there. There were chickens, guineas, turkeys, emus, and llamas. Learning and respecting the land and animals was my goal for the kids … or so I thought."

While Dawn had her own ideas of how things should go, the horse had his own idea, and Charlotte helped her work through it all. From the experience of being around that horse, she learned a valuable lessons about people—the importance of good communication with family and friends.

"We (humans) are predators and horses are prey," said Dawn. "They are naturally afraid of us. We can either force them to do something or help them understand how to do it. Horses learn from fear or respect—hmmm … so do kids."

She finds child-raising lessons from her horse, too.

"You can hold on to a horse all day and make him do something; what happens when you let go of the reins? Is the horse running off or did the horse pay attention to what you have been teaching him? You only know what you have when you let go. It's the same with our children."

The list of lessons that owning a horse has taught her is long.

"My horse has taught me a lot about respect," said Dawn, "Funny thing is … most people will let humans disrespect them, and they'll let their pets disrespect them. I have only seen a few people who command the respect of all and, in turn, respect all. Buck Brannaman, who was the inspiration for The Horse Whisperer, was one. So often when something wrong happens with the horse, the rider blames the horse, when it was the ego of the rider who could not handle taking the responsibility. This is just like when someone blames others for a wrong when that person was really at fault."

When people respect each other they don't automatically blame others—they try to work together.

"The best part of riding a horse is when you are in sync," she said. "It's when you and your horse are having a great ride together. It is both exhilarating and ultra-peaceful at the same time. Come to think of it, when you are on the same page with another person, you can get that same feeling."

How our minds can open up when we make the choice to add passion to our life. We are suddenly excited about life and feel energized. You can do this, even if it's just checking out a library book or watching a movie that you really enjoy. It doesn't have to be something big like owning a horse or going glamping. There is something that energizes you—find it.

Dawn knows that having a passion—something that gets us excited— can add more happiness to our lives. Owning a horse or other pet, like playing an instrument, can teach us responsibility, because to be successful you have to have accountability— she has to feed and groom her horse, as well as ride him. If you play an instrument and want to get anything out of it, you will need to practice and keep the instrument up, such as tuning and protecting it.

"With a horse, we have to take care of him and treat him right," she said. "He is in our care. We have to teach him what to do and what we want. Do we do it by using respect or by invoking fear? When the horse is unsure, their flight instinct is higher. This means they can move quickly, and injure us an unintentional consequence.

"So, we learn to read a horse's confidence level and figure out how to give what is needed. All horses are different. All of this applies in humans, too. With my horse, I have learned so many things about life and people, but mostly about myself."

We must always be learning things if we are going to continue having a positive life. Learning gives us curiosity. It helps instill confidence when we know things. Athletes are always learning—that's why they have coaches. If a competitor never learns a new thing, that athlete will not have much success, because everyone is learning. Have the determination to be a learner.

What are some ways you can find passion and continue learning and growing? Try something new. Figure out what you like to do. You can learn facts and you can also grow within your soul by learning more about yourself.

If you are determined, you can learn new things. One day I decided I wanted to learn guitar, so I took some lessons. I realized that might not be the instrument for me and then I found out about the autoharp. I was hooked. If you strum the autoharp, it's a great instrument for sing-alongs. Every so often when Sheryl Godsy comes to town, we get out our instruments and "jam" and it's a lot of fun.

She is really good and I haven't spent as much time at it as she has, but when we are singing and playing together, it's a lot of fun. If you are looking for something easy to get started with, the autoharp might be something fun to add to your life.

Sometimes life can beat us down, but if you want to live a happy life, be determined not to let it. When you are working on yourself or pursuing a passion—even when going through the worst of times—it opens your heart to hope.

Be Determined to Always Have Hope in Your Heart

Sometimes things don't go the way we want them to, but we should not lose hope. I've seen things like this many times on Facebook: "We're at the ER, please pray for us." So many people reply, "Praying." The next day I go to check on their update and it says something like "Praise the Lord, he (she) came through. God is good."

It always sticks with me that if the person had not made it, would they still feel the same—that God is "good"—or is He only good when things go our way?

Hope is the gift that God gives us, because if there were no hope, our suffering would be unbearable. Because of hope, God is good all the time, no matter what. We have the hope of a good life on earth; and also the hope of our future in Heaven.

WE'VE GOT A LOT TO LOOK FORWARD TO

During the period of time I was writing this book, my mother took her last breath on earth. If you don't believe there's a Heaven or that a loved one is waiting on the other side to greet you when you die, I wish you could have been in that room with us the day she crossed over. There was no doubt in our mind after that—and it gave us so much hope for the future.

On a dismal rainy Tuesday, my sister Barb and I sat by her bed. The hospice nurse had told us she felt our mother had begun "her journey" and we had been staying with her all day that week.

As we sat and drank the Hawaiian Punch and ate the Little Debbies on what we jokingly called "the bereavement tray" they set out for us, our mother suddenly started talking. This was a thing in itself, because she had Alzheimer's disease and had not been able to put words together in a sentence for a while.

But at this moment, she was smiling and talking and at one point, she said something that her dad—our grandpa—would have said and we felt his presence in the room. Then a minute later, she said something that only our dad would have said—the famous "Wow!" He had been waiting for her and she saw him!

When our parents would get dressed up to go out for the evening, as she walked down the hall, Pop would look up at her and say "Wow!" and here, all of a sudden, Mom says "Wow!" and even though it was her saying it, it sounded just like Pop.

I looked at Barb and we both had the same thought, "Are we in Heaven, or are they on earth?" It was so amazing and peaceful—and natural.

Mom had the biggest smile on her face as she talked to whoever she was talking to—but it certainly wasn't us, because she was looking up. Then she said, "Yes, yes!" so enthusiastically as if someone had just asked her to go with them. She also mentioned "the girls" so we knew Judy, Nancy, and Annie were there.

After we assured her that it was OK for her to go, we said what she had always said to reassure us: "Everyone is all right, everyone is safe, they are all where they should be."

In that moment, we felt God's loving arms around us and her—embracing us with His heavenly love and comfort. She fell asleep and did not wake up for her last two days on earth.

We tried so hard to talk to her, to get that wonderful, happy feeling we had again, but she just stayed asleep.

I likened those two days to leaving your car running. The person started the car, but got out and though her soul had left for Heaven, the car (her body) needed a little more time and once it ran out of gas, it was over. At one point, I noticed she was not breathing and I went to get the nurse, who took her pulse and then turned to me and with large arms spread in a hug for me, she said, "Your momma's gone to Heaven!"

All those days of Alzheimer's when people would tell us, "There's no hope," we were determined to see it to the end and give her the fun and respect she had given us. We were determined she would live a happy life—in whatever form it could be in. It may not have been the life we would have asked for, but we had some great days with her, connecting in ways we never would have imagined.

> *"We wait in hope for the Lord; He is our help and our shield. In Him our hearts rejoice, for we trust in His holy name. May your unfailing love be with us, Lord, even as we put our hope in you."*
>
> *— Psalm 33:20-22 New International Version (NIV)*

Don't lose hope, for if you have no hope, you will lose your determination. You might think, "What's the use?" Well, the answer to that is EVERYTHING. No matter how bleak things get or how hard it all seems, don't lose hope.

ATTITUDE MAKES A BIG DIFFERENCE

Teresa Barnes, a former television reporter who advocates for Pulmonary Fibrosis (PF) on Capitol Hill experienced a terrible situation when multiple members of her family were stricken with PF, a fatal lung disease.

"My father had been diagnosed with this incurable lung disease, and was told he needed a lung transplant," said Teresa. "He was told there was nothing they could do to stop the rapidly progressing disease. For a time, he believed them. He became withdrawn and depressed and our family grieved for the man who'd lost his hope, even though he was still alive."

Most people can relate to that feeling of being around someone who is normally optimistic and something causes them to lose hope and be depressed. It is devastating, because we hate to see someone suffering, but worse than that we hate to see our loved ones down about their situation. It can make it all the more difficult for us to be optimistic.

"Then, my father received a call from one of his doctors telling him he wanted to consider him for a life-saving lung transplant," said Teresa. "A transplant is the only known way to survive PF, but few people live long enough to get one. Though he was just over the cut-off age of 60, they felt he was an ideal candidate and possessed a positive attitude that could help him survive the difficult surgery and months of recovery."

This little glimmer of hope changed everything in her father's demeanor and outlook.

"My father's hope was renewed," she said. "Throughout the long, stressful wait, he never complained. He spoke with a positive ring to his voice and talked about the future even as his lungs showed signs of increased deterioration."

He waited 17 months and had six false alarms with possible organs.

"On the lucky seventh attempt, the organs were good and the surgery was a go," she remembers. "Though I know he was anxious and fearful of the risks associated with what he was about to undergo, all I could see in his face and hear in his voice was his hope."

As it turned out, he didn't make it, but what a gift to his family and especially his daughter that he went out with hope. He was a determined person.

With his hopeful attitude, he gave his daughter the strength she would need to continue after he was gone.

"The sadness I felt was made easier with the knowledge that my father had renewed hope. He held onto his hope and he gave it to me."

Through the sadness of losing her father, she found the strength and determination to help advocate to find a cure for PF. She started a nonprofit and though she has seen other family members die from this terrible disease, she continues fighting for a cure and helps others who are going through what she did.

"Though his entire generation was lost to the disease and mine is threatened, I look at my little girl and I see a hope in her just like the hope I grew up knowing in her grandfather," said Teresa.

Now she makes frequent trips to Washington, DC to lobby and she works alongside some of the best researchers and experts in the world searching for a cure.

"I now work to help find a treatment that can save my family and others from the deadly lung disease," said Teresa. "We have a steadfast focus on a future that will be brighter and more hopeful."

And guess what she decided to call the new initiative she started for research and patient care—HOPE (Healthier Options for Pulmonary Fibrosis).

"Hope begins in the dark, the stubborn hope that if you just show up and try to do the right thing, the dawn will come. You wait and watch and work: you don't give up."

— Anne Lamott

Are you scared or upset because someone you know (or maybe even you) is battling with a situation that seems so impossible, so unfair?

Remember this: most people will survive their surgery, most people will find another job if they lose one. Keeping a positive outlook and attitude is so important in recovery.

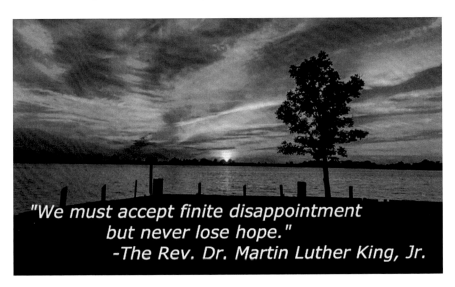

"We must accept finite disappointment but never lose hope."
-The Rev. Dr. Martin Luther King, Jr.

"To achieve anything requires faith and belief in yourself, vision, hard work, determination, and dedication."
—*Gail Devers*

GOLD MEDAL DETERMINATION

In 1990 Olympian Gail Devers was feeling sluggish and run down. After a while, she was diagnosed with Graves disease, a form of overactive thyroid disease and almost had to have her feet amputated. She was determined to live her life on her own terms so slowly as she began feeling better she started training again.

In 1991 she won a silver medal at the World Championships. She went on to win Olympic Gold several times.

This incredible example of determination shows there is always hope in life. If you are feeling weak due to your current circumstances, just know that this is not the end of your story.

There was a movie a while back called, How Stella Got her Groove Back. I loved that title, because we all come to a time where we just need to get our groove back. No matter what we go through, we can get our groove back and sometimes be even better (groovier!) than we were before.

You generally don't get your groove back by accident. You become determined to do it and it may even take some planning and preparation.

"One important key to success is self-confidence. An important key to self-confidence is preparation."
— *Arthur Ashe*

You can do anything you want, with a little bit of preparation and planning—and determination.

Some of the worst Academy Awards acceptance speeches have been made by people who "didn't think they would win," so they didn't prepare anything. Always prepare to win, always prepare to succeed, that way you will be ready for all the successes that will come your way.

"If you are watching right now, all I have to say is this [being an actor] is hard work. I have worked hard for a long time and it's not about winning. What it's about is not giving up. If you have a dream, fight for it. There's a discipline for passion: it's not about how many times you get rejected or you fall down and get beaten up, but how many times you stand up, and are brave and you keep on going."
— *Lady Gaga after winning the Oscar in 2019*

There are a whole group of people who are determined to live their life on their own terms and be passionate about it. They won't be defined by their circumstances. You see them helping people in times of need. You see them being happy. You see them on Facebook—they are the ones who don't complain, they fill the universe with positivity. You don't realize their hearts are breaking or they are afraid of something or they are having a root canal that day or whatever. They keep going—and are an example to all of us. We can all be those people—the determined, happy ones.

They are the ones who inspire us. They inspire us to be better. They inspire us to be more like them. I know I try to be around positive people as much as I can.

"You are the average of the five people you spend the most time with."

— Jim Rohn, motivational speaker

If you want to live a happy life, determine that you will surround yourself with positive people. Be a positive person that others want to be around. You don't want to be around a "downer," so if you are acting like one, why would anyone want to be around you? But if you are trying to be positive and project that on others, you automatically attract other positive people—and they in turn help you.

Think about the people you were around today. Were they whining and complaining or were they out there doing the best they could?

I have heard people say, "I surround myself with people who are smarter than I am" and for many years, I wondered why would you do that—if I surround myself with people who are smarter than I am, I will be found out! But that's not true.

BE AROUND GREAT PEOPLE TO BE GREAT

I discovered that most people, even the seemingly successful or famous ones are like me—we're all just trying to make it through life. We're all just trying to fit in and live a happy life. Why not be with people who can help you learn more, who can stretch your capabilities, and maybe even help you become better.

There's a big difference between "know-it-alls" and smart people. Know-it-alls brag about everything and tend to make us feel bad in the process. The ones I look up to are those who build each other up.

You are doing the best you can today, so why be around someone who expects more? If your best isn't good enough for someone, then move on. You are the only one who should expect more of yourself. If you see an area you can improve, then go for it, but don't let someone else's perceived opinion of you tear your confidence down.

I know someone who calls his mother every day and he says in a cheerful voice, "Good morning, Mom, how are you doing?" And every day she says something like, "Oh so-so" or "Not good." It amazes me that he keeps going with such a positive attitude, because often someone with a bad attitude can bring us down. If she would train herself to say "I'm doing great!" every time someone asked, then maybe she might see herself having a good day.

You don't have to hide your feelings, but there are ways you can try to be positive even when you have problems.

Why is it that some people like being the center of attention for negative things? Their life is going bad, they didn't get the job, they are caring for their elderly parent—you hear it every day, and Lord knows you see it all over social media. Some parts of our life aren't that fun, but don't dwell on those.

Author Anne Lamott wrote the book, *Bird by Bird*. Strange name for a book until you find out why she named it that. She told a story about her brother having to write a report on birds for a school assignment and at the last minute, he was panicking about getting it done in time. The thought of writing a full report on birds was overwhelming to him. Their dad sat down and putting his arm around the boy said, "Bird by bird, buddy. Just take it bird by bird."

Take each event in your life as one separate thing—then it won't seem so overwhelming. And have faith when you face your problems.

"Faith is indeed the greatest miracle-working power imaginable.
Faith never fails a person; we fail when we give up on our faith."
— Robert Schuller

That is why people often say "Keep the faith," when encouraging someone. If I stay the course because of my faith, then I am determined to make it.

A bump in the road, no matter how large or small is going to happen, and in fact life is pretty much a bumpy ride. How we react to our situations determines how happy of a life we will live.

We hold the key to our own happiness. It is how we view our life and our circumstances and how we react that will determine our outlook.

> *"It's faith that will take you through and determination that will drive you."*
> — **Jonathan Anthony Burkett, Author**

"Happiness would lose its meaning if it weren't balanced by sadness," said Trisha Davis, a business owner. "That quote helped me a lot when I was dealing with my grandmother's passing."

That's a good thought. How would we know we were happy, if we had never known what it felt like to be sad?

The book *Illuminated Prayers* by Marianne Williamson was the last gift my sister, Nancy, left me as I found it among her things. I was so touched by Marianne Williamson's writing, I wrote to her and she wrote me back. It was a personal note, but it was clear she was motivated by the happenings of her life and determined to help and inspire others because of it.

> *"Dear God … May a great and glorious light emerge and show us all the way. May our eyes look up at an illuminated sky and see a sign … May every tear be wiped away and every heart begin to gladden and every life be healed by love. Now, not later, now.*
>
> *We pray and say thanks for we are heard. He hears us … Amen."*
> — *Marianne Williamson, Illuminated Prayers*

Despite all you've gone through, you can say to yourself, "I'm determined to live a great life no matter what and I'm going to surround myself with a community of people who will help me do that."

"If you go looking for a friend you're going to find they're very scarce. If you go out to be a friend you will find them everywhere."
--Zig Ziglar

Chapter Five

Build Your Community—Accept the Help of Others

Look around you. Who do you see? Are you surrounded by the good people you would choose with a clear mind, or have your circumstances caused you to drift? People are all around us, willing to help us have a better life. It's up to us to figure out who the good people are and accept their help.

If you stop and think about it, you know who wants to see you succeed. If there is anyone in your life who makes you feel like you are not good enough or are not doing things the right way—if you are doing your best, then eliminate those people from the circle around you. Seek out those who think highly of you and believe in you or that you think highly of and believe in them.

Sometimes it is those closest to us—the ones who should be cheering us on—who keep us from achieving greatness, because they take away our confidence by putting us down. They may react negatively or express doubt saying, "I just don't want you to get hurt, if it doesn't work out." Remember, you can get hurt every day of your life, but don't let that keep you from trying something.

I was lucky to have a family who always supported each other's endeavors and said, "You can do it," but I know there are many of you who don't get that kind of support from those around them. It must be terrible to have a parent who hurts you, but whether or not someone loves you or believes in you should not be a factor in whether or not you succeed in having a happy life.

So how do you strive for excellence, greatness, and happiness when you constantly feel you are being put down by someone around you? You learn to create your own positive circle—build your own community of people who have your back. One way to do that is by staying open to possibilities.

Sometimes support comes from the strangest places, people you would never have thought to consider.

Whether we are looking for a job or a date, navigating through an illness, or just having a bad day, you never know where your encouragement or inspiration will come from.

THE PEOPLE IN OUR CIRCLE ARE OUR COMMUNITY— THEY'RE OUR TEAM.

We must pick our team by choosing only the positive people who can help us win in life or whom we can help. We're not talking about "using" people for worldly gain—we're talking about finding those who can bring out the best in us and we in them.

Communication is a huge key in choosing your community. We need to listen to each other so we really hear what is going on. Unfortunately sometimes in conversations, we already have our minds made up on that topic. With bad communication, we can close ourselves up to what the person is saying.

"When we hear someone say something, we hear them with our own preset receptors," said Wendell Fry, the father of four, who studied Theology at Oral Roberts University. "We take the words, and we can only attach our meaning to them."

Wendell points out that in a conversation, the more we have at stake in a matter, the more limited our hearing and our perception is. This is why there are always "two sides to the story."

Often when someone is telling us or writing something, we shut down as far as really listening and don't always get the message, as it was meant.

"We think, 'I know what you are going to say,' and then shut down," said Wendell. "The person may or may not be speaking truth, but our ears won't hear. Only the humble can hear the truth with honesty. If you are filled with the love of God, you free yourself and are able to listen better, because you are not worried about what others think of you."

You could miss out on a real friend or someone who is ultimately on your side, because you take what they say in the wrong manner or you refuse to listen and never hear it. We owe it to ourselves to listen to what a sincere person is saying, but then it is up to us to decide if we agree or disagree with it.

Sometimes a person who loves us makes a suggestion about how we are doing something and it hits us the wrong way—hurts our feelings. "What do they know?" we think. But if we take the time to carefully consider what they said, maybe they have a point—maybe their idea is a better way to do it, or at least worth trying.

CONSIDER THE LAYERS

Charlyne "Chuck" Miller, a business consultant and certified leadership coach who works with companies internationally knows a lot about communication.

"There are the facts, and then there are layers of the story," said Chuck. "The layers are how each person perceives the facts."

She says that, in general, there are many layers to people's beliefs and, therefore, many layers in how we communicate about these in our conversations. 'Facts' are only facts in the eye of the beholder.

"What those facts actually mean and represent to others can be completely different," said Chuck. "Learning to get to the same layer and then dig beyond to better understand the other layers is everything. One never gets there if they're not a good listener."

Listening to what someone says is a big part of communication. The "layers" include each person's side of the story. When you watch a crime show you might see the crime happen, but then you are able to see how two people involved give completely different stories to the police. This type of thing happens in our everyday life, and especially in divorce. Both parties lived the same life, but they both have their own side of the story.

Always try to listen to those who you know care about you, and after you consider what they said, you can make a decision about what you will do. That's what friends do—they listen.

Listening is so important, because it goes a long way in showing respect for the person trying to talk to you. We get help from so many different places—and some are unexpected.

AN ACT OF KINDNESS CAME BACK TO HIM

The Rev. Nicholas Inman is a well-known citizen in his small town of Marshfield, Missouri, for all of his community work. He has spent his life helping build up the town he lives in, as well as the people in it. He has started traditions, such as the Missouri Cherry Blossom Festival and served as the town's chairman of their Fourth of July Parade for twenty years, but his real gift is in meeting people and seeing their needs.

"When I was in high school, I had a teacher who was going through a really difficult time in her life," said Nicholas. "She was a terrific person and a great inspiration to her students and friends. I watched as she handled this struggle and I knew that it was taking a tremendous toll on her emotionally and physically, although, she NEVER complained."

Most high school students are too busy worrying about what they will be doing on Friday night to actually take notice of a teacher who is going through a tough time, but something made him want to help her.

"I have always been a great fan of the poem, Footprints in the Sand. This inspirational poem has been used at many family funerals and it has been one that has touched me throughout my journey of faith," Nicholas said. "I decided to present a copy to this special teacher and to explain to her about the Lord carrying us through the most difficult times in our journey."

So he got a copy of the poem and took it to her.

"When I gave her the poem, her eyes filled with tears as she read its simple and profound wording," he remembered. "She explained that she had really needed to hear this poem and would always cherish the words."

Years later, Nicholas became ill and had to undergo several rounds of treatments. It was a grueling treatment and a very trying time in his life. It seems his teacher was listening when he communicated to her those years ago and she became a part of his community.

"One day, a card arrived in the mail and it was on a day that I was really feeling bad and down," Nicholas said. "It was from this former teacher and I was surprised that she knew of my illness. When I opened the card, out came a copy of the beloved poem that I had shared with her, many years before.

"A simple note accompanied the poem inside of the card and it read: A dear friend once shared this poem with me and now I return this message, reminding you that you are not alone!'

"It was just what I needed. I could not have received those words at a better time in my journey and I have never forgotten the message, the friendship, or the encouragement needed during a dark valley in my life's story."

When you are going through a tough time, sometimes you are so mad you could scream and other times you feel so defeated you just want to go to bed and cry.

Those feelings are normal. In fact, if you didn't feel that way you would not be normal.

"We need each other."
--Leo Buscaglia

Whatever your beliefs are, it is during the terrible and trying times that you look for someone or something to hold on to. So often, when we are going through a tough time, the easy ways out are not always the right ways. Sometimes we just need to be still and hope the bad passes quickly.

> *If you're going through Hell*
> *Keep on going, don't slow down*
> *If you're scared, don't show it*
> *You might get out*
> *Before the devil even knows you're there.*
> — ***Rodney Atkins***

If you have tried everything you can and nothing is helping you, then you might as well try praying about it. If we have open and sincere hearts that are grateful for what we have, if we really listen for God's answer, we will hear it. Sometimes it takes a while, but He always comes through.

WHERE TWO OR MORE ARE GATHERED

"When I need help, I repeat what the Scriptures tell us," said Jack Scaife of Ohio. "In Proverbs 11:14 it says, 'There is safety in a multitude of counselors' and I always think of it as 'steering a ship' which keeps us off the rocks when we seek Godly counsel."

"Where there is no guidance, a people falls,
but in an abundance of counselors there is safety."
— *Proverbs 11:14 ESV*

A "multitude" (or abundance, depending which version of the Bible you use) of counselors" are people you can count on for Godly advice. They need not be trained counselors or teachers. They could just be people willing to join our team, with whom we can talk things over and we feel safe that they want the best for us.

"For where two or three are gathered in my name,
there am I among them."
— *Matthew 18:20 (ESV)*

There are a lot of people out there who care about you and want to help, but you have to figure out who they are. Sometimes good people who are trying to help don't know what to say so they say the wrong thing, but if they are sincerely trying to help you and be on your team let them in.

SHE GETS BY WITH A LITTLE HELP FROM HER FRIENDS

"I have learned over the years it's not for lack of caring that those words are said. Some people are just at a loss of words," said Suzanne Corbett, a Food/Travel writer who has some experience in the area of facing challenges. She went through life married to a husband who was bipolar, and took care of him as he faced cancer at the end of his life. She also went through breast cancer and several knee surgeries, herself.

"Sometimes people are fearful about what to say, while others are simply apathetic or don't understand," she said. "So, the question is, when you are in a situation where you need understanding and the ability to communicate a level of concern, where do you look? I can sum it up in up in one word—friends. Friends will get you through any situation you are in."

Your friends are your community. They are the ones who cheer you on when you try something new and they sit beside you when your world is falling apart. If they don't, get new friends.

"Nowhere else will you find that caring ear who will listen or a helping hand that reaches out to you—often unsolicited," she said. "Friends have taken me through the darkest times. Some of those friends I never knew I had until the chips were down. Yet, fueled by care and kindness, each have helped pull me through adversity and heartache; encouraging me back on my path at times when I thought the worst."

It works in reverse, too—you may be in need of a friend right now, but look around you, there is someone out there who needs you. You might actually be the answer to someone else's prayer.

Showing someone friendship to help them be strong is selfless and it is something the person you are being a friend to will not forget.

"Friends—which if you're really lucky includes your family—will always be the roses in your garden that help grow success, happiness, and peace," said Suzanne.

Throughout difficult times, even on the hardest days, she persevered and kept going. She wrote stories and books, and some of them even won her awards. She never gave up on herself or others. She kept on going, and while she accepted the help of friends, she also did things to support those closest to her.

"Friendship is a garden I get to cultivate by returning the kindness of friendship to those around me," she said. "As a result, I have enjoyed a harvest of blessings. I believe those blessings will continue, in spite of the fact I don't know the challenges that are in the road ahead. But I'm not worried—well, maybe a little from time to time—but in my heart I know I'll be fine. I'll make it. After all, as Lennon and McCartney wrote, 'I get by with a little help from my friends.' "

She Relies on Her Sisters

Once we stop feeling so alone and open ourselves up to the support of our community, we will have a better life.

Jill Sutherland suggests having "prayer sisters" (or brothers).

"Twenty years ago, my family was going through a very stressful situation," she remembers. "It was making me ill."

Sometimes when we are going through something, it does make us physically ill. Stress or worry can come out in many ways—stomach aches, headaches, even back aches.

"I was invited to join a prayer group," said Jill. "The strength of praying sisters has brought me through so much. I look forward to it every Saturday morning. It's like a reset button."

She says the group has continued over the years and everything they pray about is confidential—which could have been a challenge since she lives in a small town, but she says everyone agreed to it and they stick to it.

"I feel so blessed to have a group like this," she said. "I think I have to remind myself to give control to God."

Your community should be what works best for you. Maybe, like Jill, it is finding a group, or maybe it is confiding in a friend. You are not a bother to those who love you.

Often when we are facing a tough time, we feel like others are abandoning us. Sometimes we wonder where our friends went, but if we pay attention, there are always those who are there for us and those are our real friends.

DON'T GIVE UP ON YOUR FRIENDS

"When my wife was given the news of her cancer, it came with the prognosis that she had 24 to 36 months to live," said Paul Avery, a former youth pastor and law enforcement officer who now works in security. "That was the beginning of what would ultimately be an exhausting nine-year journey of treatments and surgeries."

When she first got sick, they were determined to continue living their lives.

"We tried our best to remember to 'live' when we would give ourselves permission," he said. "We had an extensive support group."

As her sickness wore on, they noticed fatigue within their circle of support.

"We started to notice the cards and calls tapered off from what was originally a thunderous outpouring of support."

Paul and his wife started to realize they would go days and even weeks without hearing from the dear family and friends that had rallied behind them in their journey. If you are going through something that takes a longer time than you expected or when new problems reoccur, you might begin to feel bitter towards your "community" for "abandoning you."

"In an honest conversation with a very trusted friend, I realized that we were the ones who had grown silent and reclusive," he said. "In taking care of our situation, we had fallen into the trap of not wanting to be a burden to our friends and loved ones. I learned that people desperately want to be helpful, but at the same time are terrified of saying or doing the wrong thing. People took their cues from us that we didn't want to talk about it or socialize."

If he had not thought to talk it out with his friend, he might never have realized what was happening.

"Relationships of all kinds are definitely a two-way street," he added. "We learned that we had to identify that trusted group of support people in our lives and give them permission to speak and ask, even at those times when we were silent.

"I know personally that honest support—without fear—strengthened those relationships and made the arduous journey of living life with cancer more tolerable and way less quiet."

"When we give cheerfully and accept gratefully, everyone is blessed."
                                                        — Maya Angelou

The key in your situation is to accept gratefully. I would even add accept "gracefully." It's hard to let people help, because it might make us feel weak or like we are a bother to them. There is no shame in needing help and asking for it.

Nobody wants to go through a bad situation—whether it is you who is experiencing it or if you are watching a loved one go through a tough time. Heather Berry, a successful magazine editor says, "The road of life seems to have a way of including potholes along the way.

Heather also had a difficult journey with a loved one's health. Maybe you are experiencing the difficulty of illness.

"Around 2004, my mother found a lump in her breast and went to the doctor—but the news wasn't what we wanted to hear," said Heather. "So we fought with her—and won for a while."

If you fight the battle of a disease or a very bad situation and it turns out in a different direction—you have not lost a battle, you are a winner in my book for not giving up.

Once Heather's mother was diagnosed, though they had a strong family, the journey was made more difficult due to distance.

"My sister and my mom's only sister, lived out of state; and my brother was out of the country," said Heather. "While my father went to Mom's appointments, I chose to also go with Mom every single step of the way. I served as her note-taker during appointments when she felt terrible, and was trying to understand what the specialists on her team were saying. When she forgot questions, I would ask. When she wasn't hungry, but needed to eat something, I found something she could eat."

Do you have someone like this? Or could you be that person to someone who needs you? Her mother needed help and accepted it gratefully and gracefully from Heather, and it blessed them both at the time. She was with her every step of the way—both physically and mentally. This can mean so much to a person's recovery and to their life at the time of going through something. If you are the one going through something, maybe you could try to find someone to walk the journey with you.

"I listened when she wanted to talk (or yell)," she said. "I was silent when she needed silence. I made her laugh when she was having a good day and felt like laughing. And I was there to love her through all the ugly parts of what she faced."

Heather could feel her love back and she felt appreciated, because her mom would pat her hand when she saw her trying to keep everything on an even keel in front of her.

"I tried my best to save my tears for the drive home, or when I could cry with abandon in my husband's arms. But sometimes I wasn't successful and I broke down in front of Mom and Dad—and that was OK, too. We blew through a box of Kleenex together."

Heather and her family never expected to go on the journey like this, but they were glad they were together.

"Being there for each other and knowing that God was there, too, helped us through the darkest of days," she said. "While we don't always understand, I know one day I will. And I work hard to approach each day with a grateful heart, helping others who are in their own battles—for sometimes being there to love and care makes all the difference no matter where the road leads."

We need people—even when we think we don't. We need our community and they need us.

"Love is not patronizing and charity isn't about pity, it is about love."
— Mother Teresa

SHE'S CALLING ON ANGELS

Barbara Baxter has been through trying times like everyone else. She grew up on a farm and lives in rural, Missouri, so it is nothing for her to be out in the country with not a person in sight. In a big city, there are people everywhere, yet many feel lonely.

Barb never feels alone—even if she is out in a field by herself.

"What saves me in time of distress?" she said. "I find myself turning to God and saying 'You are my Lord, my Savior and my strength.' "

From where do you get your strength? You must get it somewhere, because you are doing a great job. Even if you sometimes feel weak and defeated, if you are moving forward you're not defeated. Every day you are taking great steps to live your life.

"Think about where you gather your strength from, in times of distress," said Barb. "That is where you turn. I turn to God and my angels. They have always been there and have given me more help than anyone would ever begin to believe. I don't know if this helps you, but it is what carries me through in rough times."

Barb finds comfort in feeling that her loved ones who have passed away are always with her—she calls them her angels.

One day she walked in to her husband's office and found him non-responsive, lying on the floor. She had no idea what was wrong and an immediate panic overcame her. As she went about the process of calling 911 and then the agonizing trip to the emergency room, she began praying to calm down. As she prayed, she thought about her team of angels and it gave her strength. She felt them with her helping her.

Many reading this will know that feeling and if faced with a crisis, will find comfort in prayer.

Nobody Could Rain on Her Parade

When I was in college, I was in a car full of girls out on the town one Friday night. As our driver pulled out onto the highway, a car from the middle lane started over into our lane. You could hear screams and curse words from all of our passengers, but above all the terror came the most beautiful voice belting out in a voice more powerful than Barbra Streisand, "Don't Rain on My Parade!"

She had recently sang that song in a state-wide beauty pageant, which she had won.

Our driver laid on the horn, and the other driver went back into their lane and we all calmed down. But someone asked her, "Why did you start singing a show tune at such a crucial time?" She answered, "I want to go out singing!"

That always stayed with me. It shows how we really can control our emotions and make our situations better, if we prepare ourselves and try to go to a place of comfort. For Barb, it is angels—for our pageant queen, it was music.

But what if you feel like you are out there on an island and no one understands what you are going through? There are many times when we are suffering and we think that others are against us, because of the decisions we made—or the ones we didn't. Or sometimes, we just think our situation is too weird for anyone to understand.

HERE COMES THE JUDGE

Becky (she didn't want her last name used) was unhappy at her job and every day that she went to work, she felt the life was being sucked out of her. She was trying to fit in, but for all the efforts she was making, her spirit was dying. One day she could not take it anymore and she quit—no job, but with a house payment and other bills.

At the very moment she gave her resignation, she felt a huge weight come off her shoulders. This decision she made empowered her to seek another opportunity where she could be more respected and feel more necessary. What she had not counted on was how some people judged her for her decision—even family members. She'd had enough and she felt great about the decision, but as you can imagine, there were those who rather than trying to support and help her, expressed their disappointment in her.

She felt she made the right decision, but she could feel some friends and family members were placing blame on her. What about your house payment?

She felt judged because of the questions people asked. Was she being overly sensitive? Sometimes in our efforts to help a friend or family member, we feel the urge to fix things. Questions can sound like accusations when all you want a safe place—someone to talk to who will believe in you and side with you.

People will do things we don't agree with, sometimes they will flat out mess up, but if we are on their team, we will be there for them, no matter how many times it seems like they screw up.

A successful media executive felt this when he was going through a

86

divorce. He felt people were judging him and thinking that somehow he was happy when the divorce became final—when really his heart was breaking.

"I don't understand a divorce to some as being some type of party or celebration," he said. "It's not. It's a never-ending funeral to me—you don't just lose that person who was meant to be your lifelong best friend, but you may lose an entire family … and this can be beyond heartbreaking."

Sometimes when we are not the one experiencing the pain, we assume things that maybe aren't there. When a couple goes through tough times or in the end, a divorce, it often depends on who we are closest to as to what we think, but it's better not to judge.

Deepak Chopra encourages morning affirmations and on a recent television appearance suggested we start our day with the decision not judge anyone or anything the entire day.

> *"If you try not to judge people you will see how many times a day we are judging others and not even realizing it. When we judge others, it brings in a negative spin to our day."*
>
> — *Deepak Chopra on PBS*

If we stopped judging others, we would see the world in a whole different way—in love. Try it some time. It's not easy, because though we don't realize it, we are constantly making judgments rather than just accepting and adapting. You can't be optimistic about a person if you start with a preconceived judgement against them.

While we should support our loved-one, in any situation, there are two sides—two versions of the same story—or maybe even more.

When someone is going through a tough time they may feel their friends or loved ones have turned turn against them for no reason.

Sometimes life can seem like a Lifetime movie, but if it is someone else's movie—someone else's life you are watching, it's good to be aware that they are seeing it differently than you are. Maybe to you there is a simple fix and so you offer advice based on the layer of understanding you have. Sometimes advice is better left unsaid. Sometimes we just need our friends and family to be with us and listen, without judging or fixing.

...And when this road gets too long
I'll be the rock you lean on
Just take my hand, together we can do it
I'm gonna love you through it.

— **Martina McBride**

Sometimes the best we can do is love someone through it and do nothing, but just be there. This can apply to ourselves if we are the ones experiencing the situation. We should try to keep the lines of communications open as to how someone can help us. Try not to be overly sensitive during this time. If someone you love hurts your feelings, maybe they just chose the wrong words—cut them some slack, because they love you and you need them.

It's good to be able to express your feelings to those you love, but at the same time, respect how they feel if they are trying to help. You may want to be left alone and they try to help. If a loved one thinks you want to be alone too much and they want to help, this might be the breakthrough you needed. Don't shut yourself out from others.

SAY WHAT YOU NEED TO SAY

The actress, Glenn Close, along with singer, John Mayer, teamed up using the song, *Say What You Need To Say,* in bringing awareness to mental illness. Glenn Close's sister, Jessie, had mental illness and they participated in a Public Service Announcement (PSA) commercial where Jessie wore a shirt that said "Bipolar" and Close wore one that said "Sister."

It was a powerful message, because we can feel so alone in the world, but with better communication and understanding, we can help each other.

Are you a person who finds it hard to accept help? Often those who are the most helpful to others find it difficult to accept help when they need it.

Accepting help freely when offered at a time of need is something we should allow ourselves to do. We don't always have to be the one in control. We don't always have to be the driver with the GPS. Sometimes it's nice to just sit in the back seat, look out at the scenery, and let someone else drive.

This is how you grow your supportive community—and this is how you help someone else grow theirs. See how I turn it around: whenever I say, "Do this for yourself," then I turn it around and say, "Do it for someone else." The best way to help yourself is to help others.

Surround Yourself with a Community That Is Good for You

I remember when I was a kid and an older friend lost his father to a massive heart attack. This was the time that he needed good people around him to support and help him. Unfortunately the mother was so distraught that she basically left him to fend for himself and he ended up getting in with the "wrong crowd." Those kids were out doing things they shouldn't be—probably because their parents had other things going on. In a way, those kids were just looking for someone who loved them, who could be their community. Beware of those swooping in at an opportune time.

It's important to pay attention to those who comfort you. There are people who you have tried to avoid, because they provide negative drama into your life, but then when you are in a weakened state, they can insert themselves into your life and provide you with more negativity that you just don't need right now.

Hopefully, you can tell if someone is toxic and bad for you and avoid them, but remember to let the ones in who have good intentions and want the best for you. I'm talking about your sister, the friend you've had for 20 years, the lady at church who stops to greet you and ask if you are OK, even the random nice person you know who takes the time to ask you out for coffee.

Life is too short to spend our time with negative people and it is also too short for us to be judging people or cutting them down—or letting others put us down. If we want to be happy, we should strive to find a loving community, who will support us and keep us optimistic, no matter what.

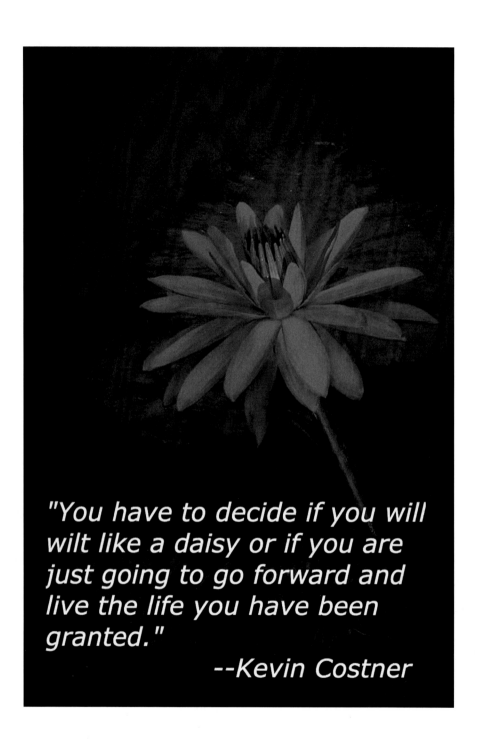

"You have to decide if you will wilt like a daisy or if you are just going to go forward and live the life you have been granted."

--Kevin Costner

CHAPTER SIX

Optimism
Don't Give Up on Yourself—or Others

Optimism is looking at something with the best possible view. If you are optimistic, you open your heart to the possibility of something good happening.

We know the power of optimism, that's why characters like Orphan Annie, Pollyanna, and the Shirley Temple childhood characters were so popular. They looked for the good in all situations.

HE KEEPS HIS EYES ON THE GOLF BALL

During Kyle McGuire's senior year of high school, he noticed his eyesight was getting blurry, but he was busy with baseball and getting ready for college. A few years later, when he went to the doctor to get his eyes checked, he was diagnosed with a progressive eye disease called Keratoconus. With the help of glasses, he was able to continue with college and go on to Florida to become a pro golfer.

Recently he had a follow-up appointment and was shocked to learn the disease had progressed. Did he give up his dream of being a golfer? No, he worked even harder.

"Kyle is the eternal optimist," said his mother, Debbie McGuire, a marketing manager for a large company. "He won't let this stop him from pursuing his goal of playing golf at a high level. Sports have been a huge part of his life and his athleticism is a strength that not everyone has."

While Debbie is thankful for her son's optimism, as a mother it is scary to think of what lies ahead. As with most parents, there are the "what ifs" and "I hope he's OK." Worrying won't help our situations, but we can't help it when it is our family. Luckily Kyle seems to have the tools he needs to help himself through troubling times.

"His faith is very strong and his will to excel—a gift that God gave him— is even stronger," said Debbie. "He is competing in the West Florida Golf Tour and when he's not on tour, he works day and night, rain or shine to do what it takes to knock strokes off his game."

Nothing is promised to us except this moment and Kyle is doing the best he can with his life today—that is the best attitude anyone can have.

"Whatever happens in the future, we know how very lucky we are and that we can face it as a family with the courage, confidence, faith and determination that Kyle holds dear."

He keeps playing golf and using the gifts he feels God has given him. Your happiness is directly related to your outlook and Kyle continues to move forward. Here's to a long, successful golf career, Kyle McGuire!

It's All in How You Look at It

"If you see a big, gray storm cloud and it looks like it's about to rain, your perception of the situation is how you will react to it," said Ryan Powell, a baseball scout living in Florida. " 'A picture says a thousand words' is a powerful message, because many people see the dark clouds and simply see a storm rolling in—but it's dependent on a person's perception that tells the tale. Within any storm, it is very much like the tough times in our life. A storm may roll in, but it also passes."

Ryan points out that there are two ways to look at a storm and we get to choose how we perceive it.

"What makes the difference is how you go through it," he said. "You see it within the context of a mission statement that defines who you are through each storm of life. Life has a way of throwing all of us curveballs—or rainstorms—from time to time, but it's up to you on how you will react to them."

Dr. Daniel Amen, the brain health doctor on PBS (Public Television) thinks that eliminating our negative thoughts will improve our health, including reversing depression, anxiety, or negativity in our lives.

Every day we are faced with "Automatic Negative Thoughts" that pop into our heads, that Dr. Amen calls ANTS. He advises us to get rid of our ants.

"Kill your ants," he advises. One way he suggests to his patients is wear a rubber band around their wrist and every time a negative thought creeps in, snap the rubber band.

What are some examples of ants? According to Amen, beating ourselves up or anticipating things, such as: assuming the worst, anticipating what someone else's reaction will be, or using phrases like "I should do this" or "I must do that." He uses the example of, "I should go visit my grandmother," rather than what he would prefer, the more positive, "I want to spend time with my grandmother."

SHE WANTS TO JUMP INTO LIFE

Carolyn Seeling is only four years old, but she is full of optimism. Her grandpa took her to the swimming pool at a hotel in Johnson City, Tennessee. The concrete was hot and her grandpa was calling to her to get her shoes on, "Get off the hot concrete!" But she just hurried towards the pool steps and didn't seem to notice her bare feet against the heated pool deck.

"I'm just so excited to be here!" she exclaimed with glee. "I'm so excited to go in the pool!"

As her grandpa helped her into the pool, she spoke in a loud voice, "This is so fun! I'm so excited!" Then she started singing. As I sat there and watched her, I was enthralled. I had just been in the pool and had felt the same way. The sun was beating down, yet the water was cool and perfect. Here was this little girl saying just what I was thinking.

Her grandfather was a bit embarrassed that little Carolyn was becoming the center of attention. As I looked up from my book, others in the pool looked at her. "Let's talk in a quieter voice," he gently told her, but she would not listen.

She made up a song and started singing it and you could see she was not in our world—she was in Carolyn's world—and having the time of her life. Optimism is seeing the cool water in the pool, not the hot concrete on the way to get there.

HE NEVER GAVE UP

Sometimes with all you are dealing with, it is hard to be optimistic. Being optimistic doesn't mean being unrealistic, it just means you try to find good in your situation—or at least try not to look for the worst. You don't give up when you have setbacks and nobody knew this better than Ray Barber who grew up in California.

"God gives us all gifts, but do we really appreciate them?" asks Ron Barber, a former TV and radio anchorman, reporter and Ray's son, who lives in St. Louis said, "For me the greatest gift was my dad—my square peg in a round hole, 'life is full of endless possibilities' dad, Raymond Hershfield Barber. He showed me what love was all about—despite the setbacks he faced every day."

Ray Barber went to Hollywood High School and rubbed shoulders with the likes of Clark Gable and Myrna Loy growing up. He had a beautiful voice and recordings still exist of him singing songs like April Showers in clubs.

It seemed he was destined for stardom himself, but that dream came to an end after he suffered a vocal cord tragedy in the late 1930s. Not being able to sing was a huge blow to my dad, as he had his life planned out as an entertainer, so he began to drink in his frustration. However, he had a brilliant mind and tinkered with inventions.

"He pioneered the strobe light beacon as a Signal Corpsman in World War II," said Ron of his father who in the early 1960s was asked to take a test and became a charter member of the newly formed MENSA. After the war, he ended up in the Midwest.

"My mother, who was as beautiful as a Hollywood actress, was on a train bound for Wisconsin in 1944, where she was to meet her fiancé," said Ron. "My dad, also on that train, took one look at her and like a moth to a beautiful flame, he wooed her away from her intended."

Ray's folks wound up in the Chicago suburb of Glenview, and by day, his wife, Mescal, kept house as Ray worked as an electrical engineer and tinkered with his inventions further, trying to perfect the strobe beacon.

At night, young and in love, they took to the bar scene with all the other young soldiers returning from war. He didn't realize at the time that his carefree evenings, paired with the frustrating daytime career struggle, would wind him up on a path of alcoholism.

"I think the drinking started to become a problem in Hollywood, when he so desperately wanted to be the singer, the performer, the star of the show," said Ron. "Then he was involved in a long, brutal fight over the patents he'd had for the Strobe beacon. At times, it seemed like he put so much effort into his life, but he was seeing no results. He ended up winning in court, but it took a toll on his life—and ours."

Sometimes we want something so bad that we get tunnel vision. Ray wanted to be a success for his family, but ultimately they would suffer.

Life can be tough trying when you're trying to make it in the work world—and many of you know that. It can be so stressful and self-defeating when you feel you are doing everything right, but you don't get the results you want. Maybe by Ron sharing his father's story, it can help someone reading this—someone who is feeling like a failure. You aren't. There are others around you who think the world of you.

"My dad was a beautiful, yet imperfect man," Ron said. "He sat many long nights with me at the kitchen table trying to interest me in math and things he knew about, but ultimately I had aspirations of following Jack Quinlan, the Cubs announcer on WGN-Radio and become a broadcaster."

Though frustrated with how his own life was going, he turned to helping others. He could not find his place in the world, but he could help Ron by sending out his audiotapes, writing letters and making phone calls on his son's behalf to help him achieve his dream.

"When I got my first job at WJBD in Salem, Illinois, you could say he was living through his son—in the entertainment world that he was not able to do, because of his voice—he helped me in a career where my voice was my biggest asset," said Ron. "Over the years, I managed to eke out new jobs in far-flung corners of the country— Lansing, Michigan, Asheville, North Carolina, Santa Maria, California—but he always managed to visit me."

His car was an old beater with questionable tires, but that didn't stop him from being there with a few bucks for the son he loved.

"He constantly sent me letters of support," said Ron. "He loved me and schlepped his way halfway across the nation to show it."

Watching his father struggle with alcohol throughout the years was agonizing for Ron, and anyone who has been in that situation knows the heartbreak.

The thing about Ray was that while things didn't seem to work out for him, he kept plugging away at it. He had a son and a family and they were looking to him. He always stayed optimistic.

"Ray Barber never gave up on himself," said his son. "He certainly had fallen prey to alcohol, but what amazed me was that he never let himself stay down long and was always tinkering, experimenting, and trying something new, something that could finally give him the breakthrough he had wanted his entire life. He'd come home with some gizmos, gadgets, ideas and plans that always made me smile, because they made him so happy. If only one had worked out, but he never, ever stopped trying."

Who knows, maybe his next breakthrough was about to happen. Maybe he didn't get his rewards on earth, but we don't know the plans that lay ahead of him.

Ron learned some valuable lessons from his dad. After making money on an investment that he made with the company that produced The Gong

Show, Ron, feeling proud of himself, told his dad.

"I'll never forget his response," said Ron. "He said, 'Son, don't put your money in frivolous investments that may make you profits early on. That is never where your ultimate happiness and goals should be. Invest your money, your time, and your life in projects where you can sit back and take the utmost pride in them—and yourself.' "

"To this day I remember that advice and I've started some successful companies, but at the core of everything I've done, I've invested my time, money, and life in things that truly make a difference. I've tried to copy his decency, goodness, and love."

Ron started companies that have made a difference in the world by providing life-saving video training and education for police, fire, and first responders. His reality-based video and online "In the Line of Duty" training for police and his "American Heat" training for firefighters are standards of excellence utilized by thousands of law enforcement agencies and fire departments across the country. He also did a video series to give young people nationwide an in-depth look at role models and realistic careers they may well have never known even existed.

When things aren't going the way you want, be persistent and don't give up. When one door closes, another one might open, and if it doesn't, keep going and keep looking for that next doorway of opportunity. Don't be afraid to try things. Be optimistic about your future.

Sometimes it seems like nothing we try works out. Believe me, I know this feeling—you feel like a failure. You think you have a great idea, so you try it, but it doesn't work out, or health problems prevent you from doing something you really wanted to do, or somebody you feel is less qualified gets the job. Keep on trying—there may be another way of achieving what you want or you might discover something else that's better along the way. How do you know your next idea won't work if you stop trying?

Sometimes our failures are taking us down a road that is going to educate us about what we need to know for a future opportunity, but if we give up, we'll never get that opportunity. We'll never know. We have to be optimistic, if we are going to succeed. Whenever you get a negative voice in your head that you aren't good enough or you are a failure, immediately replace that with, "I AM good enough and I'm going to have an amazing breakthrough soon."

Her Carefree Life Was Gone with the Wind, But She Never Gave Up

Patrisha Henson has also been touched by family member with addiction problems. She has seen her life completely change in the last ten years and she finds it tough to be optimistic at times—but keeps persevering. This Kentucky woman went from carefree wife and grandma who loved to travel and had a passion for *Gone with the Wind*, to a completely different place in life than she ever imagined she would be. She and her husband are raising their grandchildren, because she had a family member who was unable to do it, due to addiction.

It is tough to see a family member with destructive behavior and though she loves her grandchildren, it was a double-edged sword. What was it that kept her going? She had no choice.

"Our lives have been touched by addiction and it's hard to know what direction to take to make things better, but I remain optimistic," she said. Then she added, "Sometimes it's hard to positive, but I keep trying and I don't give up."

We don't always have to be upbeat every day when life beats us down, but we can always try to make the best of any situation presented to us. Viewing things in a negative way can only bring you down and diminish your coping skills. Being optimistic can actually give you more strength to do what you need to do.

Even though Patrisha didn't know what to do, she kept going. She had no idea of what a great example she was to others who were quietly watching her, because in the midst of her thinking she didn't know what to do, she kept moving forward, doing her best trying to raise positive grandchildren.

This book is not about "cheer up and move on." It's about people like her. It's about people like you and me. We face adversity, but we're not throwing in the towel. We're not giving up.

Sometimes it is hard to be positive when we are living our lives, but we shouldn't give up, because others depend on us. There are many who are counting on you and looking up to you—even if you don't know it.

Patrisha may feel lost at times and sometimes sad—because that is normal—but she is doing everything she can to give those children a good life. Even though her heart may be breaking at times, she still carries on and has the optimistic attitude that things will get better.

No matter how tough it is for you right now, you will get through this.

It will have an end—and you don't want to look back on this part and feel you gave up.

Just staying in there during times of trouble is a victory. You are amazing that you get up every day. Even if you can't jump out of bed enthusiastically, you can wake up and have an optimistic outlook for the day—no matter what it may hold.

"I grew up in a situation where you didn't really ask for help—you figured it out," said Patrisha. "And you did what you had to do. I think that is maybe why I just do what I have to do."

Just like all of us going through something, Patrisha sometimes feels all alone. It is hard for us to talk about our problems, but it is good to find a friend, confidante, or counselor—or even a volleyball like Tom Hanks did in the movie, *Castaway*—to talk to. He had no other human to talk to, so he painted a face on the ball and named it Wilson. That's how he survived.

It may seem easy to mask our feelings with bad behavior, but in the end, we will have to face the music. The old saying, "drowning our sorrows" is exactly what it is, but the problem will continue even though you may "self-medicate," because that's not a long-term solution.

Things start out going downhill and we think we can manage it, but soon we find ourselves on a roller coaster. That gentle rain we think we can control continues into a full-out downpour, unless we take the time and effort to find shelter—to find help and strength—which often can be found within ourselves or through someone else.

If you are reading this and you feel yourself spinning out of control due to a situation you are in, get help. Someone loves you so much and is counting on you.

The National Drug Helpline, 1-888-633-3239 offers 24/7 drug and alcohol help to those struggling with addiction.

I am praying for anyone involved in an addiction problem—whether you are the person who is addicted, or you have a loved one who is.

THEIR SON GAVE THEM STRENGTH

Sometimes we can get our strength from the place we least expect. Dan and Elizabeth Crum's son, Daniel II, was going through pediatric cancer and the parents were worried. Their child had an optical tumor and their future seemed so uncertain. Even though they rely on their faith, there was an unexpected source that provided strength and optimism to them.

"We were blessed to have a child with a 'never-give-up' attitude," said

Dan. "We were able to draw strength from Daniel, himself. He had such a giving heart that he was helping us when we were trying to help him."

Dan said there was one more thing that helped him and his wife, Liz—family.

"It was Daniel's strength and our family support that helped us get through it."

The family support also helped Daniel. Daniel remained optimistic throughout his cancer experience and that optimism has stuck with him, as he goes through life legally blind. Though he is visually challenged, he can see well enough to get around and even played on the golf team in high school.

His tumor is still there, but it is stable and has been for some time. He does not spend his time worrying about what could come, but he lives his life and helps others. Though his parents were a little afraid to drop him off at the airport both times—he has taken two overseas mission trips—to parts of the world he would have never imagined he would go. Their family has learned the importance of a giving spirit. They gave it to their son and he in turn gave it back to them.

"He's a person who enjoys giving back after all he has received from others," said Dan Crum. "And now he has the heart of a champion. My biggest advice is to never give up and always stay optimistic."

What if your challenge is on a big stage? What if you feel you have failed or been made to look bad in front of millions of people? There are no bigger stages than Hollywood; Washington, DC; or the professional sports arenas. Actors work so hard for a movie and if they get a bad review or worse yet, if it turns out to be a flop, everyone finds out about it. Coaches get fired, pitchers give up big runs in the ninth to lose the game for their team, and politicians lose elections.

JUST BECAUSE YOU LOSE, DOES NOT MEAN YOU ARE A LOSER

No one knows this more than former US Congressman Jack Buechner, who served ten years in the Missouri State Legislature and then four years in the United States Congress. He was a delegate to the Republican Convention a few times before he thought he'd test the waters and run for political office himself.

On his first election, he lost narrowly to the incumbent and while others may have written him off, he saw that loss as a positive.

"I remember Lesley Stahl saying, 'One of the first evidences of the Reagan coattails is that Jack Buechner of Missouri has defeated a five-term incumbent,' but it turned out I didn't." he said. "After that loss, I felt so defeated, but then I thought, 'You know what? I'm a fighter. I'm going to make it through this.' "

Like Lloyd Christmas in *Dumb and Dumber*, he thought "You're telling me there's a chance!" All he needed was that loss to push him to his next win. Don't ever feel defeated, because one loss might be getting you prepared for an even better win.

> *"I've missed more than 9000 shots in my career. I've lost almost 300 games. 26 times, I've been trusted to take the game winning shot and missed. I've failed over and over and over again in my life. And that is why I succeed."*
>
> *— Michael Jordan*

So Jack got to work.

"I worked really hard the next two years and when I won, I thought, 'Wow, this is really something.' I kept at it and then I had no trouble the next two years."

As we all experience, there are ups and downs in our life. We all have good times and then there are those periods that are not so good, but it takes all of it to make a life.

"A lot of people look at benchmarks in their lives and for me, 1990 was an unbelievable year," said Jack. "First of all, I turned 50, which is always a hallmark and in that year, I got divorced, remarried, and I lost a major election. That is a lot of things to happen in one year, all life-changing."

Jack did win his second election and went on to have a great time in Congress, doing all the things Congressmen do—work in the US Capitol, travel, meet world leaders, and serve with Presidents.

The third election was a stunner and one of the most difficult things he has endured in his life.

"This was an election everybody thought I couldn't lose," he said. "It was devastating and shocking."

Losing an election is no small thing, as elected officials have donors and people working for them on their staff—and they feel their family is all counting on them. It can be a heavy weight on someone's shoulders.

"It's not like losing an election for your senior class," he said.

Or maybe ... it is JUST like losing an election for class president, only in a different arena. I am sure most of us remember failing in our life—or what we perceive as failing. All those times you didn't make the team in high school, or didn't get that job you thought you were perfect for, or when your boyfriend or girlfriend dumped you—or whatever it is that is still in your memory, it is as important to you as losing a seat in Congress—only not on as large of a stage. But to you that stage was just as big.

"Everything is taken away from you," Jack said. "You feel numb. I had no plans, no plan B."

What happened was at the time he was declared the loser in the election, the results were not all in, but it was very close. There was still that glimmer of hope but the reality was setting in that he lost—but it took a while to happen.

"It ended up being the closest election in modern congressional election history at the time," Jack said. "You think you're going to win and then it turns out that you don't win. I lost by 54 votes."

Then it started hitting him that it just did not affect him; the loss affected others.

"Of course, it's your ego, but more than that, I felt like I had let people down. I felt worse about letting people down than I did for myself. I thought 'I'll never be able to get over this.' "

He had worked hard in the election and expected to be celebrating that night. The loss caused him to realize how much he had loved the job and that he had not planned to lose. It was a low point in his life—but things were about to change.

"Two weeks after the election, Nancy (his fiancé) and I were married."

So he went from the pits of the world to the top of the world. It was a whirlwind of excitement with the wedding and the honeymoon, but when they got back to the condo they had just bought, it was not the life they had thought they would have.

"We had to figure out what to do," he said. "Nothing was coming. In my whole life, I had never had an instance where I was literally blank. My brain wasn't processing anything. I didn't know what to do. I didn't know who to discuss it with to figure it out. My friends didn't know what to say to me—they were embarrassed."

If you are at the bottom of the well, remember this: if you can look up and see even the smallest crack of light, you know there's a way out. Jack knew he had to save himself, so he got an idea.

"I began reaching out to others who had lost elections to find out how they had handled it," he said.

He felt that talking to others who had been in the same boat as he was in, was helpful. In a way, it is the same thing as a support group. You find out you are not the "only one" going through your situation.

"A big piece of advice from many of them was, 'Don't do anything precipitately,' " Jack said. 'Don't just dive into something—take time to figure it out.' "

During a time when you are in a valley, maybe you have experienced that numb feeling, that feeling of not knowing what to do. You might even feel the world is against you.

"The toughest thing was that people treat you like a loser," he said "We live in a society where winning isn't everything, but it's pretty close. So I had people who had never run for anything in their lives telling me how I should think or treating me like I had just lost their investments. The people who worked for me, of course, lost their jobs, and a few blamed me, so I felt even worse. It was a lot of responsibility on my shoulders."

It is during these times where we feel the world is doubting us that we need to keep believing in ourselves. Every situation can be turned around eventually, but at the time, it may seem so hopeless.

Even though it was a dark time in his life on the professional side, Jack knew it would be unfair to his new wife, if he moped and gave up.

"There's that saying that if one door closes, another opens, and that was sort of how it played out," said Jack. "That loss led to a new life and relationship with Nancy—different than we thought it would be, when we thought I would be a Congressman, but we knew we could still have a great life. And then months later, we had our child and I was selected for a position that allowed me to travel the world and do so many things that being a member of Congress would not have allowed me to do."

He was glad he had not lost sight of his life as he went down another path. To be a member of Congress is an elite thing and he had actually achieved the goal of being in Congress. He had to remind himself of that—just like we should always remind ourselves of the good we have accomplished.

"I had to say to myself, 'Wow, I did it,' and focus on that. There's only been like 10,000 people in the history of the country who have gotten to be a Congressman."

Out of an extraordinary disappointment came something wonderful.

"Even though my life didn't go down the path that I thought I wanted, I got something that ended up being better," he said. "That's what you have to look at. Something that I did not expect to happen, ended up being the best thing in my life," he said. "And if it hadn't been for Nancy, it would have probably really have had some serious side effects. It's good to share your feelings with someone.

"Whenever you go through a challenging time, it helps to have someone talk to, and I was lucky to have her with me on that journey. Without having someone to talk about it, I don't know how I would have handled it."

Even so, it was a difficult time to get through.

"During that time, I was disappointed, but never depressed," he said. "You have to realize there is a difference between a tragedy and a great disappointment."

His "tragedy" came 12 years later, when after years of happiness with Nancy, she was diagnosed with cancer. He watched her suffer, once again knowing there was nothing he could do in the situation. He said this was the only time in his life he was depressed.

The greatest disappointment of his life was losing that election and then the greatest tragedy of his life came when Nancy passed away.

Once again he was numb and didn't know what to do. Once again, he was left with no Plan B. After a period of grieving, he began opening himself up to possibilities. That's called optimism. Life has a way of surprising us and three years later, he married his current wife, Andrea.

"I am so lucky I found love with Andrea" he said. "I now have Parkinson's disease, which is incurable and instead of being able to take her to Ecuador, South Africa, the Galapagos Islands and other the places that retirees dream of going, she ends up caring for me some of the time.

"I can't do the same things with her that we had planned before my diagnosis, but she is such a great friend and wife and caregiver. This life with Andrea is so great."

Jack said that if it is possible to "mature" after the age of 60, he feels he has done it and the experiences that led him to where he is today helped him. When he looks to the future, it is with a bright outlook.

"For Andrea to be able to take me as things have changed—take me as I am—that is such a wonderful thing. It has taught me that life comes in such different forms and you can embrace them all with optimism."

"It's bad enough to lose your job," he said. "But in politics, the underlying message is that somehow 10,000 people said they don't like you. Rather than think of those who don't like you, you have to find the positive—900,000 people who did like you."

Jack feels contentment in his life now, but it took all the bumps in the road to get to where he is.

"I'm a better person now," he says.

We can all try to achieve greatness even when our prospects aren't looking very good.

WE HAVE GREATNESS IN OUR DNA

Journalist Neil Cavuto said on his show: "We are the children of 'The Greatest Generation'—so it is in our DNA to be great." His comment came in the context of a World War II Veteran getting a Medal of Honor posthumously.

What a great thought that is—we have greatness in our DNA!

We may have that potential for greatness, but right now it seems like everything is so negative. We look at the past and think it was so great compared to now. When we are going through a tough time, we sometimes feel like all our happy days are over—they aren't.

These feelings are normal. That's where the saying "the good old days" comes from.

"Don't cry because it's over, smile because it happened."
— *Dr. Seuss*

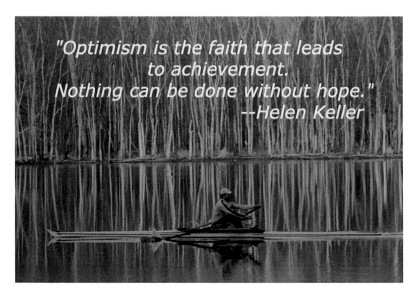

Do you have regrets and look at the past feeling sorry for yourself for something you did or did not do? Or did something that was not your fault cause you to lose a great job and your life is changed? Was there a time in your life you may not have been the greatest parent and you wonder if it affected your children? Don't have regrets. For one thing, "it" may not be over—it just may be taking a break. But if your circumstances have changed to the point that you just can't allow yourself to see happiness in the future, think of that quote.

You've had a lot of good things happen in your life, and then there were some bad times, but always keep in mind that there WERE good times and there WILL be more.

And you can be that optimistic person for someone else.

"Optimism is the faith that leads to achievement. Nothing can be done without hope and confidence."
— *Helen Keller*

How can a person who had such terrible circumstances as she did be optimistic? It's what was inside her heart. You have that, too. You have to reach down and find it though and sometimes, it's hard.

We all get discouraged. Sometimes we are having a pity party and we don't even realize it. We are so involved in how bad our life is right now that we don't realize we aren't living it. We worry too much and then we can even begin to go down a bad path.

WHAT IS KEEPING YOU UP AT NIGHT?

Or what is it that is causing that hole in your heart that you are trying as hard as you can to fill it up—whether with overscheduling activities, drinking too much, eating too much, or living a dangerous life?

We can do all those things in hopes of outrunning or getting rid of our problems, but really all it does is to cause other ones. You know, like having to lose that weight you've gained, maybe ruining relationships from the over-drinking, or elevating your stress with all those activities you wind up in the emergency room.

You don't have to try to cover up the bad or sad parts of your life—just focus on what is good. The more you try to see the good in your life, the more good there actually will be.

"Well, I don't know what will happen now. We've got some difficult days ahead. But it doesn't matter with me now. Because I've been to the mountaintop... Like any man, I would like to live a long life... But I'm not concerned about that now. I just want to do God's will. And He's allowed me to go up to the mountain. And I've looked over. And I've seen the promised land."

— Martin Luther King, Jr.

Dr. King had been to the mountaintop as he describes his experience of anticipating what Heaven is like, and then his family went to the deepest canyon a family can go to when he died. His family was comforted by his optimistic and uplifting words and we can be, too.

When we are in the deepest canyon of our lives—the "valley of the shadow of death" the thing that helps us keep going is faith—faith and optimism and never giving up.

KEEP YOUR CANDLE BURNING

When you lay your head on the pillow tonight to sleep, if you've done your best today and kept trying to be better, you are a success. Remember you don't have to be a success to others—you have to be a success to you. Striving for excellence is doing your personal best. When you do your best, it is enough, so stay on the lighted path.

The "lighted path" means where you know you should be—the path to excellence. We all know when we get off the right path, and if you find yourself either hiding what you are doing (I call that going to the dark side) or engaging in activities or a lifestyle that you, yourself are less than proud of, you might want to re-examine what's going on.

Kathy Troccoli's song, Go Light Your World says, "Take your candle, go light your world." We can light up our world every day with optimism and by treating people right.

We all have a light inside of us that is burning, so there is always hope a candle's light can give us an optimistic feeling. The flame can be so powerful. Its beauty can warm a room—its light gives hope. A prayer said when lighting a candle is punctuated by seeing the flame as a source of strength.

Have you ever been to a candlelight church service in a dark church, where one single candle was lit and then it was used to light the next one, and the person next to that candle lit their candle and so on? It is a sight to see as the entire room lights up.

"Thousands of candles can be lit from a single candle, and the life of the candle will not be shortened. Happiness never decreases by being shared."

— Buddha

One time I was watching a tape of Mr. Rogers *Neighborhood* with my grandsons. Mr. Rogers looked into his friend's eyes and said, "I see a light inside you" and the friend who was a guitar playing singer looked inside Mr. Rogers eyes and said, "I see the light in your eyes, too!" Then they started singing, *This Little Light of Mine*. Now my grandsons look in my eyes for my light and I look in theirs. "I see it! I see the light!" And then we sing that song, "This little light of mine, I'm gonna let it shine!"

When you live your daily life, do others see a light in your eye? Do you take the time to see it in others?

Just as we send light out when we are strong, we can reach down into our hearts and find that little flame that is always there in times of need. Keep it burning, even when it seems like there is no air. If all you can muster up is a flicker, then do that. Soon you will be stronger and the fire will be back to burning brightly in your life.

If you look for goodness in others, you will see their light and maybe you'll find yours.

If every day you keep trying to build yourself up, you will end up on a higher platform. Even when the chips are down, continue moving ahead, gaining wisdom. As you are in the process of building yourself up, your flame will come and go, but it will get stronger and your light will burn brighter. From a higher position, you can spread your light to more people.

Think about a flashlight. If you are lying on the ground shining it towards the rug, there is a little light, but if you stand on the bed and shine it out, the light spreads.

As I was writing this, several events were going on in my life, which could have put me in a very dark place, but I was determined not to go there. When negativity creeps in, or even hits you with a thud, think to yourself, "I have a choice to be optimistic right now. I can choose happy."

The best way out of the canyon is to believe you will get out. Optimism and a positive attitude will go a long way in your recovery and in the recovery of anyone going through an illness or a bad situation. Sometimes when things aren't working out, you just need a new idea.

"Only I can change my life.
No one else can do it for me."
--Carol Burnett

CHAPTER SEVEN

You Need a New Idea
A New Way of Looking at Things

Do you ever feel like you are just treading water with weights on your feet? You are just trying to stay afloat, let alone make any progress in any area.

Sometimes we can't seem to see a way out. Don't give up, because there is always a way. Sometimes the way out is hard to see and you need to come up with a new idea.

You can change your situation with your own creativity.

> *"The air is full of ideas. They are knocking you in the head all the time. You only have to know what you want, then forget it, and go about your business. Suddenly, the idea will come through. It was there all the time."*
>
> *— Henry Ford*

Something new is on the horizon for you, but you have to figure out how to let it in. When you are struggling, you just have to come up with a new idea—a new plan to achieve the happiness you want.

There are two ways to get new ideas—either think one up yourself or listen to others. Sometimes when we are all wrapped up in our problems, we think we are the only ones who know what to do and when things go wrong, then there must not be a solution. But if you are open to new ideas, your future can be amazing.

HER BASKET IS FULL OF HOPE

Angela Brunette is a great example that sometimes a new idea comes into our life and if open to it, we can do anything we set our mind to do. She was a regular person who has ended up running a charity and growing it nationally, but it started with a family crisis. Her six-year-old daughter, Christina, was diagnosed with a cancerous, inoperable tumor on her spine. It was a tough time for the Brunette family, as Christina endured a year of radiation and chemotherapy.

Angela is very outgoing and smiles a lot and even though her heart feels as if it were breaking as she watched her daughter go through cancer, nurses and doctors were observing how strong and positive she was and how her family's faith helped them through that time. Eventually her daughter was cured.

"When Christina completed her treatment, I was asked by her favorite nurse if I could come back in on a regular basis and visit newly diagnosed children and their families and encourage them," said Angela.

When you are going through a tough time, you may not even realize it, but others are watching. If you are doing the best you can, you may be inspiring others just by being you. She was flattered at being asked, and thought she could volunteer some time visiting with the patients.

"Right away I realized it would help to bring a gift as I went to visit the patients," she said. "So I began giving gifts that had helped us during our journey, such as a Bible, journal, uplifting music, snacks, coffees, teas, and such for the parents and toys, games, and items for the sick child and siblings."

Angela found she really enjoyed doing this and decided to put the gifts in a basket and call it Basket of Hope. Each family received a Basket of Hope along with a personal visit.

"The families were reminded that they were not alone," said Angela. "We give all glory to God for Christina's complete recovery and we wanted to help other families. Prayers were said for each child and family. We met so many amazing children and families—some were healed, some are in Heaven. We are so thankful we had eternal hope."

Her visits expanded to include families suffering from serious illnesses, as well as cancer. Angela and those she could get to help her delivered 60 baskets the first year and it went to more than 600 baskets each year. Her program was costing a lot of money and after five years, Angela felt her friends were being tapped out from being asked to contribute, when she got an idea.

"A friend suggested I send a Basket of Hope to the backup quarterback of the Rams, Kurt Warner, and ask if he could help with delivering the baskets to the kids. What a great way to make the personal visit more meaningful for them," said Angela

It was a bold move, as she didn't have a connection to him. When she didn't hear back from him for a few months, she thought she might have to try something else, but then she got a call.

"They said Kurt and Brenda Warner would love to help!" she remembered.

The Warners had started their own foundation, "*First Things First*" and chose Basket of Hope as their first charity partnership. Once Angela realized the Warners enjoyed delivering baskets and seeing the reaction from the recipient families, Angela felt it was time to get back to the drapery and design business she had been in before her daughter got sick, so she offered the program to them.

"I assumed they would take it from there," she said. "I knew they would be able to take it to the next level and I told them so."

Angela knew she needed to get back to a paying job and felt the program she had started was in good hands with the Warners, but they had a new idea.

"I was told that God had planted this seed of hope into my heart, had given me a passion for loving these children and families, and I should never quit," said Angela. "I was ready to move on, but they encouraged me to stay, even offering to pay me a salary for a year to continue working with the program, and to put my drapery business aside for a bit. It was such a boost of encouragement and affirmation that I was doing what God had put into my heart."

More and more volunteers became involved and annual fundraising events were put into place. Grants and gifts from corporations and individuals poured in and the program took off.

Angela was able to find time for both Basket of Hope and her drapery business over the years.

She knew her life was being pushed in a new direction and she went with it. That was 20 years ago, and Christina is now a married mother of three and Basket of Hope is giving out 7,000 baskets a year.

Receiving that reminder to never give up and the Warner's encouraging support, the prayers and support of friends and family, the help of the many, and the Lord's blessing, Angela was able to grow the charity and now there are chapters across the country. They have done large basket-assembling events in conjunction with the Super Bowl for the past eight years. She has even gotten Super Bowl-winning coach Tony Dungy on board.

"Tony has helped launch the program nationally and has personally delivered thousands of baskets to seriously ill children over the years," said Angela.

The next time you wonder if you can do something, believe in yourself. You never know where life is going to take you. There's always something new to try—and you can do it!

Angela felt so grateful for the way things turned out with her daughter, and when she felt God's nudge once the Warners mentioned it, she took the leap of faith. She has devoted her life and career to helping bring happiness to others.

THE CHINESE BUFFET BRINGS GOOD FORTUNE TO OUR HOLIDAYS

Life has a way of throwing us curves, both good and bad. Sometimes the outcome is not good and you lose a loved-one. When that happens it can be hard to live our normal life, but we can have happiness—by trying a new idea.

If you have lost a loved one with whom you shared your holidays, it can be tough to look forward to holiday times. After the loss of one of our family members, it was hard to think of the family dinner that had been a tradition for so long. We had already taken away one chair, but two would be too much—so we got a new idea. We went out for Chinese!

Changing it up and heading to the Chinese Buffet that year turned out to be a great idea, because everyone had fun and no one had to spend all that time cooking. We've been doing it ever since.

Many of you know the feeling, whether it's the first Christmas or Hanukkah after a loved-one's death or the dread of being home by yourself on a Thanksgiving or your birthday.

Even though I miss my family members, I always put up my Christmas decorations and Christmas trees. I usually have about 15 of them, various sizes and themes. Never was my Christmas spirit in danger, because I made up my mind it wouldn't be. I love Christmas and have always told myself that when times are tough—don't blame Christmas. Grandma died the week before Christmas—actually the night of my birthday—but I made up my mind that was not going to ruin my Christmas spirit or my birthday. She would not want me to lose my love for that time of year just because it may make me think of her.

As the years have gone by, I am so glad I keep Christmas. Some years I forced myself to go through the motions of putting out the decorations, but that's what the holiday is about to me—it's the happy memories that those decorations bring. If a family member dies, your holidays will never be the same, but then it doesn't have to be, if you try something new.

There's no point in dreading an upcoming event—Mother's Day, Father's Day, our loved-one's birthday …. I did that on the first Fourth of July in anticipation of my parents not being there. We'd had a great time the previous year with the whole family in attendance. I moped around anticipating it.

I was like Scarlett O'Hara in *Gone with the Wind* just as Rhett Butler is walking out the door, and she says, "Where will I go? What shall I do?" He looks at her and says, "Frankly my dear, I don't give a damn."

She was turning her situation around on herself and that was what I was doing. And when you are feeling sorry for yourself, frankly, people don't give a damn and why should they? They have their own life to live with their own problems.

When we lose someone, the obvious thing is to feel the loss and to miss them. I know how much it hurts when you miss someone. What if we came up with a new idea? What if instead of using our energy moping about how much we miss them, we started thinking of ways to have them with us rather than just mourning their loss.

You will have a happier life, if you stop feeling sorry for yourself. Rather than wallow in your sorrow, do something to create and promote your loved one's memory and keep it alive. I began thinking how I could do that.

I try to think, what great qualities did I love in my parents? It's my job to spread those good qualities to those I am around. Family activities were so important to them, so I decided we should still carry on our family traditions.

They were also both supportive of the community, volunteering, and also donating money to support organizations that benefited others like the Zoo and the Botanical Gardens. What better way to honor them than to collect funds to help build an "accessible" playground in their memory. We raised funds to put in a special playground at a nearby park.

You can do it, too. In order to keep your loved one's memory alive, you don't have to build a playground—plant some flowers. Write down memories of them to save for future generations. Volunteer at a place that meant a lot to them. The point is: of course, we are sad, but those who live the happiest lives are the ones who have the tenacity to keep going and sometimes that means taking a new path.

If you are missing someone, take the best from them and give it out to others. See what goodness you can put out into the world yourself.

Plans Don't Always Go Our Way— But Sometimes It's Better

Sometimes a negative situation happens, but the path we land on evolves into the plan that God has for us. Take the story of Jake Gronsky of Philadelphia, Pennsylvania. His loss was the career he had worked for all his life, but his willingness to try a new career is taking him places he never could have dreamed.

Jake was a good baseball player and worked and played at his sport with the goal of being a professional baseball player. He attended Monmouth

University in West Long Branch, New Jersey, with the goal of following his dream. He was a good student and excelled in writing with his Communications degree.

"Pro baseball is not just a dream," said Jake. "It's a goal. In college, I was having success and a good amount of teams were talking to us."

On Draft Day, it looked like he would be a mid-round pick, but the day came and went and he didn't get picked.

"I never stopped working," he said. "Sure I was disappointed, but I would be out with my dad practicing."

He signed with the Joliet Slammers of the Frontier League, an independent league, in 2014.

"I thought, 'I'm going to go to Joliet and treat it like a business trip," he said. "'I'm going to work so hard and get noticed."

He hit about .380 (which for non-baseball fans is very good). Someone from the St. Louis Cardinals organization called him.

"It was an amazing moment when the Cardinals bought my contract and I started in Rookie Ball," he said.

He played in Peoria and Palm Beach in the Cardinals minor league system. His roommate in Peoria was Harrison Bader and another close friend was Paul DeJong, both of whom went on to play for the St. Louis Cardinals.

"I got to play every day with the Peoria Chiefs of the Cardinals organization and I was starting to play well," he said. "It was what I knew I could do. I hit .320 and had more extra base hits than singles.

"I'll never forget that day I was having a conversation with Harrison," said Jake. "We were talking about my batting average and my play and he said to me, 'You're going to make it.' "

The very next day he took a fast ball to the hand and that injury ended his season. Talk about disappointment. Fans see players get injured and they are sorry they can't play, but for the player, it is their career—their life. That was a turning point in Jake's life and at least for a little while, he needed to come up with a new plan.

"I'm from the State College area and the Cardinals had a team there, so they sent me to their rehab doctor."

He packed up and went home and the first day he reported to the State College Spikes, the Cardinals short season class A team for his rehab. From here, his life changed and it was in such a dramatic way that he felt like it was a Hollywood movie.

"I remember that first day I was in the State College clubhouse and seeing friends," he said. "Then all of a sudden, I hear the elevator's 'Bing!' and I looked over, and in walks Dave Bohner and Josiah."

Josiah was a ten-year-old boy with special needs that the team had sort of adopted, and Dave Bohner was his grandpa who brought him to the clubhouse every day. Jake and Dave struck up a conversation and arranged to meet later for coffee, which turned out to be the start of a friendship that would lead to a career change for Jake.

Jake was released the following spring and his dream of baseball was gone, but in the meantime, God had been working on him and changed his heart. All that energy he had used on baseball and all that hurt of not making it had to go somewhere.

"I always saw myself as a baseball player," he said. "It's not so much that you want to play, it's that you want to 'BE' a baseball player. You grow up wanting to be a player."

He thought back on the huge disappointment of achieving his dream and then losing it—or so he thought at the time.

"I loved wearing the Cardinal uniform," Jake said. "Even on the days when they would say, 'It's hot, so you don't have to wear your uniform, just wear a tee-shirt,' I would actually realize that was one less day I got to put on the uniform. I had loved wearing that Cardinal jersey and the sense of pride that came from it, but it was over. Now what?"

During the ups and downs of baseball, he would write about his experience. Writing was an outlet for him, so even though he saw himself as a baseball player, he was constantly writing. While attending college, a professor had seen his talent and had even found literary agents for him. "Sometimes I had more literary agents than baseball agents," he remembered looking back on it.

One day, the "new idea" plan for his life became clear.

As his friendship deepened with Dave, they realized the story of Josiah and his relationship with the State College Spikes, had to be told and they were the ones who should write the book. That was how the book *A Short Season* came to be.

"If all the pain that led up to me being cut also led me to write this story, then I am lucky to get this opportunity," Jake said. "The greatest gift God ever gave me was being released from the Cardinals. It put me on the path of being a writer. My writing had kept me going throughout my career."

In its first three months, A Short Season became a best seller for the publisher—something Jake Gronsky could never have imagined during his baseball rehab—but there was more to come. You never know what will happen next in life, because David Eckstein, who had played for the Cardinals and other major league baseball teams, had been considering writing a book when he read A Short Season.

Jake and David had met before, but when David saw Jake's book, he was interested in talking to him about writing his own book. Soon they began working together and now he was writing David Eckstein's book!

Often in our life we have a plan for ourselves and it goes wrong—we end up down a different road than we started on. We just have to be patient and listen for God's voice telling us what His plan is.

FROM THE FOOTBALL FIELD TO THE NEWS ANCHOR DESK

Steve Savard is a successful news anchor in St. Louis, a major market, but who started out as an NFL player with the Dallas Cowboys. When he was injured, he was devastated. His life's work, his career, even his identity were all gone.

"I was in my second training camp with the Cowboys when I suffered a serious neck injury in a scrimmage," Steve remembered. "I had no real feeling or function in my arm or hand and spent that season on Injured Reserve and underwent extensive rehabilitation for months."

His NFL career was over, but when he went home, broken up about his lifelong dream of playing ten years in the NFL being shattered, his mom had some wise advice for him, which gave him a new outlook.

"My mom figuratively put her foot in my behind and scolded me to get on with my life," he said. "She said, 'So you can't make a living with your body—go make a living with your mind.' She reminded me that I had been a good and motivated student all my life and it resonated with me."

He had a Journalism and English degree, so he applied for a job at a TV station. Steve Savard went from an NFL football player with the Dallas Cowboys to a television job in Billings, Montana. He then did stints in El Paso, Texas, and Hartford, Connecticut, before returning to his hometown of St. Louis, where he started as a sportscaster and is now one of the stations top news anchors.

"If we are lucky, life is a marathon and not a sprint," said Steve. "What seems so important when we are young is only a small part of our over-all life experiences. My mom raised me to be more than a football player. When I lost my original career choice, I'm glad my mom had the foresight to come up with a new idea. It just goes to show you we should all have more on our life resumes than just job accomplishments."

Losing the career they thought they would have could be devastating to young people like Jake Gronsky and Steve Savard, but they didn't let their injury situations ruin their spirits. They kept the faith in God that whatever path they were being led on, it was the one on which they should be. Jake said his surrender to the circumstances given to him helped him find peace in his life—at a time that others might have crumbled or taken a bad turn and gone down the wrong path.

At the time when it seems like your dreams are shattered, it's difficult to look past that.

Steve appreciates what has been given to him and he serves on charity boards and donates time helping kids.

"I see kids afflicted with diseases and illnesses that seem to rob them of the type of childhood I had and it makes me appreciate what I have," he said. "I have no reason to complain about the hand I was dealt and I feel for those who have been given adversity."

Every day there are people spreading negativity in life and on social media, but maybe down deep, they are not really as angry as they seem. Maybe they are scared or hurt, and don't know what to do. Are you scared right now and don't know what to do? Rather than spend your time being negative, try something new.

She Embraces the Journey of Life—All of It

Amy Camie is a harpist who uses her music to bring peace to her little corner the world. We often think if we are going to contribute to the world, it has to be in a big way—but every good thing we do every day can make the world a better place.

"For those scared and lonely hearts, you are not alone," says Amy as she uses her harp as a healing tool to bring inner peace to those who hear it.

When we turn everything around to reflect how bad it is on us personally, we miss a lot of good we could be contributing to the world.

"The challenging part is to have everyone become personally responsible for how they are in a relationship with themselves—it all starts from within," Amy says.

Can we really choose to have a good relationship with ourselves, blocking out all negative forces that try to ruin it?

Amy went through breast cancer and from the moment she was diagnosed, she came up with a "new idea." Rather than just get through it, she vowed to herself to really experience everything about it—through the good and the bad, she acknowledged the feelings she was experiencing. Rather than be depressed that she lost her hair and cover her head in a scarf, she actually had a photo-shoot of how beautiful she really was.

She felt that by just getting through it with the traditional treatment and medicine, she would have missed a dimension—she would have missed the meaning of her experience.

"The loss of a loved one, a job, a relationship, or a diagnosis of a serious illness triggers feelings of fight, fear, and self-protection—reactions that resonate with our primal desire to survive," she said.

She wrote a book about her journey through cancer and how she even found joy along the way. She found joy, because she was looking for it. We often think a diagnosis or a situation is the signal for our life to stop, but she chose to keep going and out of it came her book, Loving Life, All of It, and her many therapeutic songs, which she compiled on various CDs (AmyCamie.com).

Choosing happy during a cancer journey or any other seemingly bad situation is a new idea. Even if you try to be positive, it's not going to be all rosy—part of it might be terrible. However, like Amy did, we can learn to acknowledge the bad feelings as they come, but stay focused on the positive.

FORGIVENESS HELPED HER THROUGH A TRAGEDY

It may be hard for you to imagine when you look at your life right now, that something good can come out of it. Can something good really come out of this mess? Yes, it can. We just have to be open to new possibilities. We have to trust and love ourselves.

Sally Hanson lost her son, Chris, in a car accident. It was a terrible shock to hear about this handsome, smiling young man being taken from this earth so abruptly and unexpectedly at the time his future looked so bright. Of course, she was heartbroken and there was a period of shock and disbelief. But one day, very early on, I saw this on her Facebook post:

> *"The Lord is close to the brokenhearted. He rescues those whose spirits are crushed."*
> — *Psalm 34:13*

She was sending a positive message that she was leaning on God and that she was OK. She posted of visitors who came over and they no doubt shared memories and perhaps a few laughs. There were posts of pictures of her son throughout his life, but many as a small child—the way mothers think of their children no matter what age they are. Parents always remember the sweet times when their children were young.

While Sally tried to stay surrounded by family and friends, she also soothed herself with calming words from the Bible and happy memories from the past.

"Another thing that helped us was to honor his memory in tangible ways that would last," she said. "We made a paving stone and put it at a place where he had worked, and also a cross at the accident scene, and a quilt made from his t-shirts.

She kept busy by accepting friends' invitations and working on crafty things that honored Chris, but there was one thing she felt helped the most.

"One of the biggest things that helped us was we immediately forgave the driver of the car," said Sally.

It was her family's faith that gave them the courage to do that, but they felt it was important in their recovery and to honor Chris' memory. Though we may try to do things to honor a family member who has passed away, we must also remember to save ourselves throughout the ordeal.

When faced with tough times, we have to be our own advocate. We have to love ourselves through it. Taking a warm shower and feeling the water on your body is a way to love yourself. Bend your head down to ease the tension and feel that warmth on your neck. A warm bubble bath does the same thing.

Feel the water against your skin, or go in the backyard and feel the sunlight on your back. Take a few minutes to give yourself some love.

"You can search throughout the entire universe for someone who is more deserving of your love and affection than you are yourself, and that person is not to be found anywhere. You, yourself, as much as anybody in the entire universe deserves your love and affection."
— Buddha

Learning to love ourselves through every obstacle can help us in our growth. Though Whitney Houston sang that "learning to love ourselves is the greatest love of all," she somehow could not achieve it. But you can—because you are trying.

Don't think about what can go wrong—think about what can go right—and we can try to think about the things that are going right at this very minute. There is always a bright spot.

Even in the worst of disasters, the Red Cross shows up. In our lives, there is always a proverbial "Red Cross," who is here willing to help us.

"When I was a boy and I would see scary things in the news, my mother would say to me, 'Look for the helpers. You will always find people who are helping.'"
— *Mr. Rogers (Fred Rogers)*

There are people who are helping you or new friends you are meeting during this time. You are growing in ways you won't know until later. You will look back on this time and realize why you are on this path, but for now it is up to you to try to stay strong and look for the possibilities in life.

It doesn't help you to continuously worry about the future. Whatever is going to happen will happen (and whatever isn't, won't), whether you worry about it or not. Your worries don't help determine an outcome and you could miss some great moments, if you let fear take over.

We Can Make "Today" a Great Memory for Tomorrow

The future is God's time anyway. We can't really do anything to change the future, but we do have today and we can make today be a great memory.

Can I make someone else's Thanksgiving better and, in turn, do the same for me? Can I help a young mother who needs some time off from her toddler? Is there a lonely senior citizen who would like a visitor?

So while we all face times when we feel we can't go on, maybe if we get a new idea or a new way of looking at something, it could help us keep moving.

Have you always wanted to try something, but never did it, because you didn't think you could? Think up a new way of doing it. My husband, Rob, likes to call this "going in the back door." If we can't get in the front door, we try another avenue and go through the back door. What is it that you wish would happen? What do you want to do? Get a piece of paper out and write it down and write the possible ways you could do it.

Want to be on the radio? Start a podcast. Want to become a coach? Volunteer at the YMCA. Want to learn to paint? Go to one of those wine and painting events. Want to learn to be a better cook? Take a cooking class. Don't just sit there at home and wish you'd made different choices. Try something new—now.

Sometimes if we scale our ideas down or change them a bit, we can have an outcome that is just as rewarding in different ways, but we have to put in some effort.

"Success is no accident. It is hard work, perseverance, learning, studying, sacrifice and most of all, love of what you are doing or learning to do."
— *Pele*

Every day in many ways, we can put positive energy out there. You start the minute you wake up in the morning. There is always a way to do something and your new ideas might just come in the most unexpected ways.

Keep Busy Living Your Life

When Debbie and Ross Hammond were told by the hospital that there was no more hope for their son whose liver was failing, they started researching other hospitals and found a doctor who specialized in what they needed.

They took their son, Tyler, to another state to have a multiple transplant surgery. He recently graduated from college in New York and has started his first grown-up job.

"One thing that helped us through our tough times was distraction," said Debbie Hammond. "I was recently at a charity baseball game and could not help but remember when Tyler played on that team. He was saved by people who loved on him and tried to make him feel important and valued as a team member—keeping him active and distracted. This literally kept him healthy and alive till he was called for his transplant in 2010."

When you are faced with a decision that is nothing like you would have ever expected, you might become gripped with fear. That is normal. Decisions are part of life, but they can also cause us to almost shut down with anxiety. The smallest things can become stressful.

Sometimes just making the decision can make you feel so much better—take a huge load off.

What happens when you are suddenly confronted with an option that could be life-changing, life-altering, and will affect all your family and friends? Instead of being fearful, look at it in a new way—that could be a great adventure!

A New Opportunity, Though Scary, Can Energize You

That's what happened to Dr. Debra Peppers, an educator at the time, who had won National Teacher of the Year. She was suddenly and unexpectedly confronted by a "mentor" she had known for thirty years, who boldly told her she was going to quit teaching and become a full-time professional speaker. Sounds crazy, doesn't it? Especially when she loved teaching and was popular with the students.

"I was preparing lesson plans one afternoon, in the classroom where I had taught high school for thirty years," said Debra. "Many of my colleagues were retiring, but I loved teaching and had no plans to do so. As a matter of fact, I was also teaching summers at a local university where for the past ten years I had taught in the Master's program."

Her life was going along as she thought it should and she had no thoughts of changing it, but somehow she was pushed in a new direction. This can happen to us at any time. Our lives can be pushed in a new direction in a good way (job opportunity, scholarship to a certain university) or in a bad way (diagnosis, job loss)—but no matter how it happens, there are innovative ideas to try and new ways to do things—we just always have to be open to them.

That's sort of what happened with Debra Peppers.

"As I was grading papers after school that day, in sauntered one of my former principals, Mr. Bill Coplin," she remembered. "I hadn't seen him in years and was thrilled to catch up. I knew he had taken a big risk to leave his lucrative principal position to become a professional speaker. I had loved him as our principal, but I had also attended several of his speaking conferences throughout the United States, and not only was he good, I could tell he loved it! He portrayed various characters to get the audience's attention, but then would bring his talk to the serious conclusion of 'being real' and how to help young people to find their purpose."

"Bill hugged me and exclaimed, 'Peppers, you're retiring this year!' I thought it was more in the form of a question, or a joke, so I responded with an adamant, 'No, Bill! I think I will teach until I die or until they run me off, whichever comes first!'"

Debra was surprised at what happened next.

"He laughingly replied, 'Well, I'm running you off.' Then he seriously explained to me that as an elite member of the revered National Speakers Association, he also had booking agents throughout the United States and traveled every week speaking at conventions and other such events."

Her first thought was, "But what does this have to do with me?" He stayed in her room for over an hour telling her that each member of the NSA was expected to select one younger speaker, whom they believed had great potential. They were to "pour into the new one" all they had been taught.

Speaking in front of an audience was nothing new to Dr. Debra Peppers, who had spoken to schools and civic groups gratis for ten or so years, and she was the drama teacher. She felt honored that he would come to her with this idea, but she explained to him that she could only do speaking engagements in the summers or after school hours, but he would have none of that.

Have you ever felt something tugging at you? I sure did when writing this book. One day, it became so clear to me that I was supposed to gather people's stories and put them into a book to share with others to help them get through a tough time. But I was so busy with the things that filled my days that I put it off for a short time. Then one day, I realized I was supposed to do it and I got busy. When you are being pushed in a positive direction, you will know.

"He said, 'No, Peppers, you are retiring this year to take my place! I will set you up with all of my Speaking Bureaus, my material, slides, and PowerPoints, and anything else you need to begin!' "

He even had a plan for how she would accomplish this new idea he had given her.

"My wife has been my secretary since I left the school and she will help you with bookings, flight arrangements, and the transfer of my files," he said. "But you can no longer teach, as this will definitely be a fulltime position."

Do you want to be safe and good, or do you want to take a chance and be great?
— *Jimmy Johnson, football coach*

Once he told her how lucrative her speaking career could be, she quickly did the math, and realized it would be. Then she looked at her friend and realized there was more. She asked him, "Why the urgency, why do you want me to do it now?"

"With his head lowered, he quietly told me that due to a medical diagnosis, he did not have much time to live," said Debra.

Bill Coplin wanted to leave another legacy along with all he had done—he wanted to help a fellow educator and also introduce her to the world. Bill and his wife had discussed it and Debra told him she would discuss it with her husband, Bud, that night. There was much discussion and praying involved, as this was a big decision, but in the end, she decided to do it.

"I truly believe I could have decided either way and been happy, but I didn't want to miss this once in a lifetime open door, if it was indeed God's will for my life," she said. "At the end of the following week, most of our friends and family seemed to have been on board with our decision, and I turned in my resignation at the school. Bill passed away the following year and his wife remained our secretary and assistant for five years."

His death made her realize that this change was meant to be. Fifteen years later, she and her husband have traveled in all fifty states and sixty foreign countries. She feels she has had more quality time with family and friends—and with the new change came the added fun of spending ten of those years doing radio and television.

If you ever feel something tugging at you—or if you are presented with an opportunity that you are not sure of, Debra offers this ten-stop decision-making advice:

"In analyzing the decision-making process we followed, it comes down to ten things," she said.

DEBRA'S 10-STEP DECISION-MAKING PROCESS

1. Go in with an open mind.
2. Discuss the situation with valued family and friends.
3. Search your heart for what you believe would ultimately make you the happiest.
4. Make a list of how each decision will affect your family, friends, and others around you.
5. Make two columns on a piece of paper and weigh the pros and cons of each decision. Include the timeframe, the financial repercussions, the amount of time and work it will take, and the results and rewards of each.
6. Pray over each item individually.
7. Have one or two people you truly respect review all this information and ask you pointed questions.
8. Make that final decision and close the door.
9. Don't second guess, and don't look back!
10. Go full-speed ahead, learning as you go. Make adjustments when needed, but enjoy the ride!

If presented with the opportunity, would you have had the guts to try a new idea like Debra did? It could have gone the other way. Maybe she took a leap of faith and it didn't turn out. What if she didn't get booked to do all the speaking? Things can go wrong when you take a chance—but if they do, then maybe it is leading you in the direction of an even better opportunity.

If something like that is going on with you—you took a chance and it didn't work out—then just remember there are hundreds of other chances out there just waiting for you to take them.

"It started with a leap of faith, took me to a higher place; though I wasn't ready to believe, you reached down inside of me."
— *Michael Bolton*

She did get speaking engagements and once Debra's new speaking career took off, she felt she was being tugged to move from Missouri to Florida. On one hand, it would be exciting to make a new start, but on the other hand, she would be moving so far away from her mother and brother—would she still see them? She would be leaving family and friends behind. What would it be like? Once again she took to her "Top Ten" list and she and her husband, Bud, went over each one.

"We sold our house and moved to Florida," she said. "So much would not have been possible had I said no to that open door." So you see, it's not always about seeing immediate results—sometimes it's the journey we are on.

"There's always gonna be another mountain ... it's not about how fast you get there or what's waiting on the other side. It's the climb."
— *Miley Cyrus*

"I have had many other decisions since then, but none as life-changing as this one," she said. "I am on radio in Florida, leading a women's group, volunteering at the school, and teaching in a women's jail."

Since her childhood, Debra has been thankful that someone helped her and gave her a second chance. She wrote about her life where she moved to a bad path in high school, but with help and faith she was able to turn it around, chronicled in her book, *It's Your Turn Now, From Hall of Shame to Hall of Fame.*

She always remembers someone helped her, so she has turned it around and spends her life helping others.

When you help others, you get out of your own doldrums and you feel better. Helping others even in the midst of our troubles opens up so many new possibilities to us.

"Every evening at sunset, Bud and I sit on our dock in our backyard and fish, read, and pray," she said. "Life is a banquet, so don't settle for crumbs!

And when you're ready, go back for seconds!" (pepperseed.org)

Look around you right now. There are new people you are meeting every day and some new things you are learning. You may not even realize how much you are growing at this very minute—and you were thinking you were in a bad funk.

I know someone who ended up marrying the first responding officer who came to assist her after a car accident. You just never know how a negative can turn into a positive.

Doesn't that give you something to look forward to? What is this preparing you for? What great things are ahead of you?

We all have decisions, some are small and some are large. The large ones could be anything from electing to have that surgery, deciding to leave that abusive relationship, moving a parent into your home to care for them, or moving to another state.

Have you spent too many days and nights being a slug with no feeling of accomplishment? Try being open to a new idea—even if it is just to get up and go to a matinee movie by yourself. You don't always have to have someone else help pull you out of your funk—you can do it! You just have to have the idea to do it.

A New Idea for Teachers and Parents

If you are having trouble with a certain situation, try a new way to look at it. When Laura Compton Brandt was a young teacher, she was having trouble with her middle schoolers, so she tried to figure out how she could overcome this and finally it came to her—look at them in a new way.

"When I was teaching, I often reminded myself that being 13-years-old is so much harder than dealing with a 13-year-old," she said. "It restored patience and compassion every time."

That worked so well she stayed in teaching for 30 years. After she retired, she discovered another avenue that helped her deal with people and situations.

"After I retired from teaching, I tried something new and spent a year learning massage therapy," said Laura. "I learned so much about mind/body connections, and how to be aware of holding tension and releasing it."

First you get the idea and then you get the gumption. You will be surprised at how your life will change, once you open yourself up to new

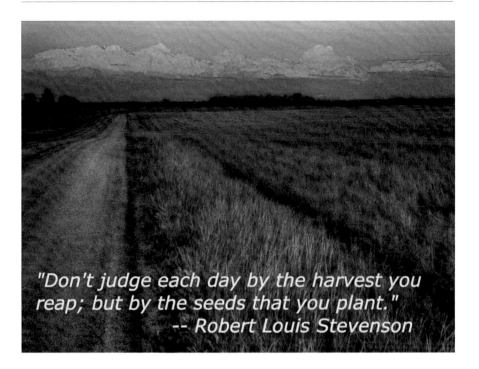

"Don't judge each day by the harvest you reap; but by the seeds that you plant."
-- Robert Louis Stevenson

possibilities. New treatments, new healthy lifestyle, new hair color, new bedspread, new book to read, or new interest like Laura had with massage. There are so many new things you can do—it makes me excited just thinking about all the possibilities out there.

There are still so many new things you can discover—despite your present circumstances. Once we are open to change and new ideas our life becomes so exciting.

If you want to be happy,
keep trying new ideas,
be tenacious—stay in the game.

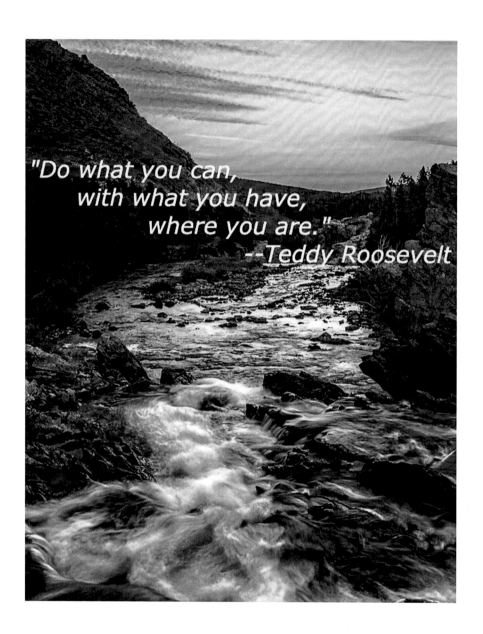

"Do what you can,
with what you have,
where you are."
--Teddy Roosevelt

CHAPTER EIGHT

Tenacity—Stay in the Game

Tenacity is that never-give-up spirit. It's the quality of being determined and being able to persist. Everybody can have a ninth inning comeback if they stay in the game.

> *"Tenacity is essential for accomplishment in anything you do. Without drive, determination and a strong-willed attitude, one's level of success at many endeavors will be limited in scope."*
>
> *— Gabriella Marigold Lindsay, author*
> Living FIT: a 40-Day Guide to Living Faithfully,
> Intentionally and Tenaciously

Tenacity is that sense of not throwing in the towel. It's having faith in yourself that you can live your life—and do it with confidence.

HOW CAN YOU HAVE FAITH WHEN EVERYTHING'S FALLING APART?

Lisa Flittner of Kansas City, Missouri, knows what it's like to have everything fall apart. She was the only child of two only children, but they were close and enjoyed family time with her grandparents.

"My family consisted of my parents and grandparents," she said. "There were seven of us until I was 30."

Then it all came crashing down. During the next decade, she lost all six of those loved-ones, with her parents dying just three years apart.

"I went from a family of seven to a family of one—me," she said.

All of this happened continually with family deaths coming every couple of years and at first, it was devastating to Lisa, but in order to survive, she had to figure out how to help herself. More than 20 years later, she has been able to do that.

"A quote from Elizabeth I helps me and explains my thought process well," she said.

> *"Grief never ends but it changes. It's a passage, not a place to stay. Grief is not a sign of weakness, nor a lack of faith. It is the price of Love."*
>
> *— Queen Elizabeth I*

Lisa said that with the frequency of her losses she learned to grieve by separating "a lost future" with "a lot of good memories."

"The way I look at life is I choose taking life's events as building blocks to create a solid foundation of positive, as opposed to accepting the weight that is the negative," she said. "That's how I am tenacious and I've been able to live my life in a positive way.

"I try to mindfully color the positive foundation as bright colors to help me visualize a bright future."

No matter what is happening to you right now, you can have a bright future if you want to. I love that she uses bright color to help her visualize it. Pastel colors can help you visualize peace, but Lisa is out there being bold and looking for those bright colors. She is going the full nine innings despite the circumstances.

One way she helps herself is by creating her own family.

"I like that saying: 'There are friends, there is family, and then there are friends that become family'" she said. "I have three close friends who supported me throughout that time and invited me to join their families. I accepted this support wholeheartedly."

This goes back to "community." When good people offer to help us and want to be there for us, we should accept it. Lisa could have withered away in her grief, not wanting to be with another family during the holidays, but she took them up on their offer. It might not be the family dinner table she was used to, but she contributed and in turn, it is a new family dinner table that she has enjoyed over the years.

"This is why I travel each year to join the holiday celebrations with a friend from college," said Lisa. "Believe it or not—this friend was my RA in the dorm my freshman year. We remained friends and kept in touch—I was in her wedding and the godmother to one of her daughters."

Lisa has no children of her own, but she has been able to share in her friend's family and they are grateful to have her.

"It hasn't always been easy—it never is," said Lisa. "But I encourage anyone who has experienced loss to keep going and realize you can still have a good life. Focus on the good memories and the love you have had—and can still have."

If you ever need faith to help keep you going, Romans is the book to turn to in the Bible. Paul wrote verses of peace, hope and faith.

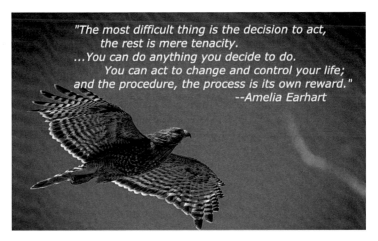

"The most difficult thing is the decision to act, the rest is mere tenacity.
...You can do anything you decide to do.
You can act to change and control your life;
and the procedure, the process is its own reward."
--Amelia Earhart

"I consider the sufferings of the present time are not worth comparing with the glory about to be revealed to us."

— Romans 8:18 (ESV)

The very first verse of Romans reads, "Grace to you and Peace from God our Father and the Lord Jesus." At the end it reads, "We may be mutually encouraged by each other's faith."

Do you have any friends with whom you are in a "mutually encouraging" situation? Try to encourage that person and allow them to do the same for you. The accountability of knowing someone is there for you can give you the tenacity to keep going. People do this when trying to lose weight, trying to exercise, and wanting to read the Bible more. Whatever it is you are trying to do, it might be easier if you were doing it with someone.

When you are sick or a family member is ill, people may ask, "Is there anything I can do for you?" Say, "Yes." Let them help. If someone asks you if they can help, they are going out on a limb, so if there is some way they can help you and you allow them to do so, then it's good for both of you.

There Is So Much Negativity These Days

If all you look for are the negatives, you can surely find them in the world today. There are those who almost seem to brag about how bad their life is—but then there are those who have a better life, because they try to be strong and positive no matter what they face. Throughout life's pain and tragedy, which we all face, those who try to live their life rather than succumb to it have a better outcome.

President John F. Kennedy's mother, Rose Kennedy, was known for her strength and tenacity as she faced tragedy after tragedy. She relied on her strong faith to get her through all the many tragedies she faced in life.

"If I collapsed, it would have a very bad effect on the family."
— *Rose Kennedy*

Patty Wilke experienced a lot of loss in her young life, including the death of her parents. One of those losses was the closing of her church—a place to which she had felt connected. When she was lonely, she turned to her faith and prayer life to help get her through the tough times.

"There's a song by Bon Jovi from the 1980s called *Livin' on a Prayer*," Patty said. "Sometimes I feel like I am praying more than usual, like the only way I'm getting by is on a prayer."

No matter what we are going through, we must keep trying, and stay in the game.

HE FOUND HIS WAY OUT FROM A BULLY

Tyler Poslosky of Wyoming did just that. He is an award-winning sports writer for a newspaper—and he was bullied when he was young. He said he endured some of the darkest days of his life, feeling like no one would help him, except his family who stood by him.

"I was in a dark place back then, with no way out," Tyler remembers. "It was hell and I really felt like there was no way out."

Things can seem so bleak, a person could think there is literally no way out, but if you keep looking, there is always a way. Tyler said he would go to the school administrators, but he got no help. He finally had to rely on his inner strength and reach down to a part of his soul that believed in himself.

This can be difficult, because when others are tearing away at our self-esteem, it can weaken our souls, but we must love ourselves enough that the bullies of the world can't hurt us.

The motivational speaker, Wayne Dyer, had a great idea for stopping bullies or people that make you mad or ruin your day. He would say to himself, "OK, who is it going to be today? Who is that person who is going to try to ruin my day?" And then he would use it as a game and when someone behaved badly towards him, he was ready for it. He was prepared for it and actually welcomed it. He stayed calm, because he was ready for it.

You can do the same things with people or situations that annoy you or set you off. No matter what you are going through, you can control how you react and you don't have to lose your temper, or give up. Believe in yourself that you can get through it.

"I just knew deep down that I would make it through," said Tyler. "I kept going and didn't give up, and eventually I became stronger because of it."

Tyler wants to encourage anyone who is being bullied or being made to feel bad about themselves.

"Be strong and stand up for yourself," he said. "I leaned on my mom and sister."

It's important to find that person who will stand by you in your time of need. These are the people whose support gives you the tenacity to keep going.

"There is always light at the end of the tunnel," he says, "Even if you can't see it right away."

One of his biggest pieces of advice is "Stay true to yourself," and he encourages others to stand up to bullies.

"If you ever see someone being bullied, stick up for them—no matter who they are. I know I would. I would stop what I was doing and stand up for them."

Sometimes in life, we have to convince ourselves that we are right—and the situation can get better. Be strong and give no credit to those who put you down. Don't let anyone tell you that you can't do something or you aren't good enough.

When you know that you are doing everything right, then believe in yourself.

He's Glad He Didn't Listen to Negative People

Richard LaMotte, SMSgt USAF is a decorated Air Force Pilot. He has had a very successful career as an airman.

On the anniversary of his thirty years in service, he posted this on Facebook: "Thank you all who helped my journey and especially those who "tried" to either stand in my way, cut me down, or doubt me—you just pushed me to a better place. Your judgment will not be mine, but another's."

That made me think about all the negative voices we hear—either from others or the voices we hear in our own head. Unfortunately, there are some whose family or friends don't believe in them, and some even see the worst in them. Richard did not get the support in his decision that he would have liked from some people in his life.

Instead of giving up on his dream, he pursued it. He had wanted to be in the Air Force and nothing was going to stop him.

"Some people didn't think I would last two to six minutes in basic training," he told me.

He didn't let their negativity stop him from pursuing his goals. As a result he had so many adventures and traveled all over the world, even living for six years in Guam.

He has served Presidents, First Ladies, and other dignitaries. He has also met movie stars and other famous people, but as he says, the best thing that happened to him was when he was stationed in England, he met Michelle, who would become his wife.

"The Air Force has literally given me EVERYTHING—my life, my wife, our child. It's taught me how to be a man, and an Airman," he said.

When Richard says the Air Force gave him everything, he also refers to intangibles. While in Guam, he was host of a radio show and developed a "Hollywood" persona, combining his love for the movies with his job.

Being on the radio helped develop his confidence, as well as his voice. Today he is a vibrant person, who adds so much happiness to the lives of others with his outgoing personality and beautiful singing voice. He goes out of his way to use his talents to help others—just as we all should. He talks to people, connects with them, and sings to them. He uses his gifts and those gifts bless others, and in turn, he has a fun, happy life.

But what if he had listened to the negative voices telling him he would not make it in the Air Force?

Have you been faced with the situation of someone putting you down? How many times a day do you put yourself down? That steals your confidence and makes you want to give up. If you feel others are putting you down, don't listen. It doesn't matter what they think—don't let them steal your joy.

You can use your own gifts to help others. Don't be afraid to let your light shine.

"Each of you should use whatever gift you have received to serve others, as faithful stewards of God's grace in its various forms."
— *I Peter 4:10 (NIV)*

Perhaps you think you don't have any gifts or talents. You have many—you just have to find them. Sometimes just being silly is a gift. When you let go and just have fun, it lightens the load of those around you and they feel free to join in.

Haven't we all gone through enough in our life that we realize down deep in our hearts that there's no time to feel embarrassed by being silly, getting excited about things, or whatever you think others try to put you down for. Get out there in life and try things, have experiences—go on adventures.

THE SISTERHOOD OF THE TRAVELING BANDANAS

I have a group of college roommates who are still friends 40 years later. We share a funny memory of going out to dinner one Sunday night in college and we decided to dress up in formals. One of the girls remarked how bad her hair looked so we all decided to wear bandanas, which were actually in fashion back then.

Five girls wearing formals with bandanas on their heads. What makes the story even sillier is that the back doors of the driver's car would not open so some of the girls had to climb through the window or hike over the front seat—in a long dress! I don't think there has ever been more laughing in one place as that night—and believe it or not, alcohol was not involved. It was just that freeing feeling you get when having fun with your friends.

Years later, we all live in different towns, but when we get together we will often bring a pile of bandanas and we put them on. Soon we are young and silly and laughing all over again. We call ourselves the "Sisterhood of the Traveling Bandanas" or the Bandana Sisters and while we love to laugh, these girls are part of my community and when needed, we are there for each other—no matter what.

NO ONE CAN RUIN YOUR LIFE EXCEPT YOU

What happens when everything in your life is going great and something happens that turns your world upside down? That's what happened to Karen Garrett, a lawyer in Kansas City. She and her husband at the time were raising two daughters, when one day she found out some things that were going on with her husband and suddenly that "happy life" as she knew it was gone.

"From the time I realized what was happening and during the time the marriage was falling apart, I was so destroyed," she said. "All I could think of was that my life is over, our happy family life is over—I'll never be happy again."

That is the most normal reaction in the world. The actions of someone else cause your life to change and you blame that person. So many things go through your mind, but it always comes back to blame.

For a while it was eating her up. She was despondent, because the life she thought she had—the life she had wanted—was no longer in existence.

"Anger is part of it," she said. "I was mad at a person. Anger can make you feel so hopeless and is part of the struggle."

Lucky for Karen, she found just the right person to talk to about it.

"I started to spill it all to a therapist," said Karen. "I told her all I had been saying that had become my mantra— 'My life is over, I'll never be happy again,' and luckily I didn't have a therapist who would let me go on talking. She stopped me right there and said, 'If this is true, your life is over, your family is ruined, and you're never going to be happy ... who does that ultimately hurt?' And with that question, I knew just what she meant."

When we carry that anger in our hearts and blame others who does that ultimately hurt? Us.

"So I made a choice," said Karen. "It's a choice you make to keep going, to be tenacious in your life. I had conversations with myself for months. I had to ask myself what is worth more, being angry and injured or figuring out how to move forward."

While the therapist helped Karen see clearly, it was ultimately the conversations with herself that helped her to change. I can't stress it enough ... we can help ourselves. You have it inside your heart to make the choices you want. Choose the good ones.

Once we decide to choose happy over sad or mad, it is a process. It just doesn't happen.

"Anger can come at any time," Karen said, "But when that happens, I ask myself who gets hurt, if I'm not happy? It's me. And of course, we hurt others in the process, but when I am angry, it is ultimately me who suffers."

This way of thinking can relate to anything you are going through. If you are so mad at cancer that it's making your life bitter, who is suffering? Is it the cancer? No, cancer doesn't care—it's you. If you are mad at your boss for passing you up for a promotion, do you think your boss is suffering?

It does us no good to keep anger in our hearts and let it rule our life and Karen realized it's her choice how her life and her family's life would go. Though at first she thought she could never be happy again, she made the choice to have a happy life with her family, and she is thriving.

Eventually she and her children's father learned to work together and raise their daughters who turned out to be strong, successful women. Both parents have remarried and have learned to co-exist—even taking a trip together to see one of their daughters.

Karen chose happiness over pity, but while it's easy to say, it's not as easy to do.

"It just doesn't happen," she said. "It always comes back to the choices we make. Life doesn't suddenly get easy—in fact with every year there are new challenges. Death of a parent can be one, but you have to think about your anger—by harboring it, you are the one who is getting hurt."

Years after that divorce, Karen is doing great and so is her family. She is enjoying her grandchildren and tries to include as much fun in her life as she can. She is choosing to stay in the game.

"To those going through something, I want to emphasize that happiness doesn't happen fast and it doesn't stick all the time," said Karen. "You have to keep working at it."

When a Problem Seems "Public"

How can you stay in the game when something so big happens to you and you don't think anyone will support you? What if you suffer an embarrassment, either publicly or within a group? This happens when coaches are fired, workers are demoted, or even when a friend or family member gets in legal trouble. Going through a divorce or losing a job can also be extra tough, because people know about it, and you wonder if they are talking about you.

It can be devastating for a family to suffer the consequence in the public's eye when something gets out on the news or the internet. Anger and hurt can get in the way of being able to cope with the situation.

When it seems like there is no one to talk to, God is always there.

"Trust in Him at all times, you people; pour out your hearts to Him for God is our refuge."

— Psalms 62:8 (NIV)

It is best if you can find someone you trust to talk to. Family and friends will be there for you. It can also be comforting to know someone is praying for you, so don't be afraid to ask. Most of the time, people feel honored to pray for their loved-ones. We should never go through anything alone; we should reach out to those who care about us.

When my husband Rob's employer, the Globe-Democrat newspaper folded, I remember having a lot of anger in my heart. Rob had his dream job, the only thing he had aspired to in his life— to be the Cardinals beat reporter for a major daily newspaper—and the rug was pulled out from under him. It was on the news and everyone knew about it.

The anger was causing me to be bitter, so I had to forgive all the bad things that had happened, if I was going to live a happy life. It takes a while, but forgiveness is so worth it, and a weight is lifted off your shoulders when you forgive someone. As it turned out, we've had many great adventures we would not have had because of that, but we had to make the choice to be tenacious rather than wilt.

SHE'S BEEN IN THE GAME FOR 31 YEARS

In an interview on BRAVO Network, the actress turned reality star, Lisa Rinna, talks about how many different things she has done in her life.

"I never pass up an opportunity to do something," she said on The Real Housewives of Beverly Hills. "All my life, when I see an opportunity, I jump at it. I very rarely turn something down."

She stars on that show now, but has done many different things, including infomercials and being a spokesperson for a product, soap operas, Dancing with the Stars, and more.

"I've been tenacious," she said on the reality show. "I just stay in the game."

Not many people in the spotlight can stay relevant for 31 years, but she knows if she lets a chance pass by, it may not come back again. She has so many gifts; many she didn't realize she had, but her agent or others see it and she takes advantage of the situation.

Your gift may not be acting or a professional singing voice, but your gift may lie in the fact that you can go out of your comfort zone to bless some-one else—which, in turn, blesses your own life. This is how you carry on. This is how you are tenacious with your life.

If we are to let our lights shine, then we need to figure out what all our "lights" are. To me, my "lights" are how I can help others, the talents I may or may not think I have, and the words I use. When I compare myself to others, I might not think I have any talents, but God gave us all talents of some sort—so we need to find them. You can be a shining light on a hill to someone, but you may have to go out of your comfort zone to do it.

Being tenacious means staying in there for the battle, but if things don't turn out the way you wanted them to—that doesn't mean you lost your battle.

No matter what trials we face, we can find joy in living life to the fullest, tenaciously overcoming battles and pressing on to the end. We find even greater joy in helping others have a great life, but in order to stay in the game, it takes energy.

"Everything we do is infused with the energy in which we do it. If we're frantic, it will be frantic. If we are peaceful, life will be peaceful."

-- Marianne Williamson

CHAPTER NINE:

Energy—Find Your Get-Up and Go

Have you ever woke up in the morning and realized all that is happening in your life and felt like just pulling the covers over your head and going back to sleep? It is the opposite of waking up in a hotel on vacation and thinking, "Oh wow, I'm on vacation, it's going to be a great day."

> *"We have a choice every morning when we wake up. We can open our eyes and say 'Good God, it's morning!' Or what I choose to say— 'Good morning God!'"*
>
> — *Anne Chapman (and others)*

That attitude along with exercise, meditation, and a giving spirit helped Anne Chapman of Denver, Colorado, survive breast cancer three times. Even into her eighties she was still going to exercise, dance and even yoga classes. She knew that staying active gave her the energy she needed to face the day.

Anne was never able to have children and it broke her heart, but instead of focusing on the negative, she made it a point to live the life she was given in a joyful way.

She knew a secret to happiness is always to be curious. Curiosity and wonder give enthusiasm, which in turn gives us energy. We become excited for the future and to see what will come next. Anne was always full of wonder.

Every time there was a full moon, she celebrated her life by going out into the backyard and dancing under the bright moonlight. Everybody wanted to be around Anne and most people wanted to BE Anne. She was that cool—and she was eighty years old!

If you wake up in a positive way like Anne did, your day will have a better chance of being great, but if you start the day in a negative way, it only puts you on a negative path. Just like on vacation, you wake up with a positive and energetic countenance, the opposite happens when you start the day off "on the wrong side of the bed." If the first thought you have is negative, it can zap you of your energy.

141

The best thing to do is to try to train your brain to wake up with a positive attitude—no matter what is going on. When you wake up, stay in your bed a few minutes and say your prayers, thanking God for all of the blessings you have. And at the end, say: "Today is going to be a really great day." If someone asks you, "How are you?" say, "I'm doing great!" It will set your tone. These are reminders of how we can determine what our life is going to be and how our day will go.

We can determine if we will have energy by choosing to do the things that keep us moving in a positive way.

If all you do is blame others for your negative circumstances or lament about all that's gone wrong, you will never be happy. Surely you know someone who does that—or maybe it's you. There's always something wrong—either mentally or physically. No one wants to hear us complain, so why do we do it?

Most of us have something we could be sad or mad about—many of us have lots of things to be sad or mad about—but the happy people are those who look for good, instead of asking, "What else can go wrong?"

"Energy and persistence conquers everything,"

— *Benjamin Franklin*

One definition of energy is the strength and vitality needed for long-time physical or mental activity. Our life is a long-time physical and mental activity, so we will have a much better road if we have energy.

WE GET HURT PHYSICALLY AND EMOTIONALLY WHEN WE'RE WEAK

Tara McMahan has seen this change in her own life. She said that in the past when someone hurt her, it would really affect the way her life went.

"I was someone who was literally crushed and often brought to tears repeatedly, because my mind would go back to the hurt," she said. "Now I remind myself to say a prayer for the person and thank God for taking the punch with me. I remind myself there are more good people in the world than rotten ones. And I keep trying my best to mimic the former—not the latter."

Sometimes when you are hurt by a person, it could be a misunderstanding or a miscommunication. There are times when we are busy, tired, run-down, or otherwise in a weaker state than we usually are, and if someone says something, it could hit you in a way it was not meant and you might take it wrong.

I was having a conversation with a friend who said some information I was not expecting in the conversation. My mind was quickly trying to process it and though I actually liked the idea, what he saw on my face was the look as I processed it.

"That look on your face proves you hate the idea," he said. That was the furthest thing from the truth, but he took my reaction wrong.

When we start feeling like the people are against us, it never ends well. Everyone is facing their own problems and they really aren't worried about finding fault with us, as we sometimes think.

> *"You wouldn't worry so much about what people think of you, if you knew how seldom they do,"*
>
> — *Mark Twain*

Every day we are faced with whatever our life hands us. Each person you come in contact with is dealing with whatever they have going on, so don't be so hard on them—and don't be so hard on yourself—it just beats us down and robs us of our energy.

Sometimes when we feel the most lethargic and just feel like going to bed—those are the times we need to grab our life by the horns and do whatever we can to get healthy and have more energy.

I know if I have not done any exercises lately, I feel more tired and the circle starts—I'm too tired to exercise, but when I don't exercise I get tired. Those are the days I need to force myself to do something.

I'm not a real athletic person and I don't belong to a gym, but I can get up and walk around the block. I can jump on my rebounder. I can turn on some music in the living room and start dancing. Don't fall into the trap of thinking that if you aren't athletic, you can't do anything. You can do something. You can do a lot of things.

One thing that can help a person stay active is one of those apps that counts your steps. They say you should aim for 10,000 steps and that's a great goal. If you have a step counter and you look at it and it says 200, it will remind you it's time to get up and start moving.

Our son, B.J., was always an athlete, but when he was younger he was not a runner. However, he started running and it gives him a sense of accomplishment, because he sets goals and is proud of himself when he meets them.

Recently, after a cold winter of being inside, he had not been running as much and he wanted to get motivated to drop a few pounds and get back to running, so he set a goal.

"On March 28, I could barely do a mile," he told me, "But I told myself I wanted to be able to do a 5K (3.1 miles) by a certain deadline in May when I was taking a trip. I lost 25 pounds and by the day before the trip, I did 3.25 miles."

He made his plan and stuck with it. We all know what it takes for our bodies to have more energy and we should make it a priority to live a healthy life.

When we do get into the shape or reach the energy level we want, we should show ourselves the respect of trying to maintain that. We work so hard to achieve that energy and the pride in doing it that we should choose to live a healthy lifestyle for the rest of our life.

NINE SIMPLE THINGS TO HELP US HAVE MORE ENERGY
(From Harvard Medical School)

1. Control stress
2. Lighten your load
3. Exercise
4. Avoid smoking
5. Restrict your sleep
6. Eat for energy
7. Use caffeine to your advantage
8. Limit alcohol
9. Drink water

HOW DOES STRESS CAUSE LACK OF ENERGY?

You could go for days working on a worrisome situation or caring for a sick person and have the energy to do it—but then all of a sudden, you have no energy at all. You want to lie on the couch and you feel like you literally can't get up.

Sometimes we don't even realize we are stressed out until our body shuts down. Ever had that happen, where you are going along handling everything thrown at you—plus some—and then all of a sudden, you either get sick or just lose all your energy and find yourself unable to do anything?

When your body shuts down, the message is clear: you need to rest. If you've been worried about something or someone, it really builds up inside you and can rob you of your energy.

This can happen to us at work when we need our energy to be at our best. These days often when an employee quits or is downsized, the company doesn't replace them, leaving those left behind with more responsibility. At first, they might be gung ho trying to do it all, but then one day, it just gets to be too much.

Another way we can experience stress at work is if we have a big proposal or sales call to do. We work so hard to prepare for it, then the night before we are to give the presentation, our body shuts down. We wonder how we will get through the next day—but most of the time, these worries were in vain, as we wake up with the energy needed to do what we need to do.

Stress can really zap us, so we must find ways to alleviate our stress. One big way to do this is to realize we can't solve every problem in the world.

IS STRESS CAUSING PROBLEMS IN OTHER AREAS OF YOUR LIFE?

Here is an example. You are worried about your child, so it is causing you stress. When you are in line to buy a coffee you are impatient, so you snap at the clerk. Then you get in the car and get irritated with the traffic. By the time you get home, you've taken on so many outside negative forces that you are crabby with your family. It was nobody's fault. You were just stressed.

"Stress can affect all aspects of your life, including your emotions, behaviors, thinking ability, and physical health."

WebMD.com

If there is any way you can help yourself, do it. Whatever it is that helps de-stress you—take the time to do it. You have people depending on you and you need to be strong.

Susan Powter, the '90s fitness and nutrition advocate had a recipe for feeling good: Eat, Breathe, Move. There really can be no better way to have energy if you think about it. Eat the right things, take time to relax and breathe deeply, and keep moving, which includes exercising.

You weren't chosen for a bad life. You were chosen to live your life abundantly—have an "even better than Hollywood ending life"—a point made by our minister at church one Sunday.

Every day we have a chance for a happy ending. When things go bad, pick yourself up, put one foot in front of the other and say "OK, so that didn't go well, but the rest of today is going to be a really great!" And it can be.

It is a lot easier to have energy to press forward when things are going well. When we feel weak and want more energy, we might decide to start exercising or go to the store and get vitamins. Don't stress yourself out, because you haven't any energy. More stress causes less energy.

LESS STRESS MEANS MORE ENERGY

Exercising and drinking water are things you can do on a regular basis no matter what your situation. Carry a bottle of water with you, so you can stay hydrated. Even if you are in a situation where you think you can't exercise, you usually can. There are halls in hospitals you can walk up and down, if you are waiting for a loved one. You can stand up and walk around the room. Move your legs, move your arms.

But what happens when you physically can't get up? How do you keep going?

DESPITE HER ACCIDENT SHE NEVER GAVE UP

Kelsey Ibach was a young woman—living an exciting life in Chicago, Illinois, until one bad event changed it all.

She was in a horrible car accident caused by a drunk driver. The crash left her with countless broken bones, but most significantly, she had a spinal cord injury at the T10 vertebrae, causing paralysis from the waist down.

"Since that day, my life has never been the same," she said. "The most obvious change is that I now use a wheelchair full-time to get around, but of course, these new challenges were beyond physical."

Kelsey said that from her experience in meeting others that have gone through similar tragedies, she sees a common thread.

"We all agree that (when something bad happens to you) you find that you have a choice. You can either choose to give up and throw in the towel or you can choose to dust yourself off, deal with the cards you were dealt, and make the best of it."

She chose happy.

"Either choice—to give up or to press forward takes the same amount of energy. It's exhausting to wallow, so I knew early on I would choose to fight."

— **Kelsey Ibach**

What a profound statement, "It's exhausting to wallow." We've all heard it: it takes more muscles to frown than it does to smile. Both smiles and frowns are contagious, so whichever you choose, that is probably what you will see mirroring back at you in others' faces.

"I am fortunate enough to have a lot in my life worth fighting for—an amazing family, supportive friends, and an exciting life living in the city," Kelsey said. "But I think that these things are just supporting roles in your journey with yourself."

From the moment her family and friends got the call about the accident, they have been nothing but supportive, but she knows that while support from others is important, one must help themselves.

"The people in your life can encourage you to be optimistic in tragic times, but ultimately you make that choice," she said. "I knew that I had no chance in having the life I lived before my accident, if I didn't believe in myself first."

Did you notice she didn't end it with "I had no chance in having the life I lived before …," she went to say, "if I didn't believe in myself first." Right there she was claiming her victory. She was saying "I WILL get my life back."

When she was in the hospital, Kelsey kept thinking, "I just want to meet someone that has been through this—someone that's the same as me … young and in their twenties."

Meeting others in your situation or reading about them can help you realize you are not alone.

"Throughout countless months and years of rehab, I met so many people in my shoes—or should I say wheels … that had extraordinary 'new' lives," she said. "I met women who went on to have children, a friend that went on to finish his medical degree and become a doctor, rock climbers, triathletes, Paralympians."

These people used what energy they had for good. It took a while of going through some rough seas for Kelsey to emerge in smooth waters—literally. She found a passion in scuba diving. She learned to dive and then began helping others by mentoring children through a rehabilitation program that involves swimming and scuba.

"Feeling sorry for yourself, and your present condition, is not only a waste of energy but the worst habit you could possibly have."
— *Dale Carnegie*

"Since the day of the accident, Kelsey has moved forward in her life and been a shining example of courage and fight," said her father Bob Ibach, former PR Director for the Cubs, "My wife and I beam with pride on her courage—I have been around athletes for over 50 years of my life, but she is the most courageous person I know."

Kelsey did not intend on being an example to others—she was just fighting to be "normal."

"When it first happened, I'd talk to people (in her same situation) and I'm always most impressed by the 'extraordinary' moments where I get to see amazing people live 'normal' lives," she said. "They like to go shopping, watch Netflix and still get annoyed with the little things in life—life didn't stop for them!"

It is often hard to believe that someone has the energy to keep going despite their situation, but Kelsey found out that sometimes just being normal in an abnormal situation can lead to super hero status.

"For those going through similar experiences, I find it's important to inspire them by just being me and living the most 'normal' life I can. I always said I just wanted to get back to the same Kelsey I was before my accident and by focusing on that, I think I came out an even better version."

What a great thought: these trials we are facing could help us emerge as an even better version of ourselves than we were before it happened to us.

SHE HAD THE ENERGY TO KEEP GOING AND DO IT HER WAY

"When I am asked how did I get through that tough time in my life, the biggest thing that comes to mind is I didn't go through it alone—I turned it all over to God," said Karen Hoffman, a business woman in St. Charles, Missouri. "He lightened the load and kept me going and kept me grounded."

In the spring of 1980, she began having stomach pains.

"I told a friend that I thought my abdominal pain was something serious," she said. "I told her I thought I had cancer or I was pregnant. My body knew something was not right."

A doctor confirmed that even though she was using the CU7 IUD, she was indeed pregnant. He told her that becoming pregnant while using this method of birth control—which was very rare—made it a dangerous and life-threatening pregnancy.

They needed to try to remove the IUD.

"The doctor tried that day and was not successful," she remembers. "He warned me that even trying could have caused a miscarriage. I came back the next day and another doctor tried to remove the IUD, and afterwards both doctors encouraged an abortion."

When faced with a major decision, the stress can grip you to the point of taking away your energy—the energy you need to fight. It was a grueling time of going over scenarios and could have drained her of her energy but she was determined and had the energy to fight.

"Once the doctor had told me I was pregnant, I knew I wanted our baby," she said.

She had made a decision and it empowered her to have the strength to fight whatever she was facing.

The chance of a septic infection and the possibility the baby could suffer a deformity made it a grueling time, because the decision could affect more than one person.

Karen Hoffman networks people together with companies she started, including City of Experts and Gateway to Dreams (gatewaytodreams.org).

She knows the importance of how people can be connected, but now she was faced with a situation where her decision could have a ripple effect, because many people were connected to the outcome.

"I sought a third opinion," said Karen, at the time a vibrant, healthy young woman with a family.

"This doctor only dealt with high-risk pregnancies and encouraged me to continue my pregnancy. Yes!" she said. "It was an incredibly hard pregnancy. I was instructed to take my temperature every day to watch that I did not have an infection.

"It was scary and painful. But, from the beginning, I put my life and our baby's life in God's capable hands. My religious grandmother even asked her sister to try to convince me to have an abortion, because she was afraid for me. I knew I would regret that decision. People have to do what is best for them at the time and for me at that time—I felt I would regret that decision."

One day it looked like the worst fear was coming true.

"That Easter, I woke up in a pool of blood," she said.

She was checked out by the doctor and told to go on complete bed rest—something that an active person like Karen might have had trouble doing, but she was determined to do all she could for her health and the health of her unborn child. She went into premature labor a few times, which of course sent everyone reeling, but this story has a happy ending.

"Thirty-eight years ago, Ricky Joseph Hoffman—who we call Joe—our miracle baby was born. He has been a huge blessing in our lives."

After all she went through in the pregnancy, she says he was "an easy child, an easy teen, and has become an amazing and loving father."

Beyond just her son, she says part of the blessing was his wife and their grandchildren who came along. They all are part of the pieces, along with her daughters who she loves very much, to make up their family—a family that might have looked different had different decisions been made so many years ago.

"Knowing that our son might not have been part of our family seems unbelievable," she said. "That our precious grandkids would not be part of our family is hard to think about."

During the time she was first in pain to when she found out the diagnosis to eventually delivering a healthy child, she had many decisions to make. We are all faced with decisions every day. No one can tell us if our decision is the "best one." We have to know it in our heart.

When Karen Hoffman was faced with that life-threatening situation, she knew she could not make the decision by herself so she asked the Lord to help her and she felt He guided her all the way.

"I give thanks to God for taking care of Joe and taking care of me," she said. "Today and every day I know how blessed I am. How blessed our family is and every year on his birthday, I think, Joe Hoffman, you completed our family."

If you are facing a decision or a turning point in your life, figure out how you can make the best decision and then make it and have faith in your choice. It might help you to pray about it; thus giving part of the burden to God and lightening your load.

There comes a time when you have to trust someone or something to help you and this trusting will give you a chance to have peace of mind while going through the storms of life.

There might be someone reading this, who ended a pregnancy due to following the advice of a doctor. The turn of events in that person's life may be just what was supposed to happen and no one should ever regret something that happened a long time ago. It happened and it is over and our lives can take new turns.

The Christmas Tree Story

When my grandparents got to a certain age, Grandpa decided he could not go out and get a Christmas tree, so they got an artificial tree, because he didn't have the energy to go to the Christmas tree lot and lug the tree back.

Because they were getting older each year, on Thanksgiving our family would help them put up the tree after dinner. We didn't want them to stop having Christmas as they wanted to, due to not being able to do it.

If you are a Christmas person, there is a wonderful feeling you get once a year when you unpack those special family ornaments that mean the world to you. It would happen for our grandparents—with their kids and grandkids at their sides and with each year, we were making memories.

After they passed away, I kept the tree, hoping I could create the same types of fond memories with my husband and children. Evidently I did, but I might not have realized it at the time. There came a time when one of our sons moved away and the other son was grown up and everyone was busy, so I was putting that tree up by myself—with a little obligatory help from Rob. Somehow it didn't have the same meaning any more. Plus it was a big, cumbersome thing to store.

One year I didn't put it up—I figured no one would notice or care. But our son, Mike, did. The following year, he told me, "I will stay over after we have our family Thanksgiving and we can decorate that tree." I was so excited, I started looking for the tree. I looked in the basement, the garage—every place you would store a big Christmas tree. When I could not find it, I got a little depressed and was just too tired to keep looking for it.

I felt awful about it, really down in the dumps, but finally after a while I just said, "It's gone, there's nothing I can do—let's get a new one." I felt a great relief once I made the decision. I suddenly became enthusiastic to find another big tree.

It goes to show you that no matter what your situation is—you will be faced with decisions and just plain old facts that happen that you have no control over.

Once you make your decision though, you can feel that energy coming back.

There is someone who is reading this book who is faced with a decision. No matter how big or small—how important or unimportant it seems to others, it is your life. The one thing about decisions is once you make it, the worry about what to do is over. A weight will be lifted.

The proverbial tree is gone, move on.

I still have the ornaments and they will look great on another tree—and if my family helps me put it up it can be another tradition, but if they don't then I can still have a happy life putting up my tree, which will make me happy and others who see it. Just coming to that realization and deciding to move forward helped, but ironically a few days later, my sister Barb mentioned "Grandma and Grandpa's Tree" and I said, "What do you mean? Do you have it?" and turns out I had given it to her the year before, but I forgot that I did. (All that worrying for nothing!)

Every day we make decisions—what to wear that day, what to eat for lunch, but with major life challenges it helps to have faith in your decisions. It helps to make a plan. It's amazing how energized you feel when you start making a plan.

My mom was faced with many challenging situations in her life, just as most people are, but a bad diagnosis didn't destroy her. She would say, "Once there is a diagnosis, you can move on with a plan. The problem was there yesterday, but now we know about it and can start fixing it. Now we have a plan."

You have to have a plan to get that gust of energy. You won't find energy wallowing in your problem or hem-hawing on your decision. Whether it is a big decision or a small one, make it and start living. If you chose to have the baby, a mastectomy, accidentally threw out the Christmas tree, or cut your hair—live the best life you can with your decision. Don't let anyone judge you.

Did you know that no one can judge us (besides a real judge in a court of law, I guess)—unless we let them. If I don't like your pink tennis shoes that doesn't mean they are bad. If you don't like my gold boots, that doesn't mean you have the right to comment negatively on them. We have to learn to accept our choices, our flaws, and our differences—and live with them. If they turn out to not be so successful, then make another choice and move on with it—but don't regret a decision you made. It was the best decision you could have made at that time and you did the best you could.

When you stop and realize that in the midst of whatever you are going through, God has blessed you richly in so many other ways, you will feel energized. Being thankful for our blessings gives us a good countenance and, in turn, the energy we need to press forward—even in times that are far from normal.

"The times when you have seen only one set of footprints ...it is then that I carried you." - -From "Footprints" by Mary Stephenson

"If you are always trying to be normal, you will never know how amazing you can be."
--Maya Angelou

CHAPTER TEN:

Normal—Achieving Normalcy When Nothing Is Normal

Sometimes life just gets chaotic. Circumstances cause things to change and sometimes it can seem like the life you are living is becoming unrecognizable. That's OK, you can make it. It's all in the way you look at your life.

There can be "normalcy" in the most un-normal of times.

HER MOTHER CHOSE HAPPY, SO SHE DID, TOO

Joanie Protzel's mother, Annette died when she was just 62. She had had a long history of health problems from rheumatic fever as a child, to heart issues as an adult. Joanie's life could have been depressing had her mother focused on her health, but she chose to make the most of the time she had with her daughter and grandchildren.

"She was one of the first ones in St. Louis to have a heart mitral valve replacement," said Joanie. "It was when I was in high school, so I felt extremely lucky to have her as long as we did."

Annette knew she was sick, but did not want it to affect her family, so she tried to keep everything as normal as it could be. Of course, it was the "new normal," because with her heart problems, the doctor would not let her drive, so Joanie did all the driving. But she wanted everything to be as normal as she could.

"When she was sick, she never made it about her," said Joanie. "She wanted to be well and didn't let her sickness stop her from doing what she wanted."

Think of all the fun Joanie would have missed, if everything revolved around an ailing mother, and worrying about the future—but it didn't. During those times, as tough as it was, Joanie continued to have family time.

"Mom didn't drive, so I would pick her up most days and she would hang out with us and the kids," she said.

Something told Joanie to begin preparing for her mom's death, so she did something that helped a lot.

"Mom had been on a ventilator for three months and I think I started grieving before she died," she said. "I made a picture of her happy and smiling and kept remembering what fun times we shared always."

"She was my best friend, so of course I was devastated," said Joanie. "I chose to remember her when she was alive and not the fact that she died."

Joanie chose happy, but her father did not.

"I had a dad who could only remember that she died—not that she lived."

"She died when my kids where in grade school," said Joanie. "They were sad, but I tried to keep things normal for the kids, as I knew they were grieving as well."

Her attempt at keeping things normal—as in going about their lives—helped her in the grieving process as well. She kept Annette's memory alive with her children and when her first two grandchildren were born, the parents named them after their grandma—using her Hebrew name.

"My kids were as close to her as I am with my grandchildren, Eli and Ayla," she said.

Today, Joanie cares for her grandchildren and keeps her mother's memory alive by trying to be the type of mother and grandmother to her children and grandchildren as her mother was to her.

We never really get over someone's death, but you can have a better outlook on life, if you focus on their life rather than their death.

"I still miss her every day, 28 years later," she said, "but I focus on the good memories and I still feel blessed I had her for a mother. That's how I choose to look at it."

Joanie was lucky she had a mother who could make the most of the situation. We all know someone who can't ever seem to "roll with the punches." They get upset at the smallest thing and their mood can really put a downer on any situation.

LIFE IS AN ADVENTURE EVERY DAY

Recently I was getting ready to take a "Road Trip" with Rob—one of our many driving trips, which always include a ballpark or a baseball destination. When you get in the car to start a road trip, you never know how it will go. We've experienced the windows being blown out by tornadoes, car trouble, hitting a deer, health problems, as well as the joy of seeing loved ones and meeting people, and wonderful scenery and fun stops along the way. You just never know how it will go, so before I left, I said a prayer and in it I asked God to give me an "adventurous spirit" for the trip.

It got me thinking, why don't we ask God every day to give us an adventurous spirit? When I am with my grandsons and we aren't sure what the day holds I say, "Let's go on an adventure!" One of the best adventures happened in a hotel workout room. Everyone went to the baseball game and I had volunteered to stay back and watch (play with) the kids. After the others left, I realized they had taken the car with the car seats and strollers—and with no car seats and strollers, we weren't going anywhere with two toddlers.

I didn't want to disappoint the boys, so I said, "Let's go on an adventure" and we went down the hall to the hotel's workout room and made silly faces in the mirror, we rolled the big red ball back and forth and played games. Suddenly the workout room was transformed into an adventure room.

SHE LOVES HAVING A POSITIVE IMPACT ON HER SONS

"I love the idea of having adventures in life and doing so with an open mind," said Karen Rains, my daughter-in-law and the mother of those two awesome grandsons. "I feel this is an important way to live life in general. I love watching my sons get to experience life with an open mind and optimism for the adventure ahead."

Sometimes as we go through life, things don't go as we planned, but we can learn to be flexible and enjoy the adventures of life. Adventures don't always turn out to be positive, but they can be fun, as long as we try to take a positive outlook on the situation.

"I am very excited about the positive impact I can have on my boys' lives," Karen says. "Everyone goes through ups and downs, but I want to teach them to look to others and vocalize what they are experiencing. I also want them to be able to look to themselves and God for strength.

"I try to live as an example for these boys as a strong Christian person serving God and others. We can all have a positive impact on each other's lives. It is my goal to provide a great life for my sons and be present both physically and emotionally."

It sounds easy to say just be positive and you will have a happy life, but we are human and every day, we face challenges. Even the strongest person we know may be going through something— plus just everyday life at large. There are dirty dishes in the sink to be washed, the trash to be emptied, diapers to be changed, and road construction, illness, and unexpected detours of life.

"Sometimes just making it through the day with the whole family being healthy and happy is a goal," Karen said. "I have learned to use my social network—those around me—to help me during stressful times of my own."

It is always good to have a positive attitude and a "social network" of those who will help you when times get tough—because they often do.

Look around you. Everyone is going through something—we just don't know what.

When we are faced with an unwelcome situation that just won't go away, it can often wear on a person. You just want your "normal" life back. It's so hard to adjust when you are hoping it will change or improve, but it doesn't.

Why, oh why can't I get a different job? Why won't this health problem go away right now? Why did this have to happen? Are you going to just be a "why-ner" or are you going to make the choice to be an "action" person? Don't get stymied in place wondering "why" you're in this situation. Keep moving forward and try to find joy in the current situation—in this current "normal" you are in.

LOVE THEM WHERE THEY ARE

"I remember the last conversation I had with my dad, when he still knew who he was—and before he forgot who I was, due to a stroke. It was about a book I was writing," said Kathy Witt, a travel writer from Kentucky, and author of several books including *The Secret of the Belles*, which she was working on at the time. "He told me he didn't like the book's cover and had some ideas to improve the layout."

Later she would look back on that brief phone call and realize her father had been short with her, almost "surly," which was completely out of character for him.

A month later, her dad had a massive stroke and the man she knew as her father was gone—but it took her family several months until this became clear.

According to the Stroke Association (strokeassociation.org), after a stroke, people often experience emotional and behavioral changes. This is because stroke affects the brain, and our brain controls our behavior and emotions. Injury from a stroke may make a person forgetful, careless, irritable or confused. Stroke survivors may also feel anxiety, anger, or depression.

If these things happen after a stroke, could his behavior towards his daughter be due to the onset of having a stroke? The brain is a strange thing, but shortly before the stroke and then after the stroke, Kathy's dad was not acting "normal."

"We had always called him the original Renaissance Man," Kathy said.

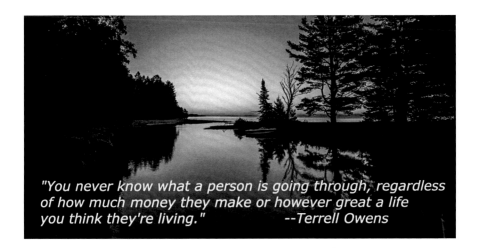

"You never know what a person is going through, regardless of how much money they make or however great a life you think they're living." --Terrell Owens

"My dad was interested in everything. He once took a computer apart to teach himself how it worked. He was an artist who painted, created a comic strip, made movies starring his five kids and once built a darkroom to develop the thousands of photographs he was always taking. He loved to read and he could spin wonderful stories—especially when we were all gathered together on summer camping trips.

"He experimented with making wine and sarsaparilla, loved a good nature hike and taught himself to make furniture—including beds so big and heavy, we had to leave them behind when we moved. He loved nothing more than going to an auction and coming home with some treasure— usually something no one else wanted, like cases and cases of sardines. He dabbled in the stock market and amassed a small fortune, which would really help later on with his care."

After the stroke, her dad spent weeks in the hospital, most of it unconscious. During that time, she along with her mom, sisters and brother read a lot of information.

"We learned that stroke survivors may be completely different than the person you knew," she said. "Some of the literature suggested looking at this as a chance to get to know a new version of this person. We learned that much remains a mystery about strokes and that having advocates on their behalf is crucial for stroke victims."

> *"We do not have a fear of the unknown. What we fear is giving up the known."*
>
> *— Anthony "Tony" de Mello, Indian Jesuit*

We like things that are familiar to us—that are normal. Kathy and her family were thrust into a situation which was not familiar. Nothing felt normal.

"Those early months—and years—were scary, heartbreaking, frustrating, humbling, full of anger, so incredibly emotional," she said. "I think everyone in my family would agree, we never cried so hard nor laughed so much."

Though his family was willing to help, they soon realized the care he needed was beyond their capability, so they moved him into a nursing facility.

His stroke had damaged his brain and left him paralyzed on his left side. He didn't remember his grandchildren or, eventually, his children. Suddenly nothing was normal, but as they went along, they realized there was a new normal that would come out of the situation.

"Though he didn't remember us, he shared stories and memories and secrets we had never heard him talk about," Kathy said. "He spoke of things like his time in Korea during the Korean War, a special place he had visited as a young boy, and a beloved dog he grew up with. He would say things that, pre-stroke, would never have crossed his lips."

At first the family was shocked by his comments, but eventually life began to settle down as they began to accept the situation they were in—their "'new normal."

"It gave way to a lot of laughs as we all got to know this new version of my dad," she said. "The love was always there, on both sides."

Whether it is due to stroke, Alzheimer's, head trauma, or whatever, it can be heartbreaking when a family member does not remember you—or their personality changes due to health situation or medicine. But this is where living in the "new normal" comes in. Expectations change and life can be sweeter when we accept people and love them where they are—not where we wish they could be.

"One day during a visit, my dad told me I looked familiar and asked me if I was an actor," she said. "I'd had a really bad day, and seeing him and hearing that comment just lifted my spirits."

Maybe in the past she would have felt bad that he didn't know who she was, but that day she saw the glimmer of hope that he knew she was familiar and that was OK with her.

"I said no, I wasn't an actor, I was a writer. He asked if I'd written anything lately. As someone who never wanted to disappoint her father, I was very happy to tell him, yes, I'd written a travel book and it was due out, ironically enough, on October 1—the same date he'd had the stroke nine years earlier."

October first—a terrible day, but nine years later October first—a great day! Life goes on and we go through things, but we get stronger. We just have to realize when we are down, that we will be back up some day.

"I brought him a cup of coffee and he was so pleased and grateful," she said. "I thought about what a long, hard nine years it has been, how acceptance had finally won in a long hard-fought battle on my family's part to bring him back. That was never going to happen. He had lost too much. So had we. But so many little miracles have happened along the way. And being with him, seeing his eyes light up—it was enough, because he was here."

What a great thing it was, to have him live his life in peace and the family learning to love him where he was. It was a blessing for Kathy and her family to experience that and share in "his world—his new normal" while he was there.

It is not unusual for a family to grow stronger as they go through a tough time, although it can also go in the opposite direction. Putting family first in tough times is important.

A MOVIE CHARACTER HELD HIS HAND OUT TO HER

"A few years after our sweet Abby was born, my husband Steve and I decided to have another child," said author and speaker Maria Rodgers O'Rourke. "The timing seemed right: Abby was in preschool; we both were content in our jobs; we lived in a happy neighborhood with good schools; we were part of a strong faith community and circle of friends; and our marriage was healthy. What better situation for a new person to come and live?"

As it turned out it wasn't as easy as they had planned. While their first child had come, within a few months this time was very different and they began praying.

"After a year or so, I consulted my surprised doctor, who explained this as a case of secondary infertility," she said. "He suggested tasks, such a daily temperature charting. Friends and family offered home remedies."

Then, as often happens, well-meaning friends offered advice.

"The most popular advice was: 'Just relax and it will happen,' " Maria remembered. "This advice was offered one too many times, and it was all I could do to keep from snapping, 'Why don't you relax?!' "

For months, they repeated the same cycle of anticipation and hope that always ended in disappointment. She stopped buying home pregnancy tests, because they represented negativity as they were expensive, and kept giving them bad news. Her doctor referred them to a fertility specialist, and as they entered this uncharted territory, the future they had imagined seemed to be slipping away.

"One night, Abby sat crying in bed, listing all the friends who had younger siblings," said Maria. "My heart ached to give her an answer, but we were confused, too. When hearing news reports of neglectful parents, we wondered why they were entrusted with a new life and we were denied. I dried her tears and insisted that Daddy and I were doing all we could to bring her little brother or sister into the world."

They endured months of hormone therapy and diagnostic tests. The turning point came as Maria was driving home from a procedure.

"The image of Aladdin, the animated character in one of Abby's favorite movies, came to mind," said Maria. "He held his hand out to me, the same way he invited Princess Jasmine onto his magic carpet. Knowing my love of movies, it was as if God spoke through Aladdin's voice and asked: 'Do you trust me?' My heart opened in response—'Yes, I trust you. I can let this go.'"

They found out that procedure had failed, so they decided to stop all extra therapies.

"With my head clear and my strength back, we started to function as a family again," she said. "One day we strolled along at the park, with Abby perched on her dad's shoulders, and I thought: 'I am happy with this. It will be okay.' "

Early the next year, she facilitated a women's retreat. Speaking on Patience, she spoke of their inability to conceive—from the sad monthly cycle to Aladdin's words. Sixty women promised to pray for her, and she felt blessed by a coincidence that only grace could have arranged.

"One of the women on the retreat was the mother of Laurie—a high school classmate of mine, who died during our freshman year," said Maria. "Hearing my story, her mom assured me that Laurie would help, saying, 'Laurie often told me she'd love to run a nursery in heaven when she got there!'"

Just three months later, their second daughter was conceived, after over four years of secondary infertility.

"'Way to go!' my doctor proclaimed. Excited and hopeful, we emerged from that painful, confusing time madly in love with the baby in my womb.

Oh, the joy of bringing her home to live with us! This tiny infant's deep blue eyes gazed at me as if to say, 'Everything is okay, Mom.'"

Out of a bad time sometimes comes a lesson and there were parts of that time that she felt helped her grow in other ways.

"Despite the anxiety and pain of that time, my husband and I believe all parents should experience some of what we went through," she said. "The waiting, the disappointments, the hormonal ups and downs and medical procedures all forced us to reassess the control we have over our lives. When we started our family, we thought it was ours to plan and execute. But, while the time seemed right for a second child, there was another path we had to take. The waiting put our priorities in line. We learned to savor our lives, not accomplish them. Sometimes, an open hand is the best way to hold on."

Throughout the ordeal, it was stressful and difficult, but they just kept moving forward and putting their trust in God. There are others who try to have a child and for some reason, it is not in their future. They suffer the same excitement and disappointments, but eventually they are left to adjust to the conclusion that they will not have children.

While we all want that happy ending, there are many areas in our life where we don't get what we prayed for. Does that mean God isn't there for us? No, He is there helping us through whatever we face. He will never leave us alone.

"Fear not, for I am with you; be not dismayed, for I am your God; I will strengthen you, I will help you."
— Isaiah 41: 10 (ESV)

When I see people on Facebook asking for prayers—say for a parent who is in the hospital—and they say, "She made it through the surgery, God is good," I get a funny feeling inside myself. I wonder if they are just praising God for all things or if the surgery had gone a different way, would they still think God is "good?"

Also there is the question that if things don't go the way we prayed they would, does that mean God loves us any less? Or if we had prayed harder, would things have gone differently? The answer to both is no. It's easy to get mad at God, if your prayers aren't answered in the way you prayed. Believe me I've prayed so many times for something and it didn't go my way, but in the end, it went God's way and God is always good. But it is not easy when it is happening.

Sometimes it gets so frustrating to keep praying for something and it never happens. People keep telling you, "Pray about it, imagine it, say it out loud, make a vision board and put it on it." You do all those things and nothing happens. Why? I don't know. You wish a million dollars could fall from the sky or the doctor would say it's all been a mistake, or you wake up and you are all together.

But instead, things happen that we can't control. We may go to college and get a job in the only field we wanted—only for that company to fold and leave us high and dry. Does God abandon us when we lose a job? Is He abandoning us when we get a bad diagnosis or struggle with finances? No. He said He will never leave us. God is good. God is good all the time.

JAMES STEWART FELT GEORGE BAILEY'S PAIN

They say money is the root of all evil but we need it to live on earth— that's why it's so hard to keep your spirits up when you are facing financial troubles.

Another *It's A Wonderful Life* mention: when George Bailey tells Clarence the Angel he needs money and Clarence says they don't have money in Heaven, George blurts out, "Well it comes in handy down here, Bub."

Years later Jimmy Stewart talked to *Guideposts Magazine* about the experience of playing George Bailey and how it affected him.

He told *Guideposts* that in the "Show me the way" scene of desperation, at the lowest point in George Bailey's life, "Frank Capra was shooting a long shot of me slumped in despair."

While reading the lines on the script, the words suddenly began to touch his heart.

"In agony I raised my eyes and, following the script, pleaded, 'God … God … dear Father in heaven, I'm not a praying man, but if you're up there and you can hear me, show me the way. I'm at the end of my rope. Show me the way, God … '"

"As I said those words, I felt the loneliness, the hopelessness of people who had nowhere to turn, and my eyes filled with tears. I broke down sobbing. This was not planned at all, but the power of that prayer, the realization that our Father in Heaven is there to help the hopeless, had reduced me to tears."

This is why all of us can be touched when watching that movie. It is a story of a situation that seems so hopeless—in this case, financial woes—but it could be anything, illness or other life change. In the end—through prayer, faith, family and friends, it worked out for George Bailey and it will work out for you.

Don't lose heart when the chips are down. If your problem is finances, examine the way you were living your life before it took an economic downturn. There are ways you can—and should—cut corners. There are things you can do. You don't have to have a certain standard to live by if it not in your means at the time. The best thing to do is try to find things that you can do that are free or cheap. Don't get depressed and stay inside—find out what is available for free and get out there and participate.

"Keep your life free from love of money, and be content with what you have, for He has said, 'I will never leave you nor forsake you.'"
                                                    — Hebrews 13:5 (ESV)

He will be there for us when we lose our job and His word encourages us to be content with what we have. So we continue the goal of trying to live our life in contentment, no matter what challenges we are facing.

If finances are a concern, there are steps that can be taken. The terror the phone brings when you are behind on your bills can leave you stressed out, on edge, and even lower your body's ability to fight sickness.

When a person finds they are out of a job, it is wise to make some changes during that time. Discount stores and "re-sell it" stores can be a lifesaver. If you have never shopped at Aldi's, try it. One thing you'll need to know is you need a quarter to get a shopping cart, but the price and quality of items in the store are a God-send during a time of financial need, and you get your quarter back when you return your cart.

I remember in our lowest financial days, getting some macaroni and cheese or some other very inexpensive meal and using the good dishes, picking flowers from the yard, and lighting candles at the dinner table. The kids often did not realize what we were going through and why should they? There are a lot of fun things you can do even when are down on your luck. Stop feeling sorry for yourself or stressed out for the future and do what you can with what you have—where you are.

You might be able to scrape up enough money to buy yourself a coffee at McDonalds and let the kids play on the indoor playground, if it's cold outside. On a nice day, take them to the park or a local pond to watch the ducks. Does your town have free events like St. Louis does? Forest Park museums are open for free on certain days. We took our kids to the Muny—the wonderful outdoor theatre—and sat in the free seats. Street parking was free, we packed some sandwiches, and what fun memories we have of those days.

Plan things that don't cost money and be sure to include family and friends. Pot luck dinners are fun and are a way to entertain when the funds are low.

There are companies who want to help you "get out of debt" and caution should be used with some of them. Consumer Credit Counseling is a not-for-profit organization that encourages cutting up the credit cards and getting on a payment plan. Hard work and diligent payments can help you get out of debt using CCC.

In an effort to work on finances, some have followed Dave Ramsey's plan for financial fitness to become better equipped at handling their finances.

They download an app and record the money they spend, and learn to make budgets. Ramsey's book, *The Total Money Makeover* has a seven-step plan to help families get out of debt.

Whether it's Ramsey's plan or another, following a financial plan can be helpful.

While we are not advocating a specific way to get back on track, we are pointing out that when you are going through a tough time, it won't last if you don't let it. With a little extra effort you can dig yourself out, and if you start early, you can even avoid debt.

One of the pitfalls of being in a financial valley is feeling desperate.

There are many companies ready to prey on that feeling, so buyer beware—or better yet, don't be a buyer, if you aren't sure of it. When a person is at a low point, it probably is not a good time to get involved in a multi-level business—unless you are extremely determined and are enthusiastic about the product. No matter how much of a success the party host or business leader is, you might not have the same results if you are not at your strongest.

The same goes for online stores. If you are up late at night with worry and you see Tom Bosley touting an online store company, turn the channel. Mr. C always gave great advice to Richie and Fonzie on *Happy Days*, but his promise of how easy it is to start an online store is not to be taken as truth. Anything that sounds easy with no work is usually not going to produce the promised results and you wind up losing all the money you put into it.

"We buy things we don't need with money we don't have to impress people we don't like."
— *Dave Ramsey*

WHEN YOU ARE IN A FINANCIAL CRISIS, NOTHING IS NORMAL

The biggest problem with being in a financial crisis is not that you may not have enough money to "start saving"—you may just be feeling desperate in trying to make it through the day. Sometimes it's best to just "let go and let God." If you can't control the situation, sometimes the best thing to do is surrender to it—live in your "new normal" —even though you are determined it will not be like this for long.

The loss of a job can create a very unwanted new normal, but with the right attitude, you can make it through.

BE AROUND FAMILY AND FRIENDS

Being around friends and family helps keep our spirits up. When we feel better about ourselves, we have more gumption to go out and find a job or do the things we should to stay on a positive path. And sometimes it's not our time to find a job. Maybe we are needed in other ways.

When you are facing adversity, it is a blessing to know your family is there to support you, but sometimes for a variety of reasons the family you wish would be there, is not. They may be unable, unwilling, or simply not there. This is when our friends step up.

We all have friends who have stepped in to help us during a difficult time and we feel so much love and gratitude for them that they seem like family. It works both ways. If a friend is in trouble, we should be willing to help them. You never know during a given situation who is going to step in to help.

"To us, family means putting your arms around each other and being there."

— *Barbara Bush*

Friends and family are the best part of life. Let those special people into your life and your heart. Include them in your adventure. Looking for the good—and expecting it—makes for a better day. The way you handle a situation can be a test of who your really are. What would you do if you had a big trip planned and when you got to the airport—due to bad weather—your flight was cancelled? Would you lose your temper? Take it out on the person behind the counter? Or do you have it in you to make the choice to go with the flow. Sometimes things are just beyond our control.

As humans, we like to feel like we can control all circumstances—especially if we are with our family we want it all to go right. Or if our family is at home counting on us getting back, we want to be there for them. But sometimes it's not up to us.

We have the decision to be a victim to our circumstances or just go with it and try to salvage any fun we can have on the trip. It may seem like everything is falling apart, but really there are just a few things—even though they may be magnified.

Once you start that "everything is going wrong" attitude— it only gets worse. But when you look on it as an adventure, you are open to the possibilities of a wrong turn—which could end up being a fun detour.

And speaking of trips, a little planning can avoid a bad hotel experience. If you find a hotel chain that works well for you, it saves the guessing to go where you know what you will get. We try to stay at a Drury Hotel because, after years of traveling, we would rather stay at a hotel that makes you dinner and provides a glass of wine at the end of the day. It makes us get off the road earlier—in time to make it for the free dinner. Even something as simple as picking the right hotel, and having reservations, can help you have a positive experience in your day.

If you are going through a tough time, your life may be far from the normal you are used to, but you can make it a "new normal" for you. Whether your life is full of chaos or you are experiencing feelings of depression, you can feel better if you can realize "normal" is over-rated.

HIS "NORMAL" VERSION DIDN'T MAKE IT, SO HE TRIED AGAIN

Speaking of normal, when Adam Sanders from San Antonio, Texas, tried out for *American Idol*, he was the most normal person you would meet— maybe even too normal. The problem was his "normal" was not what the American Idol judges wanted, so after trying out several times, he decided to try something new. Many of us can relate to that feeling of trying so hard to make something happen but it just doesn't. Maybe it wasn't our time yet. Maybe there was something we were learning for the next time.

So Adam let his "adventurous spirit" take over and he returned to the American Idol stage as a drag queen: Ada Vox. He told reporters that when he performed as himself, fans of the show were very mean to him and criticized his weight, and his singing—some even encouraging him to kill himself. Can you imagine what it was like being on the national stage, facing all of that? Would you have gone back or would you have given up? This book is about not giving up—there is always a way to do something. So Adam thought hard about it—how would he ever be noticed as an American Idol?

God had His perfect timing and when it came time to try out, Adam realized he had an alter-ego named Ada—and she had the nerve to try out again. Where Adam was quiet, Ada was bold and his Ada character made the viewers fall in love with her. Though Adam's "alter-ego" is a drag queen, he was not ashamed to take off his Ada wig and show up at the practices as Adam. How did he achieve normalcy when that is not normal? Because it was his new normal.

Things aren't always as they seem—and they don't have to be. He found a way to become a success. He didn't give up, he kept going, and tried different ways to do things.

Often when we are in the midst of a chaotic episode of life, we long for normalcy, but that is the one thing we can't get. But there is comfort knowing you can have a great life with your "new normal."

How can a guy on American Idol help you when you are facing some pretty difficult times right now? Because you can see him and say, "If he can step out of the box—that situation that was handed to him—then so can I." But how can you step out of a seemingly never-ending situation like illness, death of a loved-one, loss of job, or just feeling like you don't have a friend in the world? How can you live your life during times like this?

"A key disconnect that many people are feeling stems from their hearing, 'Go about your normal life,' when they may not really feel normal. What people need to hear is that is perfectly normal to not feel normal. These, after all, are not normal times."

— Karen Zager, PhD,
New York City psychologist, WebMD.com

What are you doing to live a happy life? Are you able to look between all the chaos and find a new normal that will work for you? If you are faced with a bad situation, would you be able to overcome it?

You can make it through any situation if you believe you can and if you want to. No matter what you are facing if you are trying your hardest then that's all you can ask of yourself.

SHE'S LEARNED TO "LET GO, AND LET GOD"

"Life isn't always perfect," said Denise Heidel, a magazine editor. "It isn't meant to be. Learning to listen to God, talking to Him, reading His Word, and really getting to know Him—along with thanking Him every day for His countless blessings, has led me to the most Grace-Full days of my life."

Denise does an inspirational blog, MyGraceFullLife.com.

"Our homes on earth are temporary," she said. "I've learned to 'Let go and let God.' His grace is sufficient, even on difficult days and I cling to that truth."

"I can do all things through Him who strengthens me."
— *Philippians 4:13*

"That is a favorite verse for many; and speaks to me" Denise said. "It can apply to anything from marriage or parenting struggles, to difficult jobs, to weight loss or health concerns."

Denise, who lives with her husband in North Carolina, calls it a "victory" verse.

"It says, nothing is impossible," she said. "And it's not about physical strength. It's strength of endurance when we're too tired to go on, strength of patience when we are running out of it, the strength of kindness in the face of rudeness, the strength of compassion to those who are different.

"It's strength of courage when we are scared. It's strength of encouragement when we feel discouraged. The Lord gives us everything we need when we let Him work through us."

One family learned this over the years as their faith strengthened during some trying times.

SHE'S HAD A LOT OF NEW NORMALS

Dixie and Mark Dawson were a young couple in love and looking forward to a great life together, but they never could have anticipated the twists and turns their lives would be taking. Her brother was killed in a car accident when she was 18 and then they were married. Not much later, Dixie's mother was diagnosed with cervical cancer, requiring much care and she passed away three years later. Soon after, Dixie felt the guilt of leaving her father and sister, as well as the support of their church, family, and support system, as they moved to Texas.

"We were blessed with many happy years, while our boys were growing up," Dixie said. "We were very involved with our church."

In 2003, she developed throat problems and started a journey that would lead to eleven surgeries, after the first one on her trachea left her with no voice. The journey involved many doctor visits.

"I couldn't talk for years, just a whisper," she said, "Our church family stepped in and were so involved when I started having my throat/ breathing issues. My friends in all the different areas of my life connected and they made sure I was covered, if I needed anything—whether I knew I needed it or not."

It was a devastating life change and a new normal, which seemed to change with the seasons, as far as her health was concerned. They moved to Missouri to start a bed and breakfast.

"I nearly died of pneumonia early on," she remembers. "They told Mark I had 30 to 45 minutes to live, but I made it and after that, I could not walk for a few months and had to go to rehab."

Imagine that, at one time she could not talk, and then when she got her voice back, her "normal" changed again as she could not walk.

When everything that used to be normal is no longer normal, it can be devastating. It sometimes feels like your life will be like this forever—but it will change.

For a healthy vibrant person to experience a life change—like first when Dixie could not talk, later when she could not walk, and then even when she developed melanoma—it can be difficult to see a light at the end of the tunnel. She had to figure out a way to live her life. We can't get a "do over," but we can get a fresh start.

"You can start over again!" says motivational speaker Les Brown. "Don't even think about quitting now! It is easy to replay in your mind how things did not work, how much you lost, what you are going through, how angry you are. There is no amount of conversation or magic that is going to wipe the slate clean. You are wasting valuable time and energy that could be used to regain a new normal and start another version of your life."

In their "new normal," Mark learned to cook, clean, iron, and make beds, because that was the part of the business Dixie had been doing while her husband ran the business part—and their faith got stronger. It was a difficult time, coupled with the fact that they had recently become empty nesters. But along with the tough times, there was the joy of grandchildren. A sort of normalcy came back and despite a very soft voice, she started feeling better, even working 14-hour days.

Dixie went from being completely dependent on others to another "new normal," where she was caring for her grandchildren and later, her dad and her mother-in-law, until they died. It was lucky she had a bed and breakfast, because they needed it, as some of the grandchildren grew up there, and later her sister moved in due to a bad situation she had been in.

Through the ups and downs of life, Dixie's faith in God has sustained her.

"God has been with me and carried me through," said Dixie, who recently started undergoing treatment again for a condition she dealt with two years ago, and was experiencing fatigue, and there went another new normal. "My faith has kept me going and given me strength I didn't know I had—even though I always thought I was a tough country girl."

She had to figure out how to live her life again—several different times. But she can do it—and so can you.

"I am not the person I used to be," she said. "Before the health issues, I was a perfectionist and was always working. I had to accept that I was not able to do things my way each time I had another."

When we are in the middle of a crisis, we are not the person we used to be. How could we be? We are slowed down by stress, sometimes sadness, and physical challenges.

As we age, the same type of thing happens, and sometimes we have to accept that we are not able to do some of the things we used to. But this does not mean we give up on life. This is where we realize our "normal" might not be what it used to be, but we can make a "new normal" life out of what we have. We don't have to live depressed lives, because we "aren't the person we used to be."

Accepting a situation you don't want to be in is often difficult to do.

"I seem to have a new normal each year," Dixie said. "As that happens, you find there are people who won't walk beside you—but your real friends will and do. And I know I'm not the only one that has problems—many of my friends lately are living a new normal. I try to check on them and see how they are doing."

Throughout it, Mark was the person who was always there for her.

"God gave me strength to be the rock for my mom and dad, but right after that He sent Mark my way all those years ago," she said. "From losing my mother and throughout, Mark has been there for me. He became strong in his faith.

"I try every day not to dwell on my negatives. Pray, eat healthy, and no stress is what I am working on. I always thought that after I got through it all, I would share my story to help others who were going through tough times. I have hope. I tell myself 'I WILL be back.' My goal is low stress and building my immune system."

"Not getting enough rest can have negative effects on your immune system, energy levels and mental alertness. Unhealthy stress can lead

to a host of health issues, from an increased risk of heart disease to an impaired immune system."

— *Dr. Andrew Weil*

Some inexpensive ways that Dr. Weil, who is a big proponent of holistic health and alternative medicine suggests to help keep your stress level down to protect your immune system include:

1. Keep a journal, which helps to release pent-up feelings that can be a burden, both mentally and physically

2. Take a "news fast," avoiding the news on TV, the internet, newspapers, and magazines

3. Practice relaxation techniques

Did you know that you can actually embrace stress and if you look at your situation in a new way, you can reduce your stress? Author Brittany Risher advocates this.

"No matter the cause of the stress—home, work, or anything else— you can find the good in it."

Brittany Risher, author
How to Beat Stress, The Scientific Guide To Feeling Happier

Examples she uses are planning a family gathering: you can look at all the trouble it will cause you to prepare for it or focus on the fun of seeing everyone enjoying themselves.

Just because things aren't normal doesn't mean they can't be great. It's all in how we see our circumstances and tell our story.

How do you tell your story? Take the time to write a few paragraphs about your life and then look back at it. What do you notice? Are there as many "ups" as there are "downs?"

We talked to many people who had been through unbelievable life experiences, but the ones who are able to enjoy their life despite their circumstances are those who realize that despite their troubles there are many wonderful moments in life. They try not to dwell on the bad. They take the time to see that there is more happy than sad. You can live with a "new normal," if you just trust yourself.

Maybe Whoopi Goldberg said it best: "Normal is just a cycle on a washing machine."

"The best way to find out if you can trust somebody is to trust them."

—*Ernest Hemingway*

CHAPTER ELEVEN:

Trust Yourself—And Others

Sometimes we feel like we are "all alone in the world." If you are in a bad way, call someone to talk about it, but there may be times you physically can't. Perhaps you want to talk to a parent who has passed away, or maybe give some great news to someone, but they have dementia or Alzheimer's disease. What if you have been waiting for a call from the doctor? Maybe you need to talk something over with your best friend and they are not answering their phone—or your child is off to college and you can't have a face-to-face conversation.

We can still endure situations by ourselves—we just have to trust ourselves and believe we are as worthy of our own attention as anyone we may choose. Of course, it's good to have a community, but sometimes in the wee, small hours of the morning when everyone else is asleep we may be up worrying.

What should you do when you are consumed with worry? Stop it. Do something to change the direction your thoughts are going. Worrying only makes our life more unpleasant. It stops us in our tracks.

"Worry is a computer that keeps buffering."

— *Bishop T. D. Jakes*

Pick up a book like this one and begin looking for encouragement. This is why there are so many beautiful photos and quotes of encouragements—to make it easy to find comfort when you really need it.

When I have a concern that is weighing heavy on my mind, I light a candle and say a prayer. I always start with thanking the Lord for all the wonderful things I have and then I ask for help on the situation. I add that "I put my complete trust in You and know You will help me." Often just sharing your burdens with God or a friend can lighten the load.

It does you no good to let your mind wander and get all worked up when you are worried. We all do it—but if you find yourself getting consumed with worry, make the choice to try and reach down into your own strength and help yourself. You can do it. You can get to a better place by having faith in yourself, faith in friends, and in God. Don't let any negativity get into your thinking.

A Car Ride Helps Clear Her Mind

Sometimes it helps to just unplug from life and try to figure things out. Samii Taylor, of Florida by way of California, who is a an award-winning screenwriter and an audio engineer has lived a very exciting life, having worked with A-List recording artists like the Bee Gees, Barbra Streisand, Joe Cocker, Prince, Kenny Loggins, Tiffany Coburn, and others.

Even though her career involves audio and video, sometimes she just wants to get away from the noise and just hear the quiet.

"When I go through a tough time, I get in the car and drive," said Samii. "No radio, no, phone, no people—just me, myself, and my problem. Only then can I begin to see and hear clearly and have any hope of resolution to my dilemma."

We live in a world where there is constant noise going on. There are the opinions on social media, commercials, and endless types of shows on television, people babbling about all their problems. It makes you want to quote the old commercial, "Calgon, take me away!"

"When the voices of my world get so loud that I can no longer hear the voice of God, I lose focus," said Samii. "Once I am a few miles away from the source of my angst, my spirit can breathe again. I can sort reality from fantasy, truth from fiction, emotional hurt from constructive criticism.

"It was tough when gas prices hit four dollars a gallon and I could only afford to drive around the block!"

What is it that clears your mind or helps you find peace? Figure it out and take the time from your day to seek it out. Many parks have hiking trails you can go on so you can walk mindlessly without getting lost and either contemplate your situation or clear your mind of it.

"When I can hear the one voice that matters, calm returns ... focus returns ... strength returns," Samii said. "I become my better self again. I can see the answer to whatever is amiss."

Driving around is good for Samii, but you may have a different way of clearing your mind. Some people go for a run, while others take a bath, a walk, do Yoga, or read their Bible. What's important is that you take the time out and find the quiet that you need so you can hear the messages that can help you know what to do ... or maybe you're not supposed to do anything Maybe you are just supposed to "be" right now. Trust your instincts, but find some quiet. Trust yourself.

When you light a candle, think of that flame as the flame that is in your heart and connect the flame to the person for whom you lit it. The flame is your faith that burns brightly—even in the darkness. You can do this thing you are faced with. You are braver than you think you are and stronger than you ever thought you could be.

HER FAMILY IS HER COUNTRY

Therese Syberg has raised her four children as a divorced single mom for most of their formative years. When she became a single mom, she said she knew it could go one of two ways—and she chose to be strong.

"I heard a quote from Winston Churchill that basically says, 'a country is only as strong as its leader,' " she said. "That's when I decided my family is my country and I am their leader. I believe our children see how the parent handles and responds to situations, and they are influenced."

She has always tried to keep positivity in her house. The décor is happy and cheerful. She knows that keeping a calm and peaceful countenance will rub off on those around her, so she does what she needs to do to heal herself, and in turn, she strengthens her family.

I enjoy talking to Therese, because she has a positive way of looking at things and when I asked her, "Have you learned anything new lately?" referring to her career path, because she is always going to seminars and trying to learn more, she surprised me. "You mean in life or with work?" she asked, so I opened it up to either.

She had an interesting perspective just waiting to come out—and if I had not posed that question, I would not have heard her answer.

"I've learned a lesson and that is when you have a problem, think about who you will talk to about it, then talk to that person and leave it there," Therese said.

So often when we get upset about a situation we tell someone, and then the next person we see asks us "how are you doing?" and we tell that person. Many people even go to the extreme of posting it on Facebook, so the whole world can comment on it.

"The more you put it out there, the more you are sending negative vibrations out into the world," she said. "You don't want to keep it bottled up inside you, so take your time and think of who is that one person who will honor what you tell them and maybe even talk you through it, and offer some advice that would be helpful."

It could be a different person for each situation. Maybe something unbearable, unspeakable, is happening to you right now and you need to talk to someone, but you don't want those around you to all be talking about it. Possibly you have a friend in another state you could talk to—who is totally neutral on the situation and can talk to you objectively—or someone who knows the people involved.

This leads us to when someone chooses you to be that one person in whom they confide. Try to think things through before you offer advice or criticism. That person is putting their trust in you for a reason. They want your support. It does not help them if you go judging them right away.

PRACTICE THE ART OF LISTENING AND THINKING

Let the situation simmer in your mind a bit and just listen, then maybe later you can offer ways to help—or maybe not. Maybe they just wanted to talk to you and have you support them.

If you confide in someone and they start giving you answers you don't want to hear—then dismiss what they are saying.

You are in charge of yourself. Don't let the negative vibes you feel control you.

ELVIS LOVED HER TENDER

If you have ever felt you were being bombarded by "outside forces," maybe the story of Ginger Alden can help. Yes—that Ginger Alden of Elvis Presley fame. I met Ginger while presenting her with an author award at the Missouri Cherry Blossom Festival in Marshfield, Missouri. We have kept in touch and I appreciate her sharing her story in hopes of helping someone.

Ginger was engaged to Elvis Presley at the time of his death. She had grown up in Memphis, but never could have dreamed she would one day end up spending time at Graceland, going on tour with Elvis, and eventually wearing an engagement ring given to her by the "King of Rock and Roll."

When he died, his death was on such a larger scale than any death you or I could imagine—the sadness was the same, but it was on an international platform. Handlers stepped in and everything was out of her hands.

"Being engaged to marry Elvis Presley and losing him when I was 20 years old, shortly after his passing, I felt like God had forgotten me," she said.

She had always had a faith in God but suddenly everything in her world changed. She wrote about her time with Elvis in her book, *Elvis and Ginger; Elvis Presley's Fiancé and Last Love Finally Tells Her Story.*

In the book she talks about the excitement of her romance with Elvis and she also fills us in on what it was like to find his body and the devastating end of it all with tens of thousands of mourners and reporters who descended on Graceland in 1977, exposing her to the reality of living in the spotlight of Elvis's short, but immortal life.

On page 361 she says, " … My mother and I said our goodbyes to [Elvis' father] Vernon and walked out to the car, and drove away from Graceland. The hopes, dreams, and plans Elvis had been sharing with me until five nights ago had vanished. It was being made clear to me by many around him that I was on my own."

The best parts of their life together serve as wonderful memories—for her, but the way it ended and some of the aftermath would be hard for anyone to take—especially since it was played out in the public.

"My depression deepened as the days slowly passed," she said in the book. "I cried often and wouldn't leave the house. My mother slept with me some nights as our family continued trying to process the tragedy."

During this time she didn't know who to trust. Complete strangers were contacting her, and the people she thought were her friends at Graceland were not supporting her. It was devastating the way the media jumped in and made assumptions.

To Ginger, Elvis' death was her personal life, but to the media, it was a worldwide story. In years to come, she would have to endure sensational stories and seeing people Elvis had been associated with giving less than factual accounts of his life as she knew it—all in the name of a "scoop."

At the time she was so devastated by Elvis' death, she was just hoping to make it through the day. She knew who she could trust—her family and herself. To aid in getting through it all, she told herself that God must have needed Elvis in Heaven more than on earth. Finally she found that memories and a thankful spirit helped her through her grief.

"I was grateful to have been able to share a part of my life and love with Elvis, and to be loved by him," she said. "I had no idea what the future would hold for me. I could only take things one day at a time."

This realization led her to say, "Now that I'd known and loved Elvis, my mind was open to new experiences. I would be forever grateful to him for that."

She went on to marry again and live a happy life with her husband, Ronald Leyser. The couple had a son, and they had a normal life, far away from the hoopla of Graceland.

In August 16, 2015, Ron passed away.

"Many years later," said Ginger, "I experienced the loss of my husband, another far too young, and on the same anniversary as the death of Elvis."

Can you even imagine this? Every year she had privately endured each anniversary of Elvis' death and then unbelievably Ron passed away on the exact same date.

"It was a double hit," she told me. "I was angry and hurt, but I had a strong family and great friends." Those were the people she trusted and they were there for her.

Throughout our lives, if we make deposits in our family and friendship accounts, there will be a reserve when we need it. We must have someone to trust—but more than that, we must trust ourselves.

Ginger knew what was true and what wasn't and she had to reach down into herself to find the trust in HER that she needed.

"Though I experienced anger and hurt, I did not give up my faith in God," she said.

"Trust in the Lord with all your heart, and lean not on your own understanding."

— Proverbs 3:5

Ginger is a very outgoing and upbeat person with friends and a great relationship with her son. How does she do it? How do you go on when you are faced with multiple challenges?

"Whenever trials come my way, I talk to God about them," she said. "I say, 'God, please make me strong.' I've also learned that the old saying, 'When God closes one door, He opens another,' is true."

She tries to sort through the noise of life to see the good, while trusting that she is doing the right thing.

"I have learned to turn tragedy around and count my blessings," she said. "I have so many blessings in the people God has placed in my life."

Because Elvis was bigger than life and his memory continues, she has had to deal with media reports—good and bad—and she just tries her best to keep the negativity out of her life.

SHE COUNTS HER BLESSINGS, NOT HER LOSSES

Inspirational Speaker, Lorraine "Rainey" Fahey, does not let the negative vibes of life into her world either and she also counts her blessings.

Rainey has endured much pain in her life including loss of family members and illness in her own life (both breast cancer and Multiple Sclerosis).

In 1987 she was diagnosed with MS. As you can imagine, she was shocked.

"I was absolutely petrified," she said. "The news nearly knocked me over. Like taking a drink from a fire hose—the fierce fast quickness of the information was almost impossible to swallow."

But as she says, "God entered with grace—abundant grace—a 'we will make it' type of grace."

"Actually, I like to call it 'ridiculous grace,' " Rainey said. "For me, ridiculous grace is when the blessings are above and beyond—way over the top—and by far outnumber the heartaches."

As the reality of MS sunk in, she was eventually able to accept it as her new life. She accepted it as her "new normal."

It took courage and strength to face the challenges day-by-day, year-by-year, decade-by-decade. She didn't do it alone. She did it along with her family and friends, but most important was she had to trust herself and she trusted God.

When her sister passed away at age 56 of breast cancer, it was a test of Rainey's strength.

"I've had many opportunities in my life to be invited to step up to the plate with courage and strength," she said. "I've certainly had many more opportunities than I would have liked."

One of the worst things that happened in her life was the death of her daughter from breast cancer at age 37 in 2006.

"My precious daughter, Susie, left behind a devastated husband, five little girls, her grieving sisters and a broken-hearted mom and dad," Rainey said. "We all limped along, helping each other try to accept what we simply could not understand."

"Blessed is the one who trusts in the Lord, whose confidence is in him."
Jeremiah 17:7 (NIV)

Sometimes that is all we can do when faced with something that we would normally think would be too much to handle. Just limp along and trust God.

But there would be more sorrow to come for Rainey and her family, as many members were diagnosed with the BRCA1 gene. They had already walked the scenario of losing loved ones and now they were facing the possibility of more. A diagnosis of the BRCA1 gene means the person has a much higher risk of developing breast cancer or ovarian cancer, compared with someone who doesn't have the mutation.

It does not mean they will get it, but nonetheless it is something that is there, that can play on your mind. But Rainey does not spend her time with "what could happen." She has a family who needs her.

"I have an attitude I got from my dad. He was really upbeat and all four of us kids chose that attitude in life. He always said "Everything happens for the best." To me that was my dad's worldly wisdom and it was rooted in Scripture."

"And we know that in all things God works for the good of those who love him, who have been called according to his purpose."
Romans 8:28 (NIV)

Rainey trusts God in all things, even death. When someone passes away, there is a thin line of wanting to preserve a person's memory and moving ahead with your life. Sometimes guilt enters the picture—like if I am out having fun, am I disrespecting the person who is gone? In your heart, you know that person would want you to live your life.

In her life, with the bad things that have happened, Rainey Fahey says there have been blessings—there always are—but she takes the time to see them. She sees her daughter, her niece (the one who lost her mother), and herself as survivors.

"When I think of strong women, I immediately picture a woman who has been knocked down by the events of life," she said. "The main point here is a strong woman is willing to get back up and try again. When I am knocked over, I cry; ask why; then look up at the sky. There I am reminded that God is large and in charge and all is well with my soul."

"When I am knocked over, I cry, Ask why, And look up at the sky."
— Rainey Fahey

"So—what is courage anyway?" she asks. "The root of the word, cor, is Latin for heart. The second part of the word, rage, symbolizes a fierceness or a passion. So for me courage is about giving it all you've got, from the heart."

Give it all you've got and trust yourself. Trust you are doing the right thing.

"Courage is the ability to take the next step when you don't want to—or wish you didn't have to— when things are very unpleasant and frightening," she said. "You get the courage, grace, and blessings to take that first step then the next and the next …

"A quote I once heard that originated by author Mary Anne Radmachder, of the book *Lean Forward into Your Life,* helps center me during those tough times.

"Courage doesn't always roar. Sometimes courage is the little voice at the end of the day that says, 'I'll try again tomorrow.'"
— *Mary Anne Radmachder*

Rainey has had plenty of opportunities over the years to use what she calls her "blessings of strength and courage" to help her through the storms of life.

"When tough things come along, the proverbial question is often, 'Why? Why God? Why me? Why now? Why this? If there's one thing God has taught me, it's that it is all such a mystery. All of it; all of life—the joy and the sorrow all rolled up together—it's just such a mystery."

And we have to have "trust" to get through it all. Trust in ourselves, trust in God, trust in the doctors, and trust in our decisions.

"I like what New Testament scholar, Luke Johnson, says, 'The purpose of mystery is not to explain it; not to understand it; not to control it. But to simply be in its presence,' " says Rainey.

"From my life's experience, I believe that strength and courage have allowed me to do just that—live in the presence of the mystery … What a story! What a life! What a ride! Thank you, God!"

"I believe if you keep your faith, you keep your trust, you keep the right attitude, if you're grateful, you'll see God open up new doors."
— *Joel Osteen*

"There is a kernel-sized piece of peace in my heart," says Rainey. "This must be the greatest gift of grace that God has given me, because it is a teeny, tiny kernel of peace in my heart … but it's there. It's that 'ridiculous grace' that He would bless me so."

Rainey gives presentations and one of them she calls, "Living in the Abundant Present."

"Taking life on life's terms," she said. "It's a choice. The day before Susie died, she could barely talk, but she managed to say, 'Mamma, I need you to promise you will be strong. You've got to pull yourself up for these kids.' "

Her daughter's words resonated with their whole family.

"My son-in-law has done a beautiful job of raising their kids," she said. "I'm not always happy … nobody is. But when I start go down that pity party road, I think, 'Thank you, God, for letting me be here.

"You can wake up every morning and say 'Good morning, God!' or you can say, 'Good God, it's morning!' (the same thing Anne Chapman said) It's your choice. I trust God and keep going."

Trusting God can be difficult for someone who is not used to being in communication with Him. For the casual "pray-er" trusting God can have a different meaning—only using it in time of desperation. But for those who build a deep relationship with their Heavenly Father, they just know they can trust Him and they talk to Him so often, they hear His voice.

HE WAS BUCKED OFF A BRONCO, BUT NEVER LOST HOPE

To many of us the "rodeo" is something fun we can attend when it comes to town, but for Clay and Lexie Ashurst, cattle ranchers in Lusk, Wyoming, the rodeo is their life. One night Lexie's trust in God was tested as she sat in a hospital emergency room waiting on Clay's condition after a devastating fall during a rodeo ride.

"In the wee hours of that first night, I sat alone in the ICU room," she remembered. "The thermostat in the room was set at an unimaginably cold temperature in an effort to control any fever Clay might run as his body's reaction to the sheer trauma he had endured. I sat there with five hospital blankets wrapped around me, shivering and unable to sleep."

She was experiencing this by herself. There will be times we have to go through something by ourselves and because of that possibility, we must be able to trust ourselves—and others. And for Lexie—though she knew she was physically alone (besides the medical staff and Clay who could not communicate with her), in her heart she knew she was not really alone.

"I began praying: 'God I have to know you are here. I can't do this. I can't hang on by myself—I have to know I'm not alone. I have to know that You do hold us in the palm of your hand.'"

Hospitals always seem so much colder when we are frightened. She sat with her husband as there was little hope at that moment, but she found that one little flicker of light in her heart to ask for God's presence. She trusted He would be there. Suddenly she felt it.

"I had the sensation of being hugged tight and wrapped up in a warm embrace," she said. "I had been shivering from the cold, but in that moment and the next few moments that followed, I was trembling. Not from the cold, but from the feeling of being held in the palm of the Lord's hand. I remember nodding my head and thinking, 'All right, I am not alone.'"

We are never alone in our darkest hours. If we look, there is always a sign of some sort, whether it is just the right person showing up at just the right time or like in the case of Lexie, just the right text.

"Not long after, my phone buzzed with a text message from a friend. It was an image of Bible verses for challenging times. Isaiah 43:2 was on that list."

"When you pass through the waters, I will be with you, and when you pass through the rivers, they will not sweep over you. When you walk through the fire, you will not be burned; the flames will not set you ablaze."

— Isaiah 43:2

I had this image in my head of Clay and I being in the river and the threat of a comatose future swelling around us and yet here was a promise from God that we would not be swept under.

"I was an avid swimmer in my early teens. Swimming was something I was confident in. I knew then that with God, I could swim harder than that river threatening me. I wasn't going to lose control or give into despair. I was going to swim and I was going to swim hard. For many days to come, I read that Bible verse to Clay and promised him I could swim hard enough for the both of us."

She was putting her trust in God. The thing about putting your trust in God is you have to let Him take you where it is He wants you to go—not where you want to go, as hard as that sounds. It's like Jan Orlando said earlier, "Put it in the lap of the Lord, and leave it there." How did they get to this point? She remembers back to that July Wyoming night at the County Fair. It started as a routine rodeo—something the family has been involved in for years.

"When that whistle blows and that crowd explodes and them pickup men are at your side, they tell you 'Good ride, Cowboy, good ride.'"
— Garth Brooks, Good Ride Cowboy

Clay was working as the "pickup man" during the bronco riding that night. He was the cowboy in charge of getting the bronc rider off the horse at the end of the ride.

AS RODEO NEWS PUT IT:

When Clay Ashurst bridled his horse, pulled his cinch tight, and stepped into his stirrup before the ranch rodeo July 29, (2017) he didn't imagine the day would play out as it did; that he would get hurt or the path for the next few days, weeks, months, and probably years would be so drastically changed.

"Clay's horse was struck broadside by the bucking horse while both were moving at top speed," remembers Lexie. "On a scale of 1-3, Clay's (brain) injury was deemed a 3-plus."

Clay was a successful competitor in ranch rodeos. The year of the accident, his team qualified for Western State Ranch Rodeo Association National Finals and Working Ranch Cowboys Association World Championship Ranch Rodeo—with Clay as the captain. They also qualified for the NILE ranch rodeo and Wyoming State Fair ranch rodeo.

It had started as a fun night, their children were there and Lexie was filming the ride at the time of the accident. Her 12-year-old was on a horse on the field also at the time. Lexie had been around Clay for 20 years and had seen him fall before, but could tell this was different.

"I knew immediately that this was bad," she said. "I have been told by others that I screamed when it happened, but I don't remember that. I just remember running as fast as I could down the front aisle of the grandstands, my camera banging around on my neck. When I reached the end of the arena closest to him, I jumped off the grandstands and onto the arena floor."

Her family took over with the children, so she could be with Clay.

"I was the second person to reach him, beating even the paramedics. I know I was praying out loud by the time I got to him. Praying over and over: 'Dear Lord Jesus, I am calling on you now, be with Clay and give him healing'—over and over and over again.

It's funny what you remember later as you go through things in your mind. When you are in your most vulnerable state, God can sweep you off your feet and put you on autopilot. It can happen on the rodeo field of Wyoming, it can happen on a football field in Georgia, or in the midst of a car accident, or in the waiting room of a hospital. If we have a relationship already built up with God and we are used to having a conversation with him on a daily basis, it can be amazing how He will step in and take over for us.

If you are used to talking to God on a day when things are going well, then you will automatically turn to Him at your most difficult time. Lexie felt terrified, but what she didn't know at the time is that there were people God would put in just the right places to help her—and Clay.

"The Flight for Life helicopter had been called before we ever left the rodeo," she said. "Living in rural Wyoming, our local hospital is quite small, but they do a great job."

"With a small town, we have the benefit of knowing most people in our area. The EMTs were friends, fellow cowboys. The ambulance driver was a friend and also owned the local tire store. He stood with me until they asked us to leave the room. When we stepped into the hall, four of my closest friends were standing there. I remember being so shocked that they came immediately. I guess that's what good friends do—come to your side whether you ask them to or not."

At this time, Clay was totally unresponsive.

"I remember his arm flapping off the side of the gurney and nearly hitting the door jam. The sight of that arm flapping off the side still haunts me. It is an image stuck in my brain forever … just like the image of my friends standing there waiting for me, ready to do whatever was in their power to help."

The medical team decided to fly him to Casper, Wyoming—100 miles from where they were and there was no room for Lexie in the helicopter.

"With the help of my friends, I made the decision to leave Clay and start traveling to Casper. My friend, Jennifer, drove me. As we were leaving, I was trying to type a text message to our friends, Trevor and Alie, and just as I was trying to type, the cell phone rang. It was those very friends calling to say they were passing through our area and asked if we wanted to have dinner. I told them what happened and where I was headed. Trevor told me to pull over, he was bringing Alie to me. So together, Jennifer, Alie, and I headed off to Casper to meet Clay."

They had no idea what to expect, but Lexie just knew she was terrified. The ride seemed to take forever, but once they got to the Emergency Room where Clay was being examined, the doctor spoke to her.

"He explained the nature of Clay's injury to me—brain stem shear with multiple other areas of bleeding in nearly every region of his brain," Lexie said. "He told me that 'Sometimes these patients wake up in three weeks, sometimes they wake up in three months, and sometimes they never wake up, and I am very concerned your husband could be in that last category.'"

Upon hearing that news, she fell back against the wall, grabbing her chest. It was incomprehensible. Her husband was in a coma with the possibility of never waking up. It was a terrible night, as Lexie tried to sleep next to her co-matose husband, with the machines beeping. The comfort she had received in the form of the warm hug from God had helped to calm her down, but what happened next gave her the strength to fight.

"The doctor came back up to check on us," she said. "He told me that he had heard me praying over Clay and that he too was a believer and wanted to remind me that though the outlook for Clay was terrible, our God is bigger than all that. He told me he never gives up on a patient until their heart has stopped and that I should not either."

"It's strange to me looking back on that conversation with the doctor," she said. "I had just heard the worst possible words I had ever been told, 'your husband might not wake up,' yet this second conversation—him encouraging me to hold onto my faith, to hold onto Clay—made those awful words not be the ones that ruled that night."

The night had been filled with uncertainty, but it was also filled with encouragement and faith and power.

"It was from the Almighty!" she said. "I believe that conversation took place at a pivotal time. At that time, when I was exhausted and weary, I was encouraged to hang on, call out to God, be in control of my emotions and advocate for Clay. And advocate for him is what I did. I petitioned God on his behalf without ceasing and I also made myself a student of Clay's injury."

Sometimes the only thing we have the control over is whether or not we will trust God and choose to fight. We can also help the situation out by being informed and either advocating or letting someone advocate for us.

Time has gone by and she's educated herself on the injury and has advocated for Clay when he could not, but during that initial stage—that time when she was cocooned up with her family and friends—that is the time she saw God working the hardest in her life. It was through the friends and family who were there for her. They were her community; her team.

"It was incredible," she said. "After our initial arrival at the hospital that night, I always had at least one very close friend in the waiting room. Those girls were there for me and managed the onslaught of visitors that came. I never once left Clay."

The friends who had driven with her stayed by her side and managed the visitors who came and went, leaving Lexie to tend to Clay.

"They made me eat, they made me sleep, they made sure I had somewhere to lie down and somewhere to shower," she said. "My family of course was amazing. I put them in charge of our boys. And because my girlfriends were able and ready to help, it freed my parents up to take care of the kids, our house, our animals, and so many other things."

During this time Lexie trusted God and she trusted her friends. Most of all, she trusted herself that she was doing the right thing and they were in the place they needed to be. Eventually—months later—Clay woke up. More about that in a minute, but Lexie has some advice for others. She is thankful that she had such a great group of friends and family who stepped in to help and encourages others to work on their friendships—and their faith.

"Take time right now and build yourself a spiritual foundation," she said. "If you do it when life is easy, it is better, because there might come a day when it gets really hard and you are going to need something to stand on."

As she looks back on that dreadful time, one of her friends told her that when she heard Lexie praying, she could feel in her heart that it was going to be OK.

"She told me that though it was so hard and very moving for her to watch me pray and cry over Clay repeatedly, when I did pray over him, she could feel something in that room. She said it was like the air changed whenever I was praying. And though she didn't know what it would look like, she knew that it was going to be okay."

"It is something I have thought about so much since she told me that. I'm thankful I had those friends with me to remind me of that, because at the time, I was too overcome with fear to realize that, but I had those girls with me to redirect my focus."

Lexie said she was not always one who relied on her religion, although her husband, Clay, made sure they went to church on Sundays.

"I was not an overly spiritual person by nature," she said. "I really like to sleep in on Sunday mornings, so church sometimes felt like an effort. I can quote maybe three Scriptures."

Many of us feel that way, but sometimes the best "Christians" aren't the ones who have the Bible memorized. God doesn't judge us by the number of Scriptures we can quote—thank goodness. He just wants us to be in conversation with Him; He wants us to read His word and know He is there.

"I am so thankful that Clay was so adamant about us going to church, because the day of the accident—before I even reached Clay in the arena, I was praying," she said, "When I felt my emotions start to spin out of control, I had one little stone of solid foundation to stand on and knew enough to seek the Lord."

"Truly I tell you, if you have faith as small as a mustard seed, you can say to this mountain, 'Move from here to there,' and it will move. Nothing will be impossible for you."

— Matthew 17:20

Despite the medical prognosis, Clay came out of the coma. He had suffered brain damage, so it was a long, bumpy road full of uncertainties.

Throughout the ordeal, he was an inspiration to Lexie, though he may not have known it. His positive attitude reflected back onto her. During the time he was critical, she kept her family and friends informed on a Facebook page.

"Clay has an amazing attitude and positive outlook. He and I both agree that he will continue to get better over the next year or two, but should he not, we know we will praise God for what we have been given back," Lexie said in one of those posts.

He worked hard day by day and more of his faculties came back. He eventually learned to walk and less than a year after his injury, he was able to see his son compete in his first junior high rodeo—because that's what they do. They are rodeo people.

There's a saying, "When you fall off your horse, you have to get right back on," and that is the type of positivity Clay and Lexie showed throughout the ordeal and recovery.

It is much easier for others to have a positive attitude, if they look to the ones who are suffering and they are staying positive. Throughout Clay's recovery, he continued being a "pickup man" to his wife, as she suffered with fear. He tried to stay positive and she was able to hang onto the love of God that he had helped her develop. A "pickup man" is defined by Cowboy Bob's Urban Dictionary as "a bronc rider's lifeguards."

If you think of any major catastrophe, there is always a pickup man— that person we look to help us, and in some instances, save us.

In your life right now, are you in the position to be the pickup man or is someone doing that for you? There are situations we find ourselves in where we don't know how we will go on. Then in sweeps the pickup man who helps rescue us during our darkest time.

MAYBE GOD CAN BE OUR PICKUP MAN.

"I would encourage everyone to start now in building your relationship with God," said Lexie who says the two lessons that stuck with her the most were the importance of a relationship with God and the importance of friends and family.

"I hold fast to the belief that you don't have to be defined by the things that life does to you," she said. "Dr. Lee Warren talks about this in his book *No Place To Hide*, He says that in life you are going to find yourself on the anvil, but the question is: are you going to be shaped and molded by these things, or are you going to let life just knock the stuffing out of you?"

Lexie says she believes the things that happen to you don't define who are—they are just things that happened to you. How we deal with them is the choice we all make. Do you want to be defined by the negatives that happen to you? Do you want to be that pitiful person that people look on and say, "And he/she was never the same after that"—or do you want to be the pickup man, the one who shines through their own tragedies, emerging as an example for someone else facing an obstacle.

Lexie uses the experience to inspire others, even when she doesn't realize she is doing it.

"It may be easy for me now, because I got my husband back," said Lexie. "He woke up when he wasn't supposed to and in the grand scheme of things, he's pretty similar to who he was before the accident."

But she knows how close they came to another outcome and it served to make her stronger and value her relationships more.

"Maybe your family won't face a life-changing accident or illness," she said. "But the fact remains, life has challenges. We face challenges every day and no matter what they are, we can choose to be molded and shaped by them, not just beat up by them."

One way of facing challenges is to live in the moment. We have some sort of adversity every day but there is no use in spending our time worrying about what could happen tomorrow. Learn to live your life with what is in front of you, right now.

Trust yourself—and others. Once we learn to do that, we will have fewer worries and be more mindful.

"The way to get started
is to quit talking
and start doing."
--Walt Disney

CHAPTER TWELVE

Mindfulness
Less Worry, More Gratitude

The world would be a better place if we had no worries; if we were just thankful for what we have. What is a worry, anyway? It is that uneasiness or anxiousness we feel thinking about something that could possibly go wrong. It is just human to worry about things, but you can also try to control your worries, that is, living in the present, and practicing gratitude.

If you are suddenly wondering if something new just happened on Twitter or if you want to check your phone to see if you have any text messages, then you are not being mindful at this moment.

DO YOU WORRY ABOUT THINGS THROUGHOUT THE DAY?

Here is a way to calm yourself down, so you can just live peacefully in this moment and be mindful.

Tense up all the muscles in your body, then take a deep breath and let it out. Now start at your toes and tense up each body part, in order, all the way up to your head. Once your body is completely tensed up, now take a big deep breath and let it all out. Breathe in, hold it, breathe out. Breathe in, hold it, breathe out.

Just by doing those simple things, you were being mindful. You were concentrating on what is happening right now. This is why taking a deep breath can be so beneficial. When a baseball pitcher is in a crucial situation, watch him, as he will usually step off the mound and take a deep breath. This is being mindful. He is trying to make his mind stop racing from "what will happen if I throw a bad ball" to "here I am at this moment, and I am present and I will do the best I can do."

THERE'S AN APP FOR THAT

Sandy Elfrink is a business owner who has many decisions to make and a lot of stress in the day-to-day operating of her company.

When she has a lot on her mind, she tries to bring herself to just being in the present.

"There are apps for everything—even for calmness. There is one mindfulness free app called Insight Timer," said Sandy. "It has several courses, guided meditation, and prayer. All the content is free and most of it is excellent." The Insight Timer has many versions including Christian meditations.

Being mindful and concentrating on where you are, rather than worrying about what might happen, is better for you.

"I am helped in stressful situations by keeping my eyes open for 'God' moments," said Karen Gore, of Marshfield, Missouri. "In the midst of all of my most troublesome times, I am amazed by the tangible evidence of God's love and attention to detail."

Karen has a good thought, because no matter how tough our times are, if we look for the good, we can find it. If we look for God we can find Him.

It's so important for us to remember we really can have control over our attitude. This is why a key to our happiness is encouraging others and being encouraged by someone. Of course, everyone gets down in the dumps every once in a while. But if you are searching for encouragement for yourself, remember there is always a way, and sometimes it involves being your own encourager.

When we engage in a pity party, we are not living in the moment. We've all done it: when we're at the end of our rope and we start feeling sorry for ourselves. But it doesn't end there. Have you ever started moping about a problem and then you start with the "and then there was the time … " and one more thing … " Just stop right there and be mindful of what is happening right now.

One time when our son, Mike, was a child, I was trying to make my point and I said, "I'm at the end of my rope!" He came back with "Well, I'm in the middle of mine!" Of course, we tried not to laugh at that comment, but it's a good point. There is always more room on the rope, so don't give up or get so upset.

If only we could live in the moment and be mindful, rather than always letting our minds wander. When I start to feel sorry for myself, I sometimes look at my sweet husband and think, "Wow, how lucky am I" that he's right there and there's someone right there for you.

This is why it would do us good to train ourselves to be thankful for what we have. It's good to just be peaceful and be grateful. Try it. Just sit there where you are and think of some things for which you are thankful.

HEARING GOD'S VOICE

One day my sister, Barb, heard the Lord tell her to plan a vacation. Her daughter, my sweet 10-year old niece, Anne, had cancer and did not have much time left. Barb heard it as plain as day: Rent a house in Florida and invite everyone. And she did. She invited her daughter's father (her ex-husband) and his wife. She invited his family and her entire family. Because it was God's plan, the perfect-sized rental house was available at a price she could afford. There were many rooms, a swimming pool, and it was just up the street from the beach.

"My Father's house has many rooms; if that were not so, would I have told you that I am going there to prepare a place for you? And if I go and prepare a place for you, I will come back and take you to be with me that you also may be where I am. You know the way to the place where I am going."

— John 14:2-4

Think about it. God gave Barb a clear path as if he had prepared the place Himself. Meanwhile he was preparing a place for Anne in His house.

Everybody had the best time on that Florida trip and a couple of weeks later, she passed away. During that week-long trip, everyone was mindful and living in the now. For that one week, we were not thinking of the bad that would eventually happen—just the fun we were having.

What if Barb had not heard God's voice? Or what if she only "thought" she heard it and disregarded it. Sometimes it is so strong, you know it and that is when you should react.

I hear God speaking to me occasionally, but it is not real obvious most of the time. Sometimes I hear him through a poem I write. I will get the urge to write a poem and "bam!" it just flows out of my head through my keyboard—kind of like this book is doing. This book is full of thoughts God put in my head at a certain time. He has blessed me, and in turn, the reader by putting all these people with stories they were willing to share in hopes of helping someone, right in front of me.

You can't hear God's messages when your life is too noisy. If your life is too busy and you don't slow down, you might miss something, so make peace in your life a daily goal.

Happy people are more mindful, because if you are appreciating this moment and feeling grateful for it, you have less chance of being depressed by a situation. Those who are depressed about a certain situation are either thinking back about how it went or feeling anxious about the future. Once you start letting your mind wander rather than staying focused, you can feel very lonely if you are by yourself.

One way to lose that lonely feeling is to call a friend who can help you cheer up or go visit someone that you think might be down in the dumps. It's amazing how when we reach out to others to help them, it helps lift our own spirits.

You will never know if you were that one person or thing that happened to save someone from killing themselves.

Some people call it the unthinkable, but I can think of it.

I can think of it, because I lost a loved one that way. My sister, Nancy, had bipolar disease and she committed suicide. I truly believe in her case, it was her illness and there was nothing we could have done, because I spoke to her at 9:30 pm and she sounded fine. We were arranging that I was to pick her up at 6 am the next morning. I was there on time only to discover she had taken her life within those nine hours. It was going to happen no matter how many times I checked on her.

It was her day to go, but maybe it's not someone else's. That's why you should try to be there for people, because you never know when you will be just the right person at just the right time. Every suicidal situation is different—many can be saved.

If you have lost someone to suicide or if you were in the position I was in, where you came upon a loved one—don't waste your life away feeling guilty. It's not your fault—it's way more complicated than that.

If you are feeling so down that you are considering suicide—don't do it! Every suicide causes many other deaths in other ways.

NATIONAL SUICIDE PREVENTION HOTLINE
(1-800-273-8255)
You are important and loved.
Get help if you need it.

PEACE, BE STILL

My next door neighbor, Dorothy, who was in a wheelchair due to MS (Multiple Sclerosis) would always say, "Peace, be still," when someone around her was stressed. Nothing upset her and she didn't feel sorry for herself, despite being in a wheelchair or in bed, and not having any family to help her.

She hired a caregiver to help her and from what I saw, Dorothy gave Cathy as much happiness as Cathy tried to give Dorothy.

Dorothy was one of the most mindful people I've ever met. The "Peace, be still," came from a story in the Bible where Jesus calmed the stormy water.

"And he awoke and rebuked the wind and said to the sea, 'Peace! Be still!' And the wind ceased, and there was a great calm."
— *Mark 4:39 ESV*

It will help us if we would look at our situation and say, "Peace, Be still."

And we should pay attention to each other and watch for messages. Is someone trying to tell you something, or maybe they are going through something that you can't even imagine. We may not know what others are going through, but if we continue to care about each other and check on each other, we might end up helping someone in the process.

One of the greatest outcomes of being mindful is that if you are in this moment you can realize how lucky you actually are. If you think about all you have and are grateful, you are being mindful. I'm thankful for you. Look around. What are you thankful for?

Every day, be mindful of the distinctiveness of that day—the uniqueness of this very minute. If we are mindful, then we can encourage others, as well as encourage ourselves.

"Do not let the behavior of others destroy your inner peace."
--Dalai Lama

CHAPTER THIRTEEN:

Encourage Yourself, Encourage Others

Do you ever feel like you are the only person in the world who has gone through what you have gone through? Well, in a way you are, because we are all unique individuals and even in the same life we have different perspectives—but be there for each other.

ARE YOU HEARING VOICES?

If you ever feel that little voice inside you telling you to do something, if it's good, you should do it. You never know how much the smallest thing can mean to someone, and that's what happened with the gift of a book.

About six months after I lost my father, I entered a period of time that was not optimistic. The day he passed away was the day before the big Eclipse of 2017. We had some family members staying with us and I had planned a Big Eclipse-themed party for them. Unfortunately I had to tell them my dad had just passed away. One of them asked, "Are we still having the party?" Well, I had all the food bought and people had traveled to get there, so I said, "Sure."

I put on a dinner party that night and had family over the next day to view the eclipse, so there was no time for me to break down and cry. It wasn't like I put it into a box to get through those two days—I just forgot to take it out of the box. Soon it was Christmas and I tried extra hard that year, buying everyone in the family matching holiday pajamas. I wanted everyone to have a fun Christmas and then a Happy New Year.

But one day in January, a big sadness came over me and I could barely function. This was not like me at all. I didn't feel like I had anyone to talk to about this, because I didn't want to upset them—I felt I was the one who should be helping everyone else. I'm sure many of you feel that way sometimes.

For several days in a row, I felt depressed and began to think, "No one cares about me."

Has that ever happened to you—where you feel bad and then you start placing blame on others for not caring about you, when in reality, of course, they did. I was not asking for help or telling anyone how I felt, so how could they have known to reach out and help me?

Then one day, my son Mike's girlfriend, Lori (who was to become his wife), gave me a book called, *Love Does: Discover a Secretly Incredible Life in an Ordinary World* by Bob Goff.

Lori said the book made her think of me, and this really touched my heart. I started to read the book—and by the first few pages of the first chapter I was in tears—tears of happiness. The box came down from the shelf and opened! All those emotions came though this Christian book full of experiences from Bob Goff's life. Just reading the book gave me great enthusiasm for things I could do. Maybe if Lori never gave me that book, I would never have written this one.

I'm not sure if it was completely the book that helped me. I think it was the fact that Lori made the effort to give me the book. The book provided just the encouragement I needed at just the right time.

She had no way of knowing that I really needed some encouragement at that time. When others saw me, I was always the happy, friendly hostess. But when everyone left, I felt I had no purpose.

I had loved being a mother to my sons, but now they were grown and didn't seem to need or want my help. I was a caregiver to my parents, but once they were gone, it was like I was experiencing that empty nest feeling all over again. It seemed everyone had their place, but there was nothing I was supposed to do, so I didn't do anything.

Then I read, "Living a life fully engaged and full of whimsy and the kind of things that love does is something most people plan to do, but along the way, they just kind of forget."

Wow, that really hit me and a huge burden was lifted. In my own little doldrums I had forgotten to be my old self—my fun-loving whimsical self.

Don't you just love that word, "whimsical"? It just makes you happy.

The author talked about how people can go along in life, but they stop "living" their lives.

"Their dreams become one of those 'we'll go there next time' deferrals. The sad thing is, for many, there is no 'next time,' because passing on the chance to cross over is an overall attitude toward life, rather than a single decision."

I am encouraging you to never pass up new opportunities. Trying new things can give us a new lease on life—it can provide us with wonder. We can be curious about things. When you are curious, you want to learn more.

Children are always asking questions, because they are curious. Everything is new and exciting for them. We must never lose our wonder—that is what makes life so sweet.

Throughout our life, in all the ups and downs, it's important that we are there for each other, and we encourage each other.

They asked the wise old man, "What is your secret for a happy and productive life?"

"Why don't they ask something more meaningful," he grumbled softly to himself, "such as, 'How do you keep from falling down?'

The answer to both is just the same: You find something substantial and worthwhile to hold on to, and HOLD ON!"
— *Jack Tippett*

My pop wrote that sentiment and he drew a picture with it. He printed it out and I have it taped to a kitchen cabinet. What a great piece of advice: Find something substantial and worthwhile to hold on to, and hold on.

Many people in this book have shared incredible stories and none are

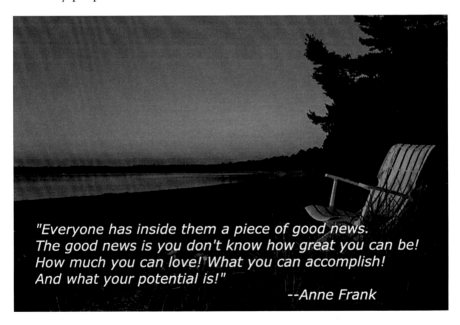

"Everyone has inside them a piece of good news.
The good news is you don't know how great you can be!
How much you can love! What you can accomplish!
And what your potential is!"
--Anne Frank

"worse" than others. Everyone's trials are just as dramatic to the person who is facing them and we can be encouraged by the strength of others.

People ask my sister Barb, "How can you seem so happy with all the loss you have faced?"

She says one of the keys to surviving a tough situation is not to feel defeated when the darkness comes in.

"Learn to give in to the waves of sadness when they come," she said. "I'm going to lie down and take care of myself today—but I'm going to get up tomorrow. It's OK to take a day, or even a few minutes. If I allow myself to feel my emotions, I know I'm not going to be crying tomorrow. It's just a day."

One thing that doesn't help a person who is grieving is to sound amazed that they are "doing so well." Everyone is just coping the best they can and we need to support each other in the place that they are.

"People say, 'How do you do it?' said Barb. They ask, 'How do you keep going?' I don't have super powers, I just do it. We all just do what we are faced with. And it's not like I have a choice."

There was a great quote, which we hopefully traced to the original author:

"She believed she could, ... but she was tired ... so she rested and you know what? The world went on and it was okay. She knew she could try again tomorrow."
— Julianne Bentler DeShayes, author

"You just wake up and face your life," said Barb.

Though she doesn't want to be held as an example, Barb is a shining example of taking what life presents us and trying to live the best possible life for herself and her family. And because she is so open to happiness, people want to be around her.

When I was 10-years-old, I wanted to have a slumber party. I gave my list to my mom and she suggested I invite Sharon Stubbe, one of my classmates. I said, "Oh, I couldn't invite Sharon, she's way too popular, she wouldn't come."

My mom said, "That's not what her mom told me. Her mom told me she cried one night, because she didn't get invited to a party. Maybe it's because people look at her and think she's too popular, so she wouldn't go." I doubt that Sharon ever cried for not being popular, but my mom had a point. I ended up inviting her and she came—and we became friends.

God Is Like a River, Always a Constant

One of my favorite old songs is *Moon River*. There's a line in it that says, "Two drifters off to see the world, there's such a lot of world to see ... " And you can imagine these two drifters off on an adventure?

Later in the song, it talks about a "Huckleberry friend" who is "waiting 'round the bend." Don't we all wish we had that special friend, who would be right there when we need them? Just go around the bend and there is your special friend. It would be great, wouldn't it? Well, the truth is you have Huckleberry friends waiting around the bend for you to call.

Did you notice that most of the meaning behind the song Moon River was about the river—not about the friend? The same thing is true with that old song, *Old Man River*—where the songwriter is taking out his anger on the river.

Both songs try to humanize the river. There are some things that will always be there for us and some that we can't always count on. The river was a source of something the writers could count on—good or bad. Moon River is wider than a mile; Old Man River just keeps rolling along.

That is how God is—He is the constant you can always count on—He's always there for you. If you have not prayed in a while or had a relationship with Him, just remember He is always going to be your Huckleberry friend—waiting 'round the bend' for you. He's there right now.

And right, now I'm with you, offering encouragement. I've said a prayer for everyone who reads this, for peace in your heart. You can do anything, even with detours in life.

"Happiness doesn't depend on external conditions, it is governed by our mental attitude."

— Dale Carnegie

A "Brand" New You

Sometimes it just takes "us"—our mental attitude to make it. Karen Fox, a sales and marketing strategist in St. Louis was talking about brand marketing at a recent seminar. She pointed out that all of us have things that are unique to us—we don't have to be famous to be special. We already are special.

"You may not know this, but celebrity ads don't sell more products than others," she said. "So there is hope for us! We can be our own celebrity!"

In talking about marketing she suggested business owners "promote what is uniquely you!"

I love that, because we can apply it to ourselves—how when the chips are down, we feel like we are all alone, but we can celebrate and encourage ourselves. We all have a personal brand and we're all unique. We can be our own celebrity. Let everybody else do them. You do you.

CELEBRATE EVERY VICTORY

"Tonight was a pretty big deal," wrote Angela Scoggins of Alton, Illinois, on her Facebook page, just above a picture of her in her cap and gown. "It may have never happened, but it did. I graduated with my certificate of proficiency in criminal justice."

The amazing thing about Angela is that she had several bumps in the road along the way to achieving that goal. While working two jobs and raising her daughter, Ariana, she started school. The first road bump was when her grandmother got sick and she dropped everything to take care of her. Then she went back to school and soon encountered another bump in her road. As she tells it, "I became a cancer mom."

Ariana got cancer and required daily treatments at the hospital, so there was no time—or gumption—to work on school.

Maybe this is like something you've gone through—you were on your way to doing something, but a roadblock got in your way—not just a little roadblock, a very difficult one to maneuver through. So now you are in the "detour"—sitting in traffic. You will get back on the road soon, don't give up. If you keep a positive attitude you will find another way.

Ariana got better from her cancer for a while, but she suffered some other problems called 'late effects' in the cancer world, like her hearing weakened, so she ended up wearing hearing aids. At times, Angela wrestled with being so happy that her little girl had survived, but also feeling inadequate, because she had not progressed in her education. She would get down on herself for many different reasons, but probably one big thing was she felt a little disappointed in herself. She shouldn't have because she was successfully raising an amazing girl, but still she had doubts about herself.

Why do we do that to ourselves? If someone else was in our situation, we would be the first to say, "You are doing a great job," but when it's us, we get down on ourselves. Think about that and try treating yourself at least as well as you treat others. You should be so proud of yourself for all you've been through and how you've encouraged yourself to stay in there.

Even though it was not Angela's fault that things had not gone along as planned in life, she felt she could have done something better or studied harder or whatever of those bad thoughts we allow into our heads that tear us down.

One day she decided not to listen to the negative thoughts, but to press forward to do the thing she started out to do. She took the support of those who wanted to see her achieve and ignored the negatives and she eventually graduated. That one little piece of paper means so much to her and you can know that feeling when you get back on track with whatever you were wanting to do, but you left it at the wayside.

Were there some classes or a degree you had started on? Was there a project you wanted to do, but you just gave up on it, because you were too tired to do it, didn't have the money to do it, or just forgot about it? Do you play an instrument but have set it aside? Figure out a way to do it and set your mind to it. It may not be the biggest thing in the world that you are able to do right now—but you can do something. Always keep moving forward, no matter what your situation.

And here was the bonus of Angela taking control of her life: her daughter had a bad MRI and they discovered her cancer had come back, but by now Angela had the strength to deal with what she had to. She became an even better mother than she had been, because she had confidence in herself. Angela and those like her are my heroes. They show up for life every day and are secretly encouraging others who are watching.

There are times in our life when we think we have no support—these are the times we must encourage others, but sometimes we need to encourage ourselves.

Her Life Continues to Inspire Others

Nancy Czaicki was a beautiful young woman who had been the drum major in her award-winning high school band. She received a scholarship for college and worked in a lab looking for a cure for cancer. She volunteered with Rainbows for Kids and wanted to help people.

Her first internship was in a lab searching for a cure for cancer. There are people working every day to find cures and treatments for so many diseases and we can all take comfort in the hope that with all these researchers there could be a breakthrough at any moment in the area we need. Nancy eventually ended up going to Africa working with Aids patients and helping to find a cure.

Her mother, Cindy Czaicki, was so proud of her, but of course missed her when she was in Africa. Cindy had raised her as a single mom and the two were very close, so the separation was difficult. She knew how important Nancy's work was and felt proud. They kept in touch—until boom! Nancy's life was cut short by a speeding, drug-impaired driver.

How do you go on in this situation? You rely on your family. In Cindy's case, she did not have that luxury, as her father had died and she was taking care of her mother, who was not in a position to help.

Her love came from an amazing group of friends.

"They took turns spending the night with me, so I would never be alone," she said. "If I had not had those friends, I don't know where I would be."

A couple of years later, her feelings are still tender and she misses Nancy every day, but she manages to go on with her life and keep a smile on her face. How does she do that? How can we keep going when we feel there is nothing to live for?

"I just kept wondering, 'Why did it happen?' " she said. "Why? She was doing so much for other people. There was still so much of her work to be done."

It is only when we stop asking that nagging question of "why" that we can start seeing clearly and live our lives, because we'll never know "why" in this life.

"I went over to Africa and met the people she had worked with or helped," said Cindy. "I was so amazed at how many lives she had touched. One man showed me a piece of paper with her handwriting on it. Nancy had written something down for him and it meant so much that he kept it. And others just shared their stories."

Remember that quote from *It's a Wonderful Life*, where Clarence the Angel tells George Bailey, "Strange, isn't it? Each man's life touches so many other lives. When he isn't around, he leaves an awful hole, doesn't he?"

Cindy didn't realize the magnitude her daughter's life had on others. We often don't see the effect we are having on someone. We may be just being there for someone, but we don't realize how much they need us at that particular time.

When Cindy searches for answers, she always comes back to one thing, which gives her peace in her heart and the strength to go on every day.

"I think about all the people that she helped," Cindy said. "And then I think that maybe by being around Nancy, those people became better people and in turn helped more people. Maybe the 100 people she touched with her life turned into 1,000 people and maybe there are people literally all over this world being better because my Nancy was here and she touched their lives."

Wow, what an amazing thought. Let's think about our own lives. Are we living the lives that others will look at and silently emulate? Are we striving for excellence in our life no matter what we are going through? It doesn't have to be something big.

It's like the earlier reference of the "celebrity" example. We don't have to win an academy award to be a success—although sometimes to live a successful life during trying times, we put on a good acting job and maybe we deserve one. I can be my own celebrity by being the best "me" I can be—and you can, too.

We can all make the world a better place by spreading love, light, and happiness to all we come in contact. And looking at it from the other side—we can take the goodness given out by those very special people who seem to put it out and turn it around to help others.

Sometimes it seems like famous people have everything and they have no problems. A baseball player who makes a lot of money seems to have the world by the tail, but really, when all is said and done, they are just normal people. They have their own problems.

"I remember one day sitting by the pool and suddenly the tears were streaming down my cheeks. Why was I so unhappy? I had success, I had security, but it wasn't enough."

— Ingrid Bergman

Fame and money are not the definition of happiness. Even though we all think it would help, the most wealthy or famous people could be the loneliest.

The old saying of, "we all put our pants on the same way," says it all. If you ever feel you aren't as good as someone or you have a job interview and you are scared to face that all-important person, remember he or she sits on the toilet and even gets constipated. No one is better than anyone else.

That's why we need to encourage everyone with whom we come in contact.

You are just as important in the eyes of the Lord as any movie star or the Queen of England—and you are also the same in His eyes as that pitiful beggar on the street corner. You are no better than anyone, but you are also no worse.

YOU DON'T NEED A TIARA TO BE SPECIAL

On May 19, 2018, when Prince Harry married Meghan Markle, people got up early all over the world to watch the wedding with all its pomp and circumstances. The glowing bride and the blushing groom wowed the crowd. This world-wide event with Sir Elton John and George and Amal Clooney in attendance as guests was full of years of tradition, yet the commentators marveled at how unique it was.

It was clear the young couple added their touch to what was required of them. Never before had gospel music been sang in such a way at the Church of England in which they were married. Never had mainstream music like *Stand by Me* been performed at a royal wedding.

In these happy moments, the royal couple was optimistic that they could change the world. And really, that feeling isn't so far from the feelings of all young couples.

They are young and energetic and their love was obvious. E Entertainment commentator, Giuliana Rancic, noticed that while they are "Royals," their outlook can be likened to all of us.

"You don't need a tiara to make a difference in the world," Giuliana Rancic said.

It's so true in our lives—although a tiara can be fun—and should be a staple on every woman's accessory shelf, no matter their age. With or without an accessory or even a person at your side, you can make a difference in the world and in someone's life—but you need to realize you hold the key.

"You need to know that you're enough," Meghan Markle told Tig Magazine before the wedding.

"That five pounds lost won't make you happier, more makeup won't make you prettier. The now iconic saying from Jerry Maguire—'You complete me'—frankly isn't, (or shouldn't be) true. You are complete, with or without a partner. You are enough just as you are."

Think about that for a minute: you are enough, just as you are. It's so easy to get caught up with what we think society wants us to be or do.

Prince Harry has always marched to a different drummer—and sometimes he was ridiculed on the worldwide stage. When there were bumps along the road of his life, he addressed them and moved forward, usually doing something to help others.

"You've got to give something back," Prince Harry once said. "You can't just stand there."

His wife agrees with that feeling. There is always something to do.

"I've never wanted to be a lady who lunches—I've always wanted to be a woman who works," she told the magazine. "And this type of work is what feeds my soul and fuels my purpose."

We all have something that feeds our souls—the challenging part is to find out what that is. The world is so loud and busy at times that we often don't take the time to be quiet and listen to what our soul is telling us.

You don't need a title. You don't need to be, "Her Royal Highness, the Duchess of Sussex."

Just be you. You can do whatever you set your mind to, as long as you take care of yourself.

"For I consider that the sufferings of the present time are not worth comparing with the glory that is to be revealed to us."
--Romans 8:18

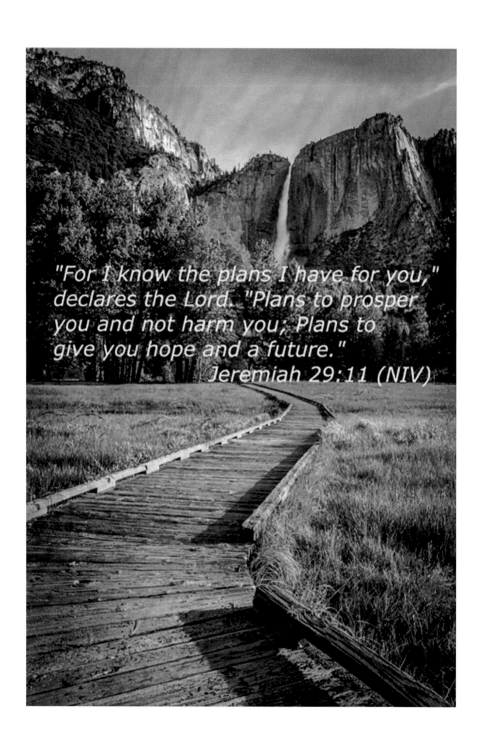

"For I know the plans I have for you," declares the Lord. "Plans to prosper you and not harm you; Plans to give you hope and a future."
Jeremiah 29:11 (NIV)

Chapter Fourteen

Nutrition and Health
Take Care of YOU

Elizabeth Kurowski of Swansea, Illinois, is a great example of "you can do anything you set your mind to," especially in the area of nutrition and health—but it could have gone either way—due to a medical diagnosis. When she was just 14 years old, Lizzie was diagnosed with Type 1 Diabetes, which she refers to as T1D.

It was a very scary day for her family, but as is the case in all of our trials, a strong family and circle of support goes a long way in acceptance of our situations and facing life full-out.

She and her family began researching the best diet and exercise plan for Lizzie to be able to live a good life. Ten years later she is living a great life—and if you didn't know she had diabetes, you wouldn't know.

"If you are just beginning your journey with diabetes, or really any new health challenge, I hope my story gives you hope that this is not 'it' for you," she said. "Once you get the disease under control—and this may take a lot of effort on your part and the part of your loved-ones—you can find out what your passions are and begin living them out."

It does take a lot of effort to take care of your health—no matter what your situation is. Many people live with a health situation where it is said to be inherited, "It runs in the family." Don't ever accept any diagnosis as final. Be your own advocate. Start a new nutrition and health plan, if it could help, and always live in hope. Remember all those out there looking for a cure.

Every day will not be a good day in the health department. This is true for someone living with a disease or just someone who may be having tension headaches lately or your tooth is really bothering you or you find yourself getting out of breath when climbing steps. Whether a serious health situation or not, there are days we just don't feel well.

"I have bad days where I feel like nothing I do can help my blood sugar and it makes me feel helpless," said Lizzie. "To overcome this, I remember tomorrow is a new day, and I can do anything I set my mind to. When I am feeling sorry for myself, I remember how fortunate I am to be alive and how things could always be much worse. I like to try and remember to look at the bright side of every situation."

One way of living a great life despite her circumstances is she makes sure her everyday life is not about the disease. Yes, she plans ahead and makes sure she is taken care of, but does not dwell on the negatives of her situation.

"I do not follow a strict nutritional plan, but I try to maintain a lower carb diet generally," said Lizzie. "I say generally, because life is hectic and that does not always happen. I try to plan ahead and meal prep, so I can have healthy lunches at work and cook dinner at home every night."

As a young professional, she has a busy schedule, so she often eats out.

"During those times, I have to make good choices, which can be hard," she said. "I love ice cream and Chinese food, so those are my weaknesses, but I try to plan when I eat these foods and mentally prepare myself for the high blood sugars that will follow."

Along with planning for a healthy diet, Lizzie sees importance in exercising and staying active.

"I have always relied on exercising to be my rock in life," she said. "Exercising is super important to me mentally, but also physically to maintain better blood glucose control. Recently, starting a career has provided me less time to work out and I have seen a dramatic impact on my diabetes control as such. I am getting back into it and each day I work out, I feel better mentally and my blood sugars are significantly more well-controlled."

Anyone who meets Lizzie sees her as a vibrant, energetic person and without knowing her, personally might not realize what she goes through "behind the scenes." Every day we meet people and we don't know their life stories; and they don't know ours. This is why we should be kind to everyone we meet and cut others some slack, if they are less than kind to us.

"I have run half-marathons and become scuba-certified to show that you truly can do anything, even with obstacles like T1D," she said. "But most of all, I have used my T1D diagnosis to become more aware that everyone has something in their life that they struggle with."

There is nothing Lizzie can't do. Rather than feel sorry for herself, because she has diabetes, she faces the disease and fights it every step of the way. She doesn't consider herself a victim of diabetes—she faces it head-on and likes to call herself a "Dia-bad-ass."

SALLY'S FOUR PRINCIPLES FOR A BETTER LIFE

- Be Careful
- Be Healthy
- Be Nice
- Be Thankful

BE CAREFUL

Did your parents ever tell you, "Nothing good ever happens after midnight?" That was their way of helping you to learn to be careful. Generally, later in the night, people who are out have either been at a party or a bar, or are tired due to work, which can lead to a bad situation. There are crime statistics to back up your parents' advice.

There are so many ways to be careful. Try to avoid accidents. Be sure your shoes are tied, wipe up spills, or use a flashlight when you walk your dog at night. Watch your children when there is any water around. Just watch your children.

Set your cell phone under your leg while driving. When you set it in your lap, you are tempted to look down—"just this once." Everyone knows they should not text and drive, but maybe it would help if I told you I personally know someone who lost a loved one due to the driver checking his phone. Don't do it. Please don't text and drive. That is a huge way to be careful.

BE HEALTHY

Some simple things can help you live longer. We know most of them, but what will it take before we actually take steps to be healthy? Will it take you getting high blood pressure before you stop putting too much salt on your food? Will it take a serious health scare before you get your weight under control?

I am not an advocate for diets, though I have struggled with my weight throughout my adult life. I am sure many of you reading this have gone on diet after diet in an attempt to lose weight. But what do we do once we lose weight? We go back to the habits we had before and guess what—it slowly creeps back, unless we are very careful.

I finally decided I'd had enough and I made a lifestyle change. I may be a little lumpy, but I feel great most of the time and that is what is most important. You can do that, too. You don't have to feel depressed, if you think you are overweight. Just start eating healthy. Don't look on yourself as being "overweight." Who is to say you are overweight—in some cultures, it is not a negative. The point is, we have to do what we can to make ourselves healthy and feeling happy. If your health depends on you losing weight, then do it in a healthy way—not a crash diet. If you feel great, keep doing what you are doing.

Find what works for you that you can live with—for the rest of your life. Don't do any more crash diets. You are worth a little planning. You can live a healthy life—if you want to.

BE NICE

How does that help you live a longer life, you may wonder? People who are nice get smiles from people and we all know smiling is good for us. People who are nice have more friends. Things just generally go better for people who are nice.

BE THANKFUL

Each day we have on this earth is a day to be thankful for.

In the midst of life we often find ourselves in a situation where we are taking care of others, but not ourselves. With the "sandwich generation," we often find ourselves taking care of our children and our parents. If someone is depending on you to take care of them (your children, your parents, your spouse, your partner), you should make it a point to be healthy, because they need you.

Isn't it crazy that a parent will worry over whether their child eats enough or eats healthy food, but they will think nothing if they skip meals or grab unhealthy food on the run. However, if the parent gets sick, who will take care of the child?

She Found a Way to Be Happy and Healthy

Kristie Breeding Scherrer, the mother of two sons, is thankful for every day in her life and she tries to make the most of them by being healthy and happy.

"I don't go a day without thanking God and being grateful for all He has done for me and my family," she says.

Her attitude could have gone the other way, because of the tragic and unexpected loss of her father when she was at a young. age His death changed her otherwise happy life and she said she did everything she could to try to make those around her happy—but the one person she forgot about was herself.

"I wasn't really happy for a long time," she said. "I was told my dad had been 'depressed,' so I wanted everyone around me to be happy. I even pretended to be someone I wasn't, but I didn't know how to make ME happy."

Sometimes we just add more to our plates, in an attempt to be distracted, so we won't notice the bad parts of our life. Maybe if I make others happy and stay busy, I won't realize I miss my loved-one who has passed away or my best friend who moved away. If I never stop to think about myself I might be able to outrun the sadness.

Many people can relate to this. I advocate an optimistic attitude, but it's important we honor our feelings and, while it's no good to wallow in our negatives, we should acknowledge there are times we get those waves of sadness. Sometimes we give into them and that's OK for a while, but when we spend too much time on negatives, it can be bad for our health. Kristie has found a way to improve her health and well-being.

"I attribute most of my happiness as coming from God," she said. "I know He sent me—and all of us—here to fulfill a purpose—we just have to figure out what His plan for each of our lives is. I am so glad I discovered Buti Yoga, because it has helped my mental focus—I feel I am helping others by teaching it," said Kristie who has always enjoyed being active with mountain biking, hiking, rollerblading, and traveling.

Buti Yoga is not the same as Traditional Yoga, which involves balance, meditation, strengthening our core and focus. Buti Yoga is higher impact, cardio-intensive, involves rotating movements of the spine and includes some dance moves.

"With Buti Yoga, we are constantly moving and doing different work-outs, to upbeat music," Kristie said. "It opens and awakens the mind, heart and soul. But one of the best things is that it has helped me love my body and myself for where I am now, and gives me more energy and strength."

Kristie sees so much value in staying healthy both mentally and physically that she started teaching classes in Buti Yoga.

"It has become a big part of my life," she said. "I wouldn't be the confident, strong, loving self I am today without it. I think it's so important for us to take care of ourselves."

Whether it's Yoga, Buti Yoga, dancing, exercising, weight-lifting, or just walking, there is something we can find that will keep us moving and will improve our health—and in turn, improve our mood and overall well-being,

"If I go a day without laughing, then the day is not over," Kristie said. "I have a love for life now and I wish more people could see how good it feels to choose happiness, above everything."

HER MOTHER DIED YOUNG, SO SHE TRIES TO BE EXTRA HEALTHY

Michele Carter has also been motivated by losing a parent at a young age and she makes the choice to be as healthy as she can—every day.

"My mom was 51 when she died," said Michele Carter, of Wildwood, Missouri. "She passed away from cancer and after that experience, it took a while, but I realized I wanted to do the best I possibly could to live a long life with my husband and children. I did not want them to experience what I had felt. I felt very alone once she died. Thankfully, I have surpassed that age."

When someone loses a parent at a young age, they usually remember the age and as we humans do, fret about that age. I remember being told Rob's father died at age 48 and as he hovered around that age, you could not deny the thoughts were there, but once he hit 48 and then 49, we realized that they were two different people. That must be how Michele felt when she turned 51 and then 52.

We are not bound by our parents' fates, as we are not them. We may have some predisposed genes, but in Rob's case, his father lived a different lifestyle, so Rob was already on a different path. Some contributing factors in his dad's death did not exist in his life. But he remembers the day as a five-year old, he looked out the living room window at the taillights of the ambulance that held his father.

Michele was just 18 years old, but she also vividly remembers the night her mother passed away. Michele was a carefree teen who thought she was invincible—that nothing would happen to her.

"The night my mother died, I was going to a party with friends," she remembers. "My grandmother told me I was selfish for wanting to be with my friends and not staying with my mother."

It's funny how these things stay in our minds. Michele had been with her mother all week. It is grueling when a loved one is sick and when her friends called, she was torn between if she should go or stay.

"My mom wanted me to go with my friends and she said that I should pay no attention to Grandma," said Michele. "When I left that night, I felt peace, because mom wanted me to go. During the party, I had a strong feeling to head home. God, I know was asking me to go to be with my mom for those last moments. When I turned down our street, the lights were on and I knew she was still hanging on."

Their family was together, and she also remembers the ambulance arriving and was thankful for her faith, which carried her through the situation.

"The main thing that I have is my faith. God is good," Michele said. "Even in the tough time, there is always hope when you have faith. I felt God swoop all of us up in His arms as the ambulance arrived to take my mom."

As a child growing up, she had never thought about exercise or nutrition or trying to be healthy, but those things soon changed. That same year, she met her husband, John.

"My parents never exercised or even took walks with us," she remembered. "The extent of my exercising was what we did with the pom-poms in high school, but I started taking fitness classes and learning about health and nutrition. Once I started exercising, it was amazing how much energy I had and how good I felt. I dropped a lot of "fat" weight and begin teaching classes. While teaching, I watched others succeed in their weight challenges and that was so satisfying.

"I try to take good care of myself physically and mentally, so I can be the best I can be for my family," said Michele, who is up at the crack of dawn every day exercising and going to Bible Study. "After my mother passed away, I asked God if it was His plan, that when I married I could have six children, and that is exactly what He provided."

Michele has always amazed me, because though she works, she builds her schedule around her husband and six children and always seems to have the energy and stamina for everything that is required of her. With six children, we can only imagine all of the day-to-day situations she faces—just as everyone else does.

"It makes my heart smile to see my children happy, but that is nothing different than any other mom," said Michele. "When I am stressed, I clean and exercise more. I like having things in order, such as my house, my finances, and my schedules."

DE-CLUTTERING CAN HELP YOUR ATTITUDE

That advice sounds like an article straight out of Shape Magazine: "How Cleaning and Organizing Can Improve Your Physical and Mental Health" by Paige Fowler. According to the article, people who feel their homes are cluttered or full of unfinished projects (those piles on the dining room table) were more depressed, fatigued, and had higher levels of the stress hormone, cortisol, than those who felt their homes were more organized, restful, and restorative.

The article points out that the piles and "To Do" lists can take a toll on your mood, sleep, and health. Taking the time to clean the house, tackle the laundry, and sort through stacks of papers can actually help you feel happier and more relaxed.

If you choose to start an exercise or workout plan to stay healthy, remember what the article also talks about: People who set short-term goals, have a plan, and record their progress are more likely to stick with an exercise program than those who show up to the gym and wing it.

This goes with nutrition also. If you want to be healthier, have more energy, and have an overall better countenance, plan ahead. A good example of this is, "Tomorrow I'm going to start eating healthy" and then you wake up and see the Frosted Flakes in the cupboard. A better approach is plan out what you will eat and either move or dispose of the foods you don't want to be tempted by.

"I also list in my head all the things that I am thankful for," said Michele. "Once I begin doing this, whatever my stressors are dissipates. I find there are always things to be thankful for, no matter what situation I am in. God is good always."

The other thing that Michele does that can actually make you more healthy is volunteer.

"I receive joy by helping others and seeing them happy," she said.

THE MAYO CLINIC'S SIX WAYS VOLUNTEERING CAN IMPROVE YOUR LIFE:

1. Decreases the risk of depression

2. Gives a sense of purpose and teaches skills

3. Helps people stay physically and mentally active

4. Can reduce stress level

5. May help you live longer
   They cited a study that found that volunteers have a lower mortality rate than those who do not volunteer and some studies have even shown that volunteers with chronic pain or serious illness experience decline in pain intensity and depression when serving others (especially when helping peers who experience the same thing.)

6. Helps you meet people and develop new relationships

"Because my mom died from cancer, as did both of John's parents, I chose a cancer charity to support," Michele said. "Working with Rainbows for Kids makes me feel like I am able to see my parents living through these young cancer survivors.

"My parents loved to dance and competed on roller skates when they were younger. When Mom died, my dad said, 'Sweet Bevie, we will dance again in Heaven.' He died on their anniversary and I am sure they danced when he arrived and are still dancing."

Along with watching what she eats and trying to get a proper amount of sleep, Michele counts on exercise and her prayer life to help her stay physically and mentally fit so she can face the world head-on.

Her advice to others, "Try to take care of the things you can control when stressed. I declutter and it helps. I develop a 'take charge' attitude with exercise—because that is something I can control. Once we do this, we can put things in perspective—we know that God is in charge."

We should be determined that our health is a priority, no matter what. We should give it our best shot.

> *"To keep the body in good health is a duty … otherwise, we shall not be able to keep our mind strong and clear."*
>
> — *Buddha*

YOU CAN FIGURE OUT WHAT FOOD MAKES YOU FEEL BEST

The food in the vending machine down the hall probably isn't the best, as it might give you a quick jolt, but planning ahead is always better. Think ahead and if you know you will be spending a long day at the hospital, in a clinic, or sitting by someone's bedside, pack some fruit, a protein bar, or whatever it is that will keep you going and keep you feeling strong.

It is not for this book to tell you what you should and should not eat, but hopefully as with everything here, you might get an idea to try. Everyone has a food regimen that is best for them—and we usually know what that is for ourselves. I remember my sister, Nancy, who owned a health food store, would say "I need to get off white flour and sugar, I've been feeling sluggish." For her that was something she felt kept her from being at her best, so she avoided white flour and sugar.

Now, years later, I realize my sister was right as far as my body is concerned.

The website, EatingWell.com, encourages five foods that can help you in your quest for good health: oats, wild salmon, blueberries, avocados, and walnuts. The site says, "As part of a balanced diet, they're proven to help you lose weight, keep your heart going strong, and promote healthy, younger-looking skin."

When you read something like that you need to read it in context, just like when they say dark chocolate or red wine is good for you. You may read that, but if you eat too much dark chocolate or drink too much red wine, it is not good for you.

That list may not work for you. If you are a low carb person, the oatmeal would be a problem.

My husband and I have discovered that eating more of a "low carb" lifestyle keeps us feeling pretty good. We also try to eat a lot of blueberries and almonds. Rob generally drinks Propel flavored water over soda, which was a big change, but worth it.

We were turned on to Quest Bars by a friend in the health food business and our favorite is the chocolate chip, which we use as a meal replacement occasionally. Each week I make carb-free waffles and cheese biscuits from almond flour. We keep them in the freezer and often we'll have one of the waffles for lunch. Dinner is usually a meat or fish plus fresh vegetables, and the occasional cheese biscuit.

I make a great low-carb crock pot lasagna using konjak noodles, which have no carbs. One of the healthiest things we've discovered is eating "whole foods" and avoiding preservatives.

We've learned the advantage of adding smoothies to our life, and sometimes will replace a meal with a Strawberry-Blueberry yogurt smoothie with kale added at Smoothie King. You have to be careful with smoothies, because they can just add a lot of calories to your diet, if you don't know what is in your smoothie. Some are meant to be a meal and some can be a healthy snack, but if you eat the smoothies full of calories as a snack that is counterproductive.

We use liquid coconut oil when cooking, because a friend whose husband has Alzheimer's disease told us coconut oil can help with memory.

None of this is an endorsement for any way of doing things, but I just want you to know you can take charge of your eating habits. Your life doesn't have to revolve around food. A little planning can make your life so much better in the nutrition department. And planning can include a cheat day where you just eat what you want.

There came a day when we decided to make some changes, and when you feel better you can face your life better. Do your research and choose what is best for you, but if you can get a hold of your eating and develop a healthy lifestyle, you will have the energy and stamina to do the things that life requires of you.

One of the best things you can do for yourself is try to choose happy, and feeling proud of your eating choices and adding some sort of exercise goes a long way towards happiness.

LAUGHTER IS A KEY TO HER HAPPINESS

Darlene Kassen, whose family owns a chain of appliance stores in St. Louis, has seen a lot of things that might get to another person, but she doesn't let things get her down to the point that she can't function. At various times in her life, she has been faced with a family member's suicide, fear of her Marine son being deployed, a public business dispute, caring for elderly loved ones, and the death of her father.

She has not only survived, she has thrived. How does she do it?

"Staying busy and laughter helped me through a lot of things in my life," she said. Darlene laughs a lot and her laughter is contagious.

Being the mother of a Marine is a great source of pride, but there is always that uneasiness about if he will be deployed or what the future holds. She does not dwell on the "what ifs"—she tries to stay in the present—enjoying her family and friends. No matter where he is stationed, she makes the effort to go visit.

One thing that has helped her find peace in her life is her family. She and her husband have built a life and a home that is open and welcoming to their family and friends—and on any given weekend, they are entertaining family.

And, of course, when family and friends are around, she is probably laughing. Choose people who laugh a lot to be in your life.

They say, "Laughter is the best medicine," and WebMd.com even has articles on the positive effect laughing can have on our health.

"Feeling rundown? Try laughing more. Some researchers think laughter just might be the best medicine, helping you feel better and putting that spring back in your step.

"I believe that if people can get more laughter in their lives, they are a lot better off," says Steve Wilson, MA, CSP, a psychologist and laugh therapist. "They might be healthier, too."

The Mayo Clinic is also on the bandwagon, encouraging more laughter: "A good laugh has great short-term effects. When you start to laugh, it doesn't just lighten your load mentally, it actually induces physical changes in your body."

According to the Mayo Clinic, laughing can stimulate many organs and enhances your intake of oxygen-rich air. This stimulates your heart, lungs, and muscles, and increases the endorphins that are released by your brain.

The Mayo Clinic stresses that laughing is not just a quick pick-me-up, but it can actually improve your immune system over time. It can also serve as a pain reliever. Our body is so amazing at how it can work to heal itself and if you are a person who laughs a lot, that can cause the body to produce its own natural pain relievers.

Another thing that helps keep you healthy is sleep.

> *"Early to bed, early to rise, makes a man healthy, wealthy, and wise."*
> *— Benjamin Franklin*

According to the American Psychological Association, sleep is essential for a person's health and wellbeing. The National Sleep Foundation (NSF) has done studies on this, yet millions of people do not get enough sleep and many suffer from lack of sleep.

The NSF found that at least 40 million Americans suffer from sleep disorders and 60 percent of adults report that they have sleep problems at least once a week.

"Getting about seven-and-a-half or so hours of quality sleep daily is important," says author Roberta L. Duyff, MS, RDN, FAND, CFCS in the book *Complete Food and Nutrition Guide*.

She goes on to say that "Sleeping less may result in eating more calories and snacking more … if you are tired you may not have the energy for physical activity."

So we should make every effort to eat properly, exercise (get up and walk, if you can—if you can't, move your body in your chair), and try to find peace. Listening to music can give you peace.

He Has the Best Disposition

Recently when I wa cleaning out a drawer, I found a folder my grandpa had kept and in it was an article by Norman Vincent Peale author of *The Power of Positive Thinking* called, "How to be Happier."

In the article, he talked about how after a dinner paying tribute to someone, the honoree's wife greeted him by saying, "I've been married to you for 22 years and every minute of it has been fun." She turned to Norman Vincent Peale, to who they were talking to and proudly said "He has the best disposition of anyone I know."

A bystander heard that conversation and asked "How do you get a good disposition? I feel I have a terrible disposition."

Norman Vincent Peale posed that question to some friends he was having lunch with and here were their answers:

How does a person develop a good disposition?

"'If you've got anything on your chest, get it off,' was the first suggestion. Then someone else chimed in with, 'You've got to have peace of mind.' A medical doctor added, 'And keep your stomach and liver in good condition' to which a dentist could not resist appending, 'and get your teeth X-rayed regularly.'"

So let's think about those things:

NORMAN'S KEYS TO A GOOD DISPOSITION

1. Get it off your chest

2. Have peace of mind

3. Maintain good stomach (gut) and liver health

4. Schedule regular dental checkups

GET IT OFF YOUR CHEST

"Getting something off your chest" is defined by the *Cambridge Dictionary* as telling someone about something that has been worrisome or making you feel guilty for a long time. Worrying does you no good and if something is gnawing at you, it can affect your health and your personality. If there is something that has been bothering you, talk to someone about it and you will feel freer afterwards.

HAVE PEACE OF MIND

The more peaceful you feel, the better you will be to deal with. When you are stressed out it sometimes comes out as impatience. Do what you need to do to achieve peace of mind.

MAINTAIN GOOD STOMACH AND LIVER HEALTH

How do you keep your stomach in good condition? It seems obvious, but your choice of food is one of the biggest ways. Exercising, drinking water, adding fiber to your diet, and living a healthy lifestyle can contribute to good digestive health. When talking about a healthy stomach, the terms gastrointestinal and gut health are often used. Stress can impact the gut in many ways, causing it to malfunction, including decreased oxygen or blood flow to that area. Besides a stomach ache, digestive problems can affect the brain and cause anxiety, brain fog, depression, and more.

How do you achieve good liver health? According to the Liver Foundation there are 13 suggestions: maintain a healthy weight, eat a balanced diet, exercise regularly, avoid toxins like aerosols and chemicals, use alcohol responsibly, avoid illicit drugs, avoid contaminated needles, get medical care if exposed to someone else's blood, don't share personal hygiene items, practice safe sex, wash your hands, follow directions on all medications, and get vaccinated.

SCHEDULE REGULAR DENTAL CHECKUPS

The dentist was right too—your oral health is more important than you think, because poor oral health can lead to many negative conditions.

There's a pattern here—the more we take care of ourselves, the better we will be for others. If we want to have a happy life, it's important to try to live a healthy one. You might not even realize you are having dental issues, as sometimes a symptom could be a headache. Regular checkups and cleaning will help with your overall health.

There are ways we can try to help ourselves and our family to be healthy and happy, but what if we suddenly can't?

One of the worst things we face is watching a family member go through a terrible situation. We watch helplessly as they seemingly turn against all that is healthy and good for them, as they go through destructive behavior.

What if someone you love is making bad choices and it seems downright unhealthy—but they won't listen?

Whether it is drug addiction or mental illness, which requires medication, many families experience both of these and both are difficult to talk about. As each day goes by, more and more people experience family members with drug or alcohol dependencies and mental illness, so hopefully the stigma is going away.

Those who speak out to help others or ask for help should be commended for their courage. If you think you need help, please find someone to talk to. And if someone comes to you, try not to judge them—try to be a safe haven and help them if possible.

Sometimes it is difficult to tell the difference between "the blues" and "mental illness" as many times people refer to a "down" mood as depression. There is the situational depression that happens due to an experience, such as death of a loved one. One can also get depressed when they go through a traumatic or stressful situation or for any number of reasons when life seems to be beating us down.

A diagnosis of bipolar disease, which is also classified as depression, may require medicine. We are not downplaying a very real disease that could be occurring, but the truth is, there is so much negativity in the world today that many people are depressed and it's not a mental illness—it's just life.

So when we get depressed, the only way out of it is to look for the exit doors. Even if you are feeling overwhelmed, look for a way to get out of it. You can do it and you don't need to use destructive behavior, have constant anger, or stay in bed due to feeling too tired.

A GOD-SIZED HOLE

Lesia Waggoner is in the healthcare profession and she has spent her life taking care of people. She had patients to take care of, and she would do anything she could for her children, but the one place the care seemed to end was with herself. She was a participant in the field of destructive behavior.

She was experiencing addiction in her life and she felt helpless, until there came a day that something changed for her and she wanted to help herself and others. This day can come for you, too. It could be something small that helps you turn your corner, but you can get out of the bad situation you are in, if you really want to.

"You have to realize that having a hole inside that you try to fill with destructive antidotes and behavior is a never-ending cycle, because the hole will never really fill up," she said. "If you are lucky, one day you realize the hole is 'God-shaped' and the miracle of recovery begins. Thank you, God."

"There is a God-shaped vacuum in the heart of each man, which cannot be satisfied by any created thing but only by God the Creator, made know through Jesus Christ."

— **Blaise Pascal**

Blaise Pascal was a mathematician, physicist, and religious philosopher in the 1600s, who laid the foundation for the modern theory of probabilities.

Isn't it amazing a guy who was thinking of probabilities realized in the 1600s that we all have that need to fill our heart. Once you learn to find other ways to fill that vacuum, you will experience more happiness.

HEALTHY PEOPLE HAVE GREAT POSSIBILITIES

Once you get healthy in life, whether it is through real food nutrition—or nutrition for your soul—your possibilities open up.

If you are unhealthy or there are things you would like to do to change, it's your choice about making that change. The older we get, the less we have choices, so it's good to start now. We are the author of our life. How are you writing it? Are you writing about a poor pitiful person who has faced adversity, someone who has every reason in the world not to be a success?

Are you writing it with excuses—because it really wasn't your fault, it was your parents, or your teacher, or the coach that cut you. Are you writing with bitterness? Are you writing it with fear?

Natasha Bedingfield sang a song called "Unwritten," which gives hope that we are all "staring at the blank page before us" and that "this is where our book begins … the rest is still unwritten."

Write your book filled with strength, hope, and possibilities.

We can feed our soul the nutrition needed to write our book in a powerful and excellent manner.

"We must never stop dreaming. Dreams provide the nourishment for the soul, just as a meal does for the body."

— **Paulo Coelho, writer**

Sometimes we feel so helpless in an emergency situation. One of the worst is being called to the hospital to sit beside a loved one, who is coming in and out of consciousness. Have you ever wondered what are they thinking as they lie there hooked up to wires. Are they even able to think at all?

SHE SAW A GLIMPSE OF HEAVEN

Karen Kroger encourages people with her story. She had what is commonly called a "near death" experience and what she experienced can help others.

She was in her bedroom and she called for her husband.

"I said, 'David, I am dying,' and he called 911," she said remembering that day six years ago. "That's all I remember about what was going on, I felt like I was up looking down on myself."

While the paramedics were enroute, she said she could see herself lying there. I asked her what it looked like. What do we see when we are looking down on ourselves—if we are in a heavenly state. Do we see a person who is terrified or passed out or sick? She said she just saw peace.

"It was very peaceful," she said. "It's OK. I used to be afraid of dying and now I'm not. I share my experience when I think it will help someone. I had a friend whose daughter died and I told her about it to give her comfort."

Karen said she has read a little about the near-death phenomenon.

"If something catches my eye about after death, then I'll read it and it's all pretty much the same," she said. "You are generally up in the corner of the room. People describe the eerie calmness of the situation and how it is totally peaceful. Eerie sounds like a negative word, but it isn't in this instance."

While she was not breathing, she felt calm and at peace, but when the paramedics arrived, they started working on her and she came back.

"I remember coming back on the floor in our bedroom when the paramedics were working on me," she said.

They took her to the hospital, but she was still in very bad shape. She had to be put on a ventilator and was septic.

"I remember being in intensive care. I remember wanting to be touched. My friend came in town and spent the night and I remember waking up and holding her hand. I wanted human touch."

There are several things we can take away from this story—the biggest being how wonderful and peaceful it is when we are released from our bodies and begin to ascend into Heaven. We can take comfort that our loved ones who have passed away are peaceful and we can be peaceful when the time comes.

Another thing was when she looked down on herself, she saw nothing negative. She did not even see her husband who was upset—she only saw herself in a loving and peaceful way. This helps comfort us so if we feel like we didn't do the right thing in the person's last few hours or if we have any regrets or guilt—the person will not have any negative feelings towards us. They will just look down on us in a loving way.

TAKE A PERSONAL SABBATICAL

In a chapter about remembering to take care of YOU it can't be stressed enough that you're worth it. I heard a pastor took a three-week sabbatical leave, with the (1) first week a vacation, (2) second week working on himself, and (3) third working on his relationship with God. I decided to take a sabbatical and you can too.

Even if you can't take a "vacation" you can design your own two or three week sabbatical using the three ideas. I did fun positive things, read books, listened to Ted Talks and inspirational YouTube videos, lit candles and prayed.

The biggest change was very limited cell phone and computer time and avoiding CNN or FOX News. I could literally feel a change. I felt free and happy. Plan your sabbatical. Make an effort to do things you enjoy that make you better; check out positive books at the library; learn things. Look at people in a more loving way, and maybe when it's over you will continue doing some of those things.

If only everyone on earth would look at each other in loving ways, no matter what. One of the keys to seeing things in love is having a clear mind and the tranquility needed to be at peace.

"Peace is the result of retraining
your mind to process life as it is,
rather than as you think
it should be."
--Wayne Dyer

CHAPTER FIFTEEN

Tranquility
Learning to Relax and Be at Peace

One of the most important keys to living a happy life is to be able to carve out times of peace. Stop and look up at the moon, gaze at a sunset, or watch an earthworm wiggling across the driveway. There is a real art to being able to stop in the midst of your busy day and calm your mind.

There are so many ways that sleep, health, and happiness go hand-in-hand. Eating the right foods can help you sleep—and, in turn, getting good sleep helps you not eat too much, and you feel better, so you are more content.

"Unplug to unwind. The bright screens of phones, tablets, televisions, and any other electronics can mess up our sleep cycles … if you usually watch TV before bed, swap that for reading a book or listening to relaxing music."

— *Dr. Mehmet Oz*

There are so many great things about social media, such as keeping up with family and friends by looking at pictures. However, there is also the danger of disconnecting from people when you actually think you are connecting.

Too much screen time of any type can be detrimental to our well-being. Our parents sat us in front of *Leave It to Beaver* and then warned us not to watch too much TV. We sat our kids in front of *Sesame Street* and then warned them not to watch too much TV. Now we worry about the next generation with too much time in front of the iPad or other devices—the devices we are giving them.

Seeing your friends posts on Facebook or Twitter isn't the same as calling that friend and talking. We need the human connection to really feel at peace.

My husband, Rob, had a great point about social media.

"Years ago they had diaries, and people wrote in them," he said. "There are diaries of Civil War soldiers, and diaries of pioneer women. These people had some of the same types of thoughts that we have today, but they wrote it in their diaries and then went about their lives.

"Nowadays, people air their life on social media and this can do several things. They may tend to dwell on their problems and hardships more, because they put it out there. We also lose the history that is gained when an old diary is discovered."

Can you imagine a pioneer woman who is traveling with her family across the country, checking her Facebook every few minutes? They used their time to live a real life in the real world—not the social media world.

"Calm mind brings inner strength and self-confidence, so that's very important for good health."

—*The Dalai Lama*

With each scroll you see so many unhappy people crying out into cyberspace about their problems. If you are upset about something in the news, making a negative post won't help. Why not look up their address and send them a well-thought-out letter. People have been known to change their minds on policy over the years, but nothing good happens from a negative post (or comment) and it only upsets others, creating more negativity. I advocate keeping social media happy.

If you are one of those who post your problems, why not contact a friend and confide in them, instead of putting it out on social media for whoever is online at the time to see. Call a real person. You matter. Your life is so much more important than a random social media post.

Another thing about using our devices, constantly checking our social media, is the fact that it can be insulting to the person you are actually sitting with—but are ignoring because you are looking at your device.

Yes, I know that is the way of the world these days, but it still hurts my feelings when I am giving of my time to a friend or loved one and they are sitting there on their phone texting another person.

I don't mind a quick check if you are expecting news or if your work calls for you to be up on social media, but there are people who actually keep running conversations going and text continuously, even when sitting with someone else.

Are you one of these people? Are you texting with someone on your phone, while also having a face-to-face conversation with someone else? Put your phone down. Talk to the person you are with and later, call the person you might have been texting with.

Being with someone is such a blessing. If you don't believe me now, you will when you lose that opportunity due to life changes. Accept the peace of just "being."

There is something to be said about the old *Andy Griffith Show* and how much peacefulness they seemed to have. Andy and Opie would sit out on the porch and talk—or not. And sometimes Andy played his guitar. And sometimes Aunt Bee brought out plates of pie and they all sat and ate it together. They never seemed to be in a hurry, and maybe that's why it is so enjoyable to watch the old reruns. Yes, they are hilarious, with some of the memorable performances of Don Knotts as Barney Fife, but it's also nice to just remember simpler times.

These days, we often feel too busy to sit on the porch and enjoy life. Did you know that frequent use of electronic devices can actually make you nervous or irritable and that just setting them down and sitting outside can calm you down?

Sometimes we display symptoms of nervousness, anger, or stress and it is not a medical situation—we just need to slow our life down. Sometimes we just need to "sit on the front porch" and give our time and attention to people and not make them feel our devices are more important than they are.

An article in *Psychology Today* said we as a society are displaying stress-like symptoms that could be caused partly by overuse of electronics. The article goes on to say parents and doctors could be mistaking these symptoms for deeper problems in their children, when really if they turned off their phones and gave the child more attention, maybe they would not be displaying the negative behavior.

There have been countless articles pleading with parents not to give their children devices in their formative years when they are developing. Children need to know their parents are there for them. While an i-Pad can help occupy a child at a restaurant, engaging with the child and trying to talk to them teaches the child valuable social skills, and besides, it makes them more fun to be around.

If we leave our children with electronic devices, we can't expect them to be friendly or know manners. It's up to us to take the time to be with them and guide them. So remember to hug your child and talk to them often—don't just leave them with an electronic device.

"Experts say that what's often behind explosive and aggressive behavior is poor focus ... by depleting mental energy ... screen time contributes to low reserves. One way to temporarily 'boost' depleted reserves is to become angry, so meltdowns actually become a coping mechanism [for too much screen time]."

— Psychology Today

For those who need an expert, there you have it. Your own meltdowns or rising stress levels could very well be due in part to not having peaceful quiet time. Remember, when a toddler starts acting crabby, we automatically think or say, "Someone needs a nap," so the next time you get crabby, maybe you need a nap.

Don't let electronics steal your joy. Don't let Facebook or Twitter steal your peace. You are in control. Choose Happy.

SOFT MUSIC CAN GIVE YOU PEACE

To achieve peace, we need to want it in our lives. We need to try to achieve it.

"I have found that music can calm me down, and it started with my dog," said Laura Sleade of Champaign, Illinois. "I know this is strange, but we have a very anxious dog. The vet gave us a copy of a CD that is piano music specifically for calming dogs. The tempo is supposed to do things like slow a dog's heart rate."

She tried it on her dog with mild success, but later she found a better use for the musical CD—herself.

"Last year, I was dealing with some health issues and feeling anxious myself," she said. "I began playing the dog's CD in the car for myself. It was a nice pace to take some deep breaths and I felt calmer and more centered when I arrived at my destination. It was great and worked better for me than for the dog."

HE TREATS HER LIKE A SECOND WIFE—BECAUSE SHE IS

Jan and Sam Orlando and their five kids were a normal, happy family.

"We were a Christian family who did all the sporting events and school events for our children," Jan said "We went to church every Sunday and many times during the week, with no problems to mention."

Or so it seemed to the outside world. Though Jan was doing all she should be doing to make it look like a happy successful family, she did not feel happy and successful herself. She felt that with all that was going on in their lives, she got lost in the middle. The family owned a successful business and her kids were all active, but something was not right inside her.

She started growing more distant from Sam and things got swept under the rug that maybe should have been said. As time went by, they realized how broken their marriage was and it seemed headed down a bad path. They tried to talk about it, but finally felt it was too late. The result was a divorce.

When they separated, Jan stayed in the house with the kids for a time and Sam stayed in an apartment above their business. Though they were sad it had come to this, they tried to have "family" activities celebrating special events together.

"During this time I realized something," said Jan. "I felt I had no identity. I had always been someone's child, then someone's wife, then someone's mother. Who was I really?"

She did some soul searching. Many women feel like this at times, especially those who work at home. They see their husband going off to work and imagine him having a really interesting day while they stayed home and did the laundry, picked up the kids from school, and made dinner.

Then there is the other side of the story, where the wife with the full-time job feels left out, because she has been working so hard all day and feels she missed so much with the kids. There is never a happy medium. But there is way to be happy in a situation you don't feel fulfilled in: change your attitude. It's the old "I have to watch the kids" vs. "I get to watch the kids." or "I have to work" rather than "I get to work."

Most things that you complain about doing, there is someone, some-where who would give anything to be doing that.

Sometimes we work so hard just making it through life that we liter-ally lose our identity to ourselves. We think of the high hopes we had when we were young and mope about the situations we may be in. That's how Jan felt at the time.

Well, guess what? While you are thinking you are living a mundane life, someone is watching you, thinking you are pretty amazing. You may not realize it, but you are everything to your kids. Even though he or she might not show it, your spouse loves the way you cook or thinks it's great you work out, or likes that you are always trying to learn new things—or just loves laughing at your jokes. Whatever you are doing, someone that you don't even realize is paying attention to you and thinks you are pretty swell.

During her separation, Jan took the time to get closer to God and have conversations with Him.

"Since I saw my identity as being attached to someone else, I really had to figure out who I was," she said. "I just wanted to find 'me.' I got a new job and tried to work on myself as a separate person."

"I've been to Paradise, but I've never been to me ... Paradise ... it's a fantasy we create about people and places as we'd like them to be. But ... it's that little baby you're holding, and it's that man you fought with this morning, the same one you're going to make love with tonight ... that's love."

— Songwriters: Ron Miller, Kenneth Hirsch
Sung by Charlene

We are never going to be able to explore who we really are, what our hopes are, or what our dreams are if we keep ourselves so busy there's no time. It's very important to take some time out of each day for peace and tranquility and maybe that is how you will "find yourself."

Jan had always been a Christian since childhood, but she had not had so many personal conversations with God, as she had during that time. She also learned a valuable lesson.

"I learned the value of 'dumping my troubles in the lap of the Lord,' " she said. "It's easy to say 'give your burdens to the Lord,' but most of the time, we take them back. During that time, I learned to put my troubles in the lap of the Lord and not take them back."

So often we try to trust God and we think we are trusting Him. We say, "Lord help me, I'm upset because my life isn't going as planned," but then we come back with, "If you could just do this or how about this?"

No. Leave it be. He's got this.

"Put your troubles in the lap of the Lord, and then leave them there. God does not need our help. We need His. We need to give our troubles to God and then trust Him."

— Jan Orlando

"I hung on to God and we talked a lot during that time," Jan said. "And I continued to pray."

If we want to live a peaceful life, we have to have trust. We have to believe. When we start trying to orchestrate the happenings of life that is not leaving it with God—it is trying to control it the way we want it to go. Jan probably had ideas about what she wanted to happen, but in the end, God changed her heart.

"Even though being separated and then divorced was a sad time in my life, some of it was good," she said. "I was finding myself. So the newness of finding out who I was, was the healthiest part of this change in our lives."

From the very beginning of their separation, Sam and Jan had put their family first and never became bitter towards each other. At one point, Sam moved back into the house and she moved out for financial reasons, but they always stayed united for the kids.

"It was heartbreak for many years, but our love for each other and our children held our family together," she said. "On the day our divorce was finalized, I remember leaving the courthouse and going home to my little house, and the realization struck that I would not be able to live with my children anymore. I was devastated. I cried and moped around—and then my phone rang. It was my kids wanting to know if they could come over tomorrow and play games. That was God's way of saying, 'It will be all right. I am with you.'"

With the realization that the divorce was final, Jan knew she had to figure out a way to live her life.

But God Changed Her Heart

"I prayed a lot and finally it happened," she said. "God put a big question on my heart: why are we doing this to our family? With all those prayers, He had turned my heart. So I took the first step."

She asked Sam to dinner, which wasn't such a stretch, because they had tried to maintain a civil attitude towards each other.

"I brought him an African Violet with a note that said, 'Roses are Red, Violets are blue, Will you marry me again?' It didn't rhyme, but it got the point across. He broke out in a big smile and said, 'I thought you would never ask!'"

That Thanksgiving was a special one, as they spent it with just the seven of them and after going to Mass, the family deacon came over to join them in matrimony—again.

"It was a wonderful occasion," she said. "That was six years after our separation. Six long years, yet in that time, we both learned a lot about ourselves and each other. Now when people talk about having been married twice, I always interject, I've been married twice, but to the same man."

They went through a lot, but now they have a new respect for each other. You could say he treats her 'like a second wife' and vice-versa.

"I am so grateful to the Lord for never leaving me and always being there no matter how wrong I was or how low I got, He was always there and I know he always will. That's the peace that surpasses understanding."

Peace is different for different people, just as happiness and love is. We sometimes think we want a different life than the one we have, but learning to accept what is placed right in front of us is a key to peacefulness and being happy.

Bloom where you're planted and one of my favorites that could never be repeated too many times: Do what you can with what you have where you are. Sometimes when our life isn't the way we want it, so maybe we should pray that God will change our hearts and we will see it in a new way and thus be at peace.

Is having a calm, peaceful mind important to your health? Yes, it is, but it goes the other way, too—we need to strive for good health in order to have a calm mind.

DON'T HAVE A MUDDY MIND

You must rest your mind to rest your body. Bad thoughts and worries "muddy up the mind." Have you ever had a day where you just don't seem right? Nothing is really wrong, but your mind is foggy, you are in a bad mood, you feel heavy, but can't quite figure out what's wrong. You have a "muddy mind."

One of our sons' teachers used that term and it can apply to all of us. Some days when the kids were out of sorts, or if a particular child was acting out or in a bad mood, she would say, "Do you have a muddy mind today?" Somehow they understood what she meant and she was able to redirect their behavior, because she taught them ahead of time what to do when they had a muddy mind.

I love that term, because it was something the kids could understand—and so can adults. We all get muddy minds every once in a while and we need to take the time to clear them. Do something different, try to relax, jump into a swimming pool—do whatever it takes to calm your mind, so you won't be looking at the world with a crabby, negative outlook.

Wouldn't it be great if we could see ourselves and each other in a positive, loving, peaceful way, instead of always having an opinion or judging? All the bad-mouthing and self-criticism we have and the flaws we see in ourselves (and others) will mean nothing on the Last Day.

Why do we waste so much time on unimportant and negative things? They don't matter. The only thing that matters is love. That is really the only thing that matters.

HE FELT GOD TELL HIM TO PRAY WITH THE PRESIDENT

Seeing someone as God sees them—seeing them in love—is something that former Alabama punter, JK Scott, saw when his team was welcomed to the White House by President Donald Trump in 2018 after they won the National Championship. Scott, who went on to play in the NFL for the Green Bay Packers, said while on the airplane going to Washington, he felt a strong message from God telling him to talk to the

President. When he got there, he looked at the President and what he saw was odd—not the typical picture of Donald Trump.

He told the SEC Network that when he arrived at the White House, he saw the President in "love" and felt the strong urge to ask him if he could pray for him.

"I said, 'Hey, Mr. Trump, would you let me pray over you?' He said, 'Yeah, come on,' " the football player told both the SEC Network and AL.com, the online version of the *Birmingham News*.

So Scott took a bold step. He put his hand on the President of the United State and began praying. Soon other members of the team joined in.

In that moment, he did not see Trump as a Republican or someone who he might have disagreed with on topics or policy. He saw him in love. God doesn't see us as a Republican or Democrat—He sees us in love.

As mentioned previously, the political climate of the country is one thing that is making people stressed and angry. Isn't it interesting that a young person had so much faith in himself and in God that he went out on a limb like that—and with the President of the United States no less!

That chance he took led to peace in his heart at the time. What power we have when we see each other in love. Try it sometime. Is there someone in your life who is the bane of your existence and drive you crazy? Maybe they are even mean to you. But if you try to look at that person in a different way, in a loving way, you might be able to find some peace in the situation.

TOO MUCH STRESS CAUSES A BAD MOOD

When you are under stress, you might be in a bad mood and for no reason, lash out at someone. And likewise, if someone was rude or mean to you and you think it was uncalled for, try not to let it bother you. Try to see them in love.

The bad thing about our moods is we have the power to ruin someone else's day, if they let us. It's their choice. When we are on edge and pop off at someone, who did that help? Take a nap and you will feel better. When you wake up, why not brighten someone's day and go visit a shut-in, whether in their home or a facility?

People come up with many reasons for not visiting a loved one, but actually when you take the time out of your busy day to go visit someone, it relieves your stress, because you see what it's like to just "be." A person who is a shut-in might have been very active when he or she was younger, but they are forced to learn to live a simpler life.

REASONS NOT TO VISIT A SHUT-IN FRIEND OR LOVED ONE

1. I don't want to remember him/her this way.
2. I don't have time.
3. It feels weird going to that place, everyone there is old (out of it, crazy—fill in the blanks).
4. They don't recognize me, so they won't care if I go or not.

REASONS TO VISIT A SHUT-IN FRIEND OR LOVED ONE

1. If you love the person, there are a million reasons to visit them and no valid reasons not to.

After you have come up with every excuse there is not to visit—turn the tables. Do you think that person would ever have said any of the above, when it came to loving you? If they would, then by all means don't go, but if you know in your heart they were always there for you, now is the time to be there for them.

If you are going through having a person in a facility, you have my deepest prayers. It is a very difficult place to be, but it's important that you go and be there for them. If it is hard for you, come up with some coping mechanisms.

You can help by giving them a big smile. Touch them, give them a hug, or rub their back. We all need that human touch and though, because of medication or age, sometimes it seems like patients don't have feelings—we have to remember they do. The human brain is strange and we can never really know what a person is thinking. As mentioned earlier, you can give someone peace through music. Maria Rodgers O'Rourke played music for her mother.

BEING AROUND PEOPLE WHO ENERGIZE YOU RELIEVES YOUR STRESS

The other day I saw a picture from a trip I had taken years ago. We had stopped to visit several friends and their smiling faces greeted me on that picture. As I looked at each one, I realized how each one of these friends energize me and make me happy just being around them. It made me want to go visit them again.

Once we find people—or even just one person—who makes us so happy it energizes us, we should make an effort to keep them in our lives. We all know people who bring so much drama into our day that when we leave them, we feel more stressed out than before. There are also those who give us great peace by just being there for us. We are that person to others, too.

Think about who makes you happy, who energizes you, who makes you feel good just being around them? Now make an effort to get in touch with them.

Every day we have stress and problems—that's just part of life, but the happiest people choose to do what they can to eliminate whatever negatives they can. When things seem to be crashing down on us, it all seems magnified. These are the times we have to learn to manage our fears. I read somewhere that it says something like, "Don't be afraid," 365 times in the Bible—that's one for every day.

WE CAN BE PEACEFUL EVEN DURING TURBULENCE

When I am scared, I light my candle and find my Bible verses to help me stay calm and grounded. I look for those songs that have comforting messages.

There was a time I was fearful on an airplane every time it shook due to turbulence. Now I keep little Bible verse cards in my purse and when that happens, I take them out.

My favorite card says, "For I know the plans I have for you," declares the Lord, "plans to prosper you and not to harm you, plans to give you hope and a future." (Jeremiah 29:11) When I read that Bible verse, I think to myself, "God has plans for me. He wants to see me prosper. If he has plans for my future then I'm going to get through this turbulence and any turbulence that life throws at me."

A side note about turbulence on airplanes. The pilots and crew take these flights every day, several times a day. They know there will be a little turbulence when flying into certain areas, such as Denver, even on a clear day, so they are prepared for it and it doesn't scare them. Picture the path an airplane take as a road. Sometimes the road is bumpy, so enjoy the bumps. It will soon be smooth and tranquil—just like the bumps in our life.

> *"Do not be anxious about anything, but in every situation, by prayer and petition, with thanksgiving, present your requests to God. And the peace of God, which transcends all understanding, will guard your hearts and your minds in Christ Jesus."*
> — *Philippians 4: 6-7 (NIV)*

If you are going through a difficult situation, you will have bumps along the way, but remember, this isn't your last hurrah. You have a lot of life left in you—and a lot of things to accomplish, so keep going and while you are at it, keep trying to find things that give you peace.

WITH HER FAMILY'S HELP SHE TOOK THE BAD NEWS AND FOUGHT WITH A POSITIVE ATTITUDE

How can we live our lives when we never know what tomorrow will bring? That's where our faith comes in.

One day Wendy Powell was sitting at her computer. The successful author and radio host was having a normal day and suddenly she found she was unable to speak.

"I literally could not talk," she said. "Luckily, my son and husband were at home and noticed something was wrong, so they were able to get me to the hospital."

After evaluating what the problem was, the hospital diagnosed her with a brain tumor. One minute, she's working on something and the next minute, she is looking at her future with a brain tumor.

"It was a bad type—glioblastoma," she said. "Not that there is a good type, but this is a particularly bad diagnosis."

The Mayo Clinic says, "Glioblastoma, also known as glioblastoma multiforme, can be very difficult to treat and a cure is often not possible."

Wow, what a terrible thing to read or hear.

So what do you do when you can't find any comfort from anybody? The doctor could not give it to her with the diagnosis. Her Google search could not give it to her. So she had to give it to herself.

Whatever you are facing, you can do it, too. Don't give up—get in gear and get ready for the fight of your life—that's what Wendy did.

"The message here is you need to take the bull by the horns and make a conscious decision to fight with all your might," said Wendy. "Cancer treatment can be difficult, so we must fight."

Wendy and her family hunkered down and started learning and praying. No matter how hard a person tries, even if they don't get well, they were not beaten—they went down swinging—and the Powells were out there swinging.

But she didn't go down—her positive attitude and her family's support gave her the strength she needed to get up every morning. There were days she was sick and she accepted those days, but she never gave in to what the diagnosis said or what the internet said.

The only person who knows the outcome of your story is God, so don't ever take someone's negative diagnoses or gloom and doom talk as gospel. The "Gospel" was already told—and it holds great promise.

The thing Wendy stressed that helped her is to learn to be at peace with your life.

"Relax and make all of your time with the people you love as valuable as possible," she said. "I was looking at a very tough diagnosis, but I wouldn't accept it. It was necessary to keep going and make it work for my family. I was the lucky one—perseverance and drive is in my DNA."

Her family researched and found the treatment they thought would be best and then she put it in the hands of God and the doctors. She tried to be as peaceful and calm as she could throughout.

"After three years of that perseverance, treatment, and pure grit, I have graduated 'cancer free,' " she said. "They refer to it as remission or any term that would make me feel better. What I heard was I was healing. I wouldn't take 'no' for an answer—and you shouldn't either."

No matter what life throws at you, it does you no good to be all stressed out and running scared. Do everything you can to calm yourself down. Do things that make you happy.

We don't know if we will be hit by a truck on any given day, so if you look at the big picture, there are no "death sentences"—only scary proclamations that try to take away our joy.

If your doctor says you have three weeks to live—that's more time that is promised to you on any given day. Enjoy every day, but don't believe anything negative—don't allow bad thoughts into your head—only positive thoughts. Think about it, even a prisoner facing a midnight execution can get a "stay" from the Governor.

NOTHING IS EVER FINAL UNTIL IT'S FINAL.

"Family, friends, and anyone that is struggling with health issues, need to hear this," Wendy said. "You must trust in God. Understand what troubles you have been going through and realize what you have learned and then give yourself credit if you handled it like a champ."

I'm looking at you and you are doing a great job. I hope you are realizing that, and give yourself some extra love today. How about wrapping your arms around your shoulders and giving yourself a big—and well-deserved hug.

The thing that mentally saved Wendy was her positive attitude, her family's support, and her love for and trust in God.

"Love runs deep and with hope and prayer, we can learn from our tough experiences," Wendy said

Maybe the situation you are facing is not as drastic as cancer—maybe you have to give a presentation at work and you are scared. At any given time in our lives, we are facing a different challenge. There was a day that Wendy's biggest problem was getting her book turned in on deadline.

Don't be afraid. Have faith in yourself. You can do it. So often the way we carry ourselves gives way to the way others see us. If we are walking in confidence and love, the others see us that way. Pray for God's love and for confidence and then feel it, and be at peace.

"There is no better feeling than you get with God's love," said Wendy, "I remain positive, peaceful, and I keep smiling. And it's true—as they say, 'When you're smiling, the whole world smiles with you.' "

FAITH HELPS HER THROUGH A TOUGH TIME

Diane Heckenkamp says that when a major problem is happening in her life, one way to get through is to sit back and rely on her faith, to give her the peace she needs.

"What gets me through a tough time is faith," said Diane. "It seems so simple to say 'faith,' because to me it is fundamental to my Christian beliefs."

In times of trouble, those who have faith seem to go into autopilot.

"For me, it just happens and I look back on it in amazement. When I was going through just the most seriously worst time, a soul-crushing time, something that seemed insurmountable, something I felt was killing me—it turned out that miraculous things happened. When I look back on it and in hindsight, it reinforces my faith."

She says that having a strong Christian faith is what helps her, but at the time, she may not even realize it.

"At the time, I prayed so hard to get through something," she says. "The answer to my prayers is that my brain slams shut like a steel trap door to block out everything else, except what I am thinking about. This allows me to focus only on pushing through the situation.

"My faith comes from my mother and grandmother and I hope to pass it on to my children or anyone who needs it. It is the difference between life and death, when darkness and heartbreak threaten me."

Having a quiet faith can help us stay grounded and at peace. There are people who seem to just be content all the time. They seem to not let anything bother them. They sail above all the silliness and noise of everyday life. They only engage in what is important.

ARE YOU GETTING THE MESSAGE?

Every day we are bombarded with messages—some good and some bad—and many steal our peacefulness and tranquility. Why is it that we let the bad messages take over our minds? I could be having the greatest day and everything is sailing along, but then someone says something negative to me, which makes me feel inferior, and everything goes out the window. Why can't we let the negativism slip by and keep remembering the positive things that happen?

Not long ago I got a massage (not message this time—a "massage") and it was the best massage I have had in a long time. Sometimes when you get a massage, there are parts of your body that hurt or the massage therapist doesn't realize you don't like a certain technique and you have to tell them. Well, this time it was amazing. I left the place feeling so relaxed and I longed for that feeling to continue.

Well, guess what? When I got home, I had all sorts of emails and people expecting me to get right back to them. However, this time, instead of letting the stress take over and ruin my peaceful countenance, I decided to wait until the next day to deal with it. With instant messaging, emails, and text messages, we often feel the stress to do everything right now. The "instant" world we live in is often the cause of stress.

As I am sitting here peacefully writing this, I heard a little "ding" on my phone. Immediately I looked up saw a Facebook message and felt the need to write the person back. If this was 20 years ago and someone wanted to contact me, they would call at an appropriate time and I would answer, we would have a pleasant chat and it would be over—or leave me a message and I could return the call the next day.

Now with the cell phones, email, and social media, we get interruptions all the time. This can be a big source of nervousness. Have you noticed that there is less and less time for quiet?

Reading a book seems to be becoming a lost art and it's too bad—but, hey, thanks for reading this one.

We pay big bucks to get a massage, so we can have an hour of quiet time with lights turned down and peaceful music playing. Why don't you do that on a daily basis—take time out, turn down the lights and play some soothing music? Happy memories from my childhood are of my parents every night sitting by the fireplace in our family room listening to music.

Loss, whether it's loss of a friendship, loss of job, or loss of a family member, it can all bring about stress. Are you really cursing, because your computer is slow today? Did you really just cut that guy off because the check didn't arrive in the mail and you are in a bad mood?

We get so mad but we need to find better ways to cope with life.

"And then all the noise, all the noise, noise, noise, NOISE!"
— *Dr. Seuss, author*
The Grinch in The Grinch Who Stole Christmas

That's how it can feel sometimes. It can almost be too much. You can't live a contented life, if you are in the middle of all that noise.

FIND PEACE IN NATURE

What is the answer to all the negativity and how do we unplug ourselves from the things that can drag us down? Go outside.

Nature is a place where you can lose your stress, feel like a kid again, and just regroup.

Next time you feel people pulling you in all directions, take the initiative to remove yourself from the situation. Get up and walk away from that device; politely excuse yourself from that person or leave the situation that is causing you stress. You have to do this to save yourself. Take a walk, take a bath—do something for yourself.

"We need to find God, and he cannot be found in noise and restlessness. God is the friend of silence. See how nature - trees, flowers, grass- grows in silence; see the stars, the moon and the sun, how they move in silence... We need silence to be able to touch souls."

—*Mother Teresa*

Any way you look at it, your life will be better if you have more peace in it—and trying to achieve that peace is a choice we can make.

The people who went out on a limb and shared their stories in this book are survivors. They are out there living their lives and striving for excellence. They are the type of people who energize me, because they are doing the best they can and choosing happy over self-pity.

There are two types of people, and you make your choice which one you will be: those who make up excuses why they can't do something and those who keep trying until they do it.

"Ninety-nine percent of the failures come from people who have the habit of making excuses."

— **George Washington Carver**

George Washington Carver, who invented peanut butter, started as a slave in Diamond Grove, Missouri. After the Civil War he learned to read and write eventually graduating from college and he even got his Master's Degree. He became a scientist who worked on sweet potatoes and peanuts to come up with more uses for them, to help poor southern farmers vary their crops and improve their diet.

George Washington Carver's gravestone reads: "He could have added fortune and fame, but caring for neither, he found happiness and honor in being helpful to the world."

WE SHOULD ALL FIND HAPPINESS AND HONOR IN BEING HELPFUL TO THE WORLD.

That was to be the last sentence in this book, but as it came to an end, I couldn't seem to let it go. I couldn't bring myself to give the book to the editor—because I felt there was something missing, but what?

I got up to clear my head and while I was up, I decided to move some books around and dust off a shelf. In the process of taking a few books down, a paper literally dropped right in front of me.

It was three pages typed and stapled together by my father. My parents had experienced much loss, including death of two grown children and a granddaughter—yet not a day went by that they weren't spreading joy to others and living as happy a life as they could.

Though Mom had kept diaries for as long as I'd known her—date books with the days happenings written on each page, Pop selected the one from 1999—a turning point year in our family's life. He quoted some of the days and summarized it down to three pages. It was 2015 when he did it, and he wanted us to remember that year and what our mother had written down about it.

On these three pages were listed events that happened that year. She listed the "highest highs" (which included a party celebrating a book I had written that year) and the "lowest low" (Annie's diagnosis and surgery).

"Annie's illness changed all of our lives in one way or another," she wrote. "We have learned so many things, including how much family and friends mean to us and how much we are blessed to have each other. My hope is that we remember what is important."

She listed her fifteen things that she felt are important to live a happy life.

MARGIE'S FIFTEEN THINGS
THAT ARE IMPORTANT FOR A HAPPY LIFE

1. Be with people you love.

2. Do some good in the world.

3. When you do a good deed or help someone, do it from the kindness of your heart and don't expect to be repaid.

4. Accomplish whatever you are capable.

5. Do what makes you feel fulfilled.

6. Take out time for others.

7. Take the time to listen to kids and adults who come to you, because if you don't respond, they might not come to you again and you will miss what they had to say forever.

8. Learn that each person is important. Each person in each household is as important as the other.

9. Realize that you are not always right.

10. Give praise where it is earned is very important. It doesn't have to be something big to deserve our praise.

11. Tell people that you love them. This is very important. No one knows what tomorrow may bring and if you wait until tomorrow, it might be too late.

12. Appreciate what you have—every day. Jack and I tell each other four or five times a day that we love each other, and we mean it. He tells me (at my age) that I am cute or pretty, or beautiful, or funny, or smart nearly every day—and I believe it, because Jack would not lie to me. I don't know how I was lucky enough to get Jack—how are any of us lucky enough to get those good people God has put around us? But I am very grateful and can never thank God enough.

13. Realize that love and respect is a two-way street.

14. Don't worry about things you can't control. In 1999, midnight came and went without any of the dreaded Y2K computer problems and it was fun watching all the New Year's celebrations all over the world. All those worries were for nothing.

15. Be thankful for your family and friends—that is the way to have a happy life.

Make up your mind that you will find contentment in your situation, no matter what it is. You can have a happy life—I believe in you.

POSTSCRIPT

When Pop died, we buried him in the gold-sequined vest he'd bought for their 50th Wedding Anniversary Party. When Mom joined him a couple of years later, it was fitting that it was the week of their anniversary and Valentine's Day, so we sent her off in her sparkly party dress and made "favors" for our friends who came to the funeral home. We had her memorial service at a park and did the Hokey Pokey—

Because, after all, that's what it's all about.

About the Author

Sally Tippett Rains is a writer, producer, author of 12 books, Volunteer Executive Director of Rainbows for Kids, a charity for families of children with cancer. She met her husband, Rob Rains, in the press box at Busch Stadium in St. Louis, while covering the Cardinals for KMOX Radio. She worked fulltime raising their children and writing books. In 2011, Rob and Sally Rains founded STLSportsPage.com where they both work.

Sally Tippett Rains sees her most worthwhile role as a family member and friend. She has always tried to stay positive and encourage others to live a happy life.